You Don't Know How Lucky You Are

You Don't Know How Lucky You Are

An Adoptee's Journey Through The American Adoption Experience

Rudy Owens

BFD Press

Portland, Oregon

Published in the United States of America by BFD Press, Portland, Oregon.

First printing 2018

Author: Owens, Rudy
Title: You don't know how lucky you are: an adoptee's journey through the American adoption experience / by Rudy Owens

Includes bibliographical references and index

ISBN 13: 978-0-692-82156-5 (paperback edition)
ISBN 10: 0-692-82156-2 (paperback edition)

ISBN 13: 978-0-692-12440-6 (ebook edition)
ISBN 10: 0-692-12440-3 (ebook edition)

Cover photo of author, taken at his childhood home in Clayton, Missouri

Dedication

To all adoptees who have been denied their most basic human rights simply because of their status at birth—you, your families, and your hidden stories will never be forgotten.

Contents

Preface

My story begins with a meeting between two family members, separated by the chasm of adoption, yet bound together by blood. One represented the villain in the other's family lore, because he was denied, illegitimately born, and relinquished for adoption. I am that person, the bastard son of a man I never knew.

As an adoptee, my understanding of my own story has changed over time, particularly after this encounter. Yet my lifelong tale has always unfolded as a mythical hero's journey. It is also one of many adoption stories among the millions of US adoptees, their birth parents, and their collective biological and adoptive families. This work will weave these experiences together to highlight a national social-engineering experiment that remains mired in discriminatory laws and partisan divisions—not equality and fairness for those most impacted by the institution of adoption.

Throughout my memoir, I intentionally challenge stereotypes and practices that have treated the mostly powerless groups of birth mothers and adoptees with disregard, prejudice, and impunity. My story is also strongly grounded in evidence-based public health research, using population health and peer-reviewed scientific sources. I also draw from government statistics, government publications, personal accounts by adoptees and birth parents, original records from archives, my personal archives, my correspondences with adoption officials, and other sources. This evidence, data, and research are cited in footnotes and cross-referenced in my bibliography.

My relation to my biological and adoptive families is central to my story. Writing about an adoptee's family relationships requires using words to describe an adoptee's relations to multiple families and especially to an adoptee's two mothers—or in some cases for adoptees, guardian or other parent figure. I will use the term "birth mother" to describe the woman who brought me into this world as a mother. Numerous birth mothers who are active in advocacy for other mothers who relinquished their children prefer the term "first mother." However, even those working in this advocacy field will use the terms interchangeably. I also have chosen to call the mother and family who adopted me "adoptive mother" and "adoptive family." Because sections of my work make many references to both families, these terms clarify for readers the family and family members who raised me.

I deliberately omit the names of individuals from my adoptive and biological families and hide their identities throughout my work—even for those who are deceased. My memoir, however, includes interviews with past and current public officials, who are all named. I also reference documents they produced for public agencies or in their professional capacity as public employees. All of these documents and statements are public records, as are documents shared with me concerning my birth records from the State of Michigan, my adoption agency, and the courts.

Finally, I will draw from conversations and interviews with the many people I have met on my journey and with those who I contacted for this book. They range from the man who literally brought me into this world—in a hospital at the epicenter of the American adoption experience—to the family members who reluctantly accepted me more than four decades later. My journey is also a shared experience, and it would not be complete without their voices contributing to that story.

Introduction

During the nearly three decades since I first found my biological family in Michigan, I frequently thought about sharing this tale with others. The decision to tell such a story in public, or even among friends, weighs heavily on an adoptee. The storyteller must directly confront social taboos, rooted in our long human experience and evolutionary psychology, that punish children born into bastard status.

A story on adoption also involves some of the most intimate, and in the case of birth mothers, traumatic moments of life: the birth of a child and the relinquishment of one's flesh and blood to other kin or to strangers. For many decades, including the 1960s when I was born, this life-changing experience meant a strong likelihood that the mother would never see her child as long as she lived. In many ways, this is a story as old and as powerful as the abandoned hero, prophet, and adoptee Moses.

An adoption tale also confronts prejudice. Adoption laws, and especially those who enforce those laws in most US states, cast adoptees who dare ask for equal, legal rights to their records as outsiders and bad actors. This stigmatization takes place in unconscious and overt ways. Outdated adoption laws represent the most obvious form of overt discrimination. They allow state agencies, courts, and adoption agencies to treat adult-adoptee citizens like mentally and emotionally undeveloped children. Most state laws make clear that adult adoptees are not worthy of having what is theirs by birthright: records of who they are and of their biological kin.

The word "adoptee" also carries a second and unspoken meaning, which adoption supporters, adoptive parents, and many adoptees wish to ignore. It provides a polite way of identifying a human as a bastard. The word remains a meta-insult, attacking the very nature of a person as cursed from his or her inception. Its very meaning connotes an obscenity, something vulgar, but also dangerous and outside the boundaries of all societies.

Therefore, my story will use the word "bastard" frequently. It is a word that only a bastard like myself can own and appropriate, robbing other users of its historic meaning to demean those conceived out of wedlock. As evidence shows, there are measurable health and public health consequences to being conceived out of marriage. To ignore those outcomes is to ignore the power of the stigma of illegitimacy, which helped to fuel the institution into which millions of Americans were placed.

Most sociologists agree that virtually every known society has created ways of defining legitimate and illegitimate births. In nearly all cases, societies have favored and still favor legitimately born children. In the decades before and after my birth through the mid-1970s, birth mothers and adoptees in the United States bore the brunt of this social calculus. My life as an adoptee is a product of that societal shame. Therefore, I reject how those who created and sustain the system would prefer to speak about the adoption experience. They do not define how I identify myself and my experience rooted in that shame. I will use the word bastard through this tale as a way of diluting its sting as a common slur.

Bastards, like myself, are also reminded constantly of their often-pariah status in popular culture. Arguably one of the most popular television shows in the world from 2010 to 2017, HBO's *Game of Thrones*, has taken bastard stereotyping to an entirely new branding level. Two of the show's most pathologically twisted villains—a sadistic bastard king, Joffrey Baratheon, and an even more sadistic usurper, Ramsay Bolton—personify the terrors bastards conjure up in popular imagination as demon seeds and destroyers. My own story includes similar fearmongering by some biological family members who created harmful urban legends around me that seem straight from pop culture or Victorian fiction.

Taking on the adoption status quo in the media, in popular culture, or in bureaucracies that manage birth records, remains a fool's errand. Some states like Oregon have opened records. Alaska and Kansas never took the right away from adoptees to see their records. After the late 1940s most states began restricting adoptees' access to their original birth documents. Oregon, where I now live, passed a state referendum in 1998, Ballot Measure 58, allowing adult adoptees to access original birth certificates. It was implemented in 2000 with success. This is the exact opposite of my birth state, Michigan, which fought me over decades to give me what is mine by birthright. It refused to give me a copy of my original birth certificate in 1989, even when I knew my birth name and knew my birth family. When I finally demanded my original birth certificate in March 2016, no less than nineteen officials in the governor's office and state public health system collaborated to reject my request and tagged me in their records system as, what Michigan's State Registrar Glenn Copeland called, a "problem."

As of late 2017, only nine states allow adoptees to access birth records without any restrictions. Another sixteen states have laws that limit the rights of adult adoptees to access their birth records. These restrictions are in the form of birth-parent disclosure vetoes, the redaction of an adoptee's information found in birth records or a birth certificate, or restrictions that are placed on access to an original birth certificate because of an adoptee's birth year. This was what I experienced in Michigan because of when I was born. Michigan's statutes even criminalize anyone who releases such records without a court order to an adoptee born after World War II through 1980. The other twenty-six states, including the District of Columbia, have statutes restricting access rights of adoptees to their original birth certificates, except by hard-to-obtain and cumbersome court orders. In January 2017, New Jersey was one of the latest states to open up original birth records to adoptees. However, its law also allowed more than 550 birth mothers to hide their names forever, setting a precedent that could harm future adoptee-rights advocacy for full, equal treatment under the law in states where they are denied equal rights to access their original birth records.

State adoption laws and the larger culture promoting adoption are also shaped by a conservative and right-leaning Christian worldview. The groups who promote secrecy at all levels of the adoption record-keeping system view advocates and adoptees asserting their right to equal treatment under the law as an existential and political threat. Opponents of open birth records have too much money and political capital invested in the global transnational adoption trade to allow US adult adoptees to achieve equal treatment by law. The global market of adoption and child welfare services is estimated to generate $14 billion a year. Symbolically, those who support adoption need to keep adoptees powerless. This posture advances many powerful pro-adoption groups' larger political goals in the decades-long culture war over abortion, and the supposed, but imaginary "adoption alternative" that is formally endorsed in the Republican Party platform.

For these political and religious interests, an adoptee's original birth certificate is the talisman through which this symbolic power is channeled. One never surrenders a magic object without a battle. Look at the decades of fighting over the flag of the slaveholding Confederacy.

Larger cultural conflicts are often intertwined in fights over symbols that are loaded with meaning and power. If adoptees were like everyone else, then adoption as a special, life-giving act—similar to the "rebirth" one experiences through a Christian view of redemption—would lose its intended meaning.

The closed nature of American adoption contrasts sharply with many modern democratic nations that allow adoption. In 1975, England passed a national law that gave all adopted persons eighteen or older the right to have full access to all of their birth records, with no exception. This duplicated what Scotland had been doing successfully since the 1930s. France, Germany, Denmark, Iceland, Norway, Sweden, Finland, Israel, the Netherlands, New Zealand, and Norway also have long-practiced open systems that are working for adoptees, birth parents, and adoptive parents. As of June 2016, Hawaii was the latest state to pass a law that grants all adoptees unrestricted access to their records when they are eighteen, duplicating what other countries do without harm to nearly anyone at the national level. At a population level, open records pose almost no societal harm but provide uncounted benefits to adoptees seeking their own records and to adoptees' biological relatives. A public health approach using these metrics should have won widespread support among nearly all medical and public health groups in the United States by now, yet almost no one in these fields dares to speak publicly on behalf of the country's millions of adoptee residents.

Writing a personal story about adoption also means risking harm to one's adoptive family. For each individual and family, adoption is a unique experience. Data show these experiences are rockier and even unhealthier compared with the experiences of children who are not adopted. Some families may feel aggrieved by an adoptee sharing family tales. Some may feel deep anger. Adoptees risk harming those relations by helping others know about this experience that touches nearly all Americans through their personal, work, and community relations. Adoptees know they could disrupt their family ties forever. In my case, I knew I could begin telling this tale only when my adoptive mother's memory and mental health status had changed. I could do her no personal harm by bringing our story to a wider audience because she would never remember it or even read it.

My story, however, will not be given a formulaic storyline that frames adoption in the same way the media cover the subject—as a human-interest spectacle, for momentary entertainment. Those made-for-media tropes usually involve good, decent, and usually white families whisking away adopted children from their true kin, filthy orphanages, and corrupt countries to the United States. Or the stories focus on adoptees reuniting tearfully with birth parents later in life, but without the messy details of closed records and discriminatory laws that kept them apart for decades. Media spectacles that grab good ratings usually avoid the backstory about how laws are made and how bureaucracies and institutions deny rights to individuals because of their status at birth.

This will *not* be yet another tale in a long series of adoption reunion narratives. I wrote it to provoke anyone who reads it and to force readers to ask questions. I seek to challenge thinking that has prevented people from seeing adoptees as a group subjected to bad laws because of discrimination and stereotyping. Instead I use public health concepts that focus on laws and systems that have an impact on large groups of people. A public health lens lets one look at outcomes, including the health of adoptees and those born illegitimately. This approach points out flaws that can be fixed, particularly if we look at evidence and science as well as how adoption systems work best. I will do this by writing honestly and openly about the issues using my own personal experience.

Compared with the most common adoption genre of autobiography, this story will avoid sentimentalism. Many adoptees—including the latest ones coming of age in transracial, international, and gay adoption family configurations—have embraced a style of self-absorbed, multimedia storytelling that suggests adoptees do not master their emotions, destinies, and life stories. The content and issues are vastly different between a friend who is a Korean-American adoptee of my age and the teenage, Chinese-born daughter of another friend. But many adoptee storytellers today gaze only in the mirror at themselves. My story will focus more on issues affecting millions of adoptees and the practices and laws that have shaped adoption.

My memoir will be different from the established adoption genre in several other ways. It will be a man's, not a woman's, story. It will not challenge the assumption that adoptees are unhappy with their adoptive family. It will not obsess over the so-called pain of relinquishment. There will not be a climax of the search for one's birth mother. It will not affirm the larger Adoption Rights Movement's philosophy that knowing one's past heals the pains of the present. Finally, it will not end with a reunion as the center of an adoptee's quest.

This story of American adoption will include studies by experts relevant to the issue, and my own ideas as an adoptee who is looking both at his life's experience and trying to make sense of a system I was born into. Ultimately, it is about me looking at how to live life well and making a difference for myself and the larger world around me, particularly those impacted by the American adoption system.

As an autobiography, it includes real people—including some whom

I have never met, or may have only met briefly. I have intentionally not used the names of family members, to mask their identity. But the characters I describe are genuine and honestly portrayed. I keep real names of the public officials in my story. They are fully accountable for their actions. They act in the name of serving the public, while being paid by the public.

I believe that focusing on research relevant to the debate over open records and best practices can lead to better outcomes for adoptees, birth mothers, and adoptive families. My story about being born in an unwed mother's wing of a hospital in Detroit in the spring of 1965 is a classic adoption tale. That facility was named after a movement that was created to help single, unwed women, like my birth mother. I was part of a larger American story dating back to the late 1800s. This meta-story involves millions of mothers, mostly absent biological fathers, and their offspring—children who were then raised by relatives and unrelated new families.

My adoptive family, however, was not especially healthy and normal, though I admit I may not truly know what healthy and normal mean. My adoptive father, a Lutheran minister, was abusive and an alcoholic. He had a serious drinking problem before I was even placed in his and my adoptive family's middle-class, two-story brick home in metro Detroit. He treated my adoptive mother, my adoptive sister, and me very poorly. At times, when he was drunk, he could have killed my sister and me on more than a dozen occasions—when he would drive us in a total stupor. My adoptive family's struggles were not pleasant, but they are also things no one could have predicted, and their meaning and purpose may still not even be clear to me. However, the way I confronted these challenges was uniquely my own, and I own how I addressed my reality and the conditions of my life. No one else is responsible for that.

Adoptions often do not work out as supporters of adoption hope. So my story will not support advocates or their organizations who want imaginary adoption stories that end happily. Still, my family experience does not excuse me from making the most of what life provided for me. That canvas on which I painted my life's story was determined through the intersection of players who defined some key life events. These were my adoptive family, my birth mother, and my absent and denying birth father. They were also the Christian social service agency, medical, and government actors who transferred me from my birth mother to a foster family, and ultimately to an adoptive family during the peak period for adoptions in postwar America. As I kept discovering throughout my life, these decisions had a lasting impact, for more than five decades. This is our story. I hope you enjoy this uniquely American tale of just one adoption among millions.

Chapter 1

Meeting My Half-Sister

I'm not surprised to see you. It's as if you were meant to come.

—Rudy Owens's Paternal Half-Sister

Once again I found myself in San Diego on a perfect, warm day. A quarter of a century earlier, it felt like it did that sunny morning. During both trips to this sprawling, coastal city, I was hoping to meet someone I never really knew.

At best I expected to leave a note on her door while she was away at work. Maybe she might meet me for coffee after the workday, during my four-day trip. She likely would ignore the letter, and our lives would go on as they always had. I had planned almost entirely for this outcome.

But the events unfolded differently.

Less than two hours after landing, I had parked in front of her modest adobe-style house, located a mile from Balboa Park. She was home on a weekday. Her car sat in the driveway.

Clearly things were not going as expected. I had no choice now. I sucked in a gulp of air and then knocked. With the door still closed, she asked for my name, and I told her it was Rudy Owens. Instead of turning me away, she invited me into her living room.

And there I sat on her couch, across from a woman two years younger than me. She had dark, shoulder-length brown hair and a chin and lips that very much resembled my own.

"You don't know how lucky you are," she said, with a sigh of resignation. I did not expect this outcome. Her comment caught me off guard, almost speechless.

I planned the trip on a whim forty-eight hours before, from my new home in Portland. I had previously found that improbable journeys with little possibility for success had always opened doorways to the unexpected. This was most true when it came to this lifelong quest that brought me to Southern California with the early morning flight on September 29, 2014.

The stranger sitting across from me shared half of my DNA. She was both my half-sister and a mystery. She looked tired that morning, and she showed every one of her forty-seven years. Dark bags hung under her eyes. She appeared healthy for her age.

That early fall day she wore a black tank top and black yoga pants. She had dressed expecting to be home alone. She was not expecting to be in the company of a visitor who was also her half-brother. Yet, there I was, the forty-nine-year-old man now facing her with her Chihuahua on his lap.

Up until that day I only existed in her wider family's narrative as a liar, bogeyman, criminal, possible blackmailer, and family disruptor. I embodied every fearful stereotype societies have assigned to bastards and illegitimate children for centuries. They told themselves and others I was not related to them and was an impostor, not of the same blood. None of her family really knew who I was. I always thought that she and her family knew I was the bastard son of her deceased father, which only exacerbated their uncertainty.

In the end, I only existed in her imagination. Years of suspicion and likely fear and anger from the people closest to her created an imaginary threat.

If she harbored those feelings that morning, I could not see them. She had opened her house and treated me as a guest.

By coincidence that Monday morning, she was taking a day off work. She worked as an attorney for a local government. "I'm not surprised to see you," she said. "It's as if you were meant to come." I could not agree more.

For nearly three decades, chance and intuition had been my strongest allies searching for my family history and meeting my biological relatives. My first meeting occurred just after my twenty-fourth birthday. I embraced blind faith when I bought a round-trip ticket to Detroit, in April 1989. On that fateful journey, I met my biological mother and my cousin, son of her twin brother. I realized that I could tap what I called providential energy. The more I worked on this mystery puzzle, the more synchronicity patiently helped me find the missing pieces of my ancestry slowly through the years.

At that point in my life, the words "how lucky you are" flipped from sounding laughable to sounding improbably wise.

Up to that exact moment in time, I often had looked critically at my life, as an adoptee who was placed in a family with an abusive and alcoholic father and an emotionally distant mother. By all accounts mistakes were made. My future adoptive father was already an alcoholic and had received treatment in Chicago to address his disease before my adoption was completed—when I was five and a half weeks old. His status as a Lutheran minister who also worked at Wayne State University in Detroit likely kept the Lutheran social workers from probing too deeply into whether he was a fit parent.

Even with this sadly familiar familial situation, I always did my best to count my blessings being born in a wealthy country, where I never knew war or crisis. Still, there were countless times I selfishly thought good luck had eluded me. So, for decades, I occasionally thought that plain, dumb bad luck chose me by chance.

I long thought being placed by faceless, unknown adoption intermediaries of Lutheran Child and Family Services of Detroit into an already dysfunctional home was an added insult to having been caught up in the United States's growing adoption system. It was during the mid-1960s, when such bastards and unplanned children as well as their birth mothers were hidden from view until those problematic kids were placed with a new adoptive family, giving them a supposedly happy, new life.

That system forced me to sever all ties from my genealogical history, my ethnic identity, and the woman who brought me into this world. That system forced me to lose my first name on my original birth certificate. It made it illegal for me to get records of my biological identity—a practice that negatively impacted millions of adoptees from the 1940s through the 1970s. Unless I or any other Michigan adoptee had a court order to compel the state to release my original birth record, an adoptee like myself is still forbidden from seeing that document by the State of Michigan's confusingly written adoption laws. In my case, the state had refused to share my original birth certificate with me over a twenty-seven-year period, even though I had known my birth family during that time. I am one of an estimated twenty thousand adults born in Michigan between 1945 and 1980 who have their birth records closed—a figure that the state cannot confirm to this day.[1]

Adoption, as it was organized nationally, was supposed to allow me to be born anew into a new family and to be accepted as if I were a biological child. The champions of adoption promoted utopian thinking from the start, without any real idea how their new system would affect the infants who were adopted, or their birth mothers. Today we know from significant research, particularly of stepchildren, that parents in most cultures do not treat children equally who are not their genetic progeny. They may love these children. They may give them homes. But they are not provided the same degree of filial bonding as offspring who are biologically related. The issue of whether these problems experienced by stepchildren also extends to adoptive children remains white-hot, because it asks if kinship by means other than blood relations can be replicated through modern adoption practices. Modern US adoption is founded on the premise that families can be formed without true biological connections.

There have been more than 150 published and so-called "psychopathology studies" on adoptees since the 1930s. These publications on the "pathological symptoms" among adoptees have asserted adoptees, or tried to show that adoptees, are different because they do not have a biological bond with their adoptive parents.[2] This research, often with statistically invalid sample sizes, has allegedly shown or seeks to show that adoptees are prone to developmental and behavioral problems.[3] These studies have not answered if these risks are a result of how nurturing occurs because of a child's adoptive status. What is known from public health research, however, is that being adopted correlates with many health risks later in life, if adoptees as a group are compared to the entire population. Such findings suggest early experiences in life in a family setting have measurable and lifelong health impacts.[4]

However, those promoting adoption for the hundreds of thousands of adoptees from the 1940s to the 1980s sold a message that creating families with placed adopted infants was equal to creating families through natural birth. Children who were adopted were expected to accept that myth as well, without having any choice. But most of these children never accepted that story. They have been dealing with much greater archetypal yearnings that the adoption system still discounts in the United States. We continue to see the consequences of this failed model through societal norms that stigmatize adoptees for "not being grateful" and for asking too many questions about who they are and where they came from.

I routinely experienced those norms. They usually came as critical judgments that I was being ungrateful to my adoptive family because I wanted to search for my biological kin, and know my family and birth history. From the 1950s through the 1980s, mental health and social work professionals had routinely called this most basic of desires a mental health disorder, and to this day professional groups in these fields have never apologized for the harm they caused promoting these bogus theories. This stigma persists today, supported by the enforced secrecy in statutes in more than half of all states that keep biological relatives from meeting one another. That was my story, and sometimes it became the chip on my shoulder. It was the story I told myself.

Perhaps like many adoptees, I wondered about my alternate universe—the one where I was not adopted. What if I had lived with my birth mother? What if I had stayed in Detroit? Would that have been better or worse for me? Did I come from a family with problems, drug addictions, mental illness, genetic disease, and poverty? Perhaps I had a famous parent, like birth mother Joni Mitchell, and I was given up because I came at the wrong place with the wrong man? I sometimes wondered if my birth father was more of a sinner than a success. These are usually the private thoughts an adoptee will keep to himself or herself. Like many fellow adoptees, I chased all of these ideas over the decades, often playing the same record over and over again in my head.

Then, with a tectonic shift, things changed when my half-sister uttered those words. In a matter of seconds, I had to reexamine my decades of thinking about the twists of fortune that had brought me into this world as an "illegitimate child," outside of a traditional American family, through an unapproved, unwanted, and out-of-wedlock pregnancy.

This seemingly random trip was turning out to be much more. By chance that morning on my flight down, I was reading psychiatrist Viktor Frankl's classic Holocaust memoir, *Man's Search for Meaning*. It describes his experiences surviving German concentration and death camps. In it, Frankl explains the meaning of misfortune and tragedy. Looking at his own harsh experiences as a prisoner, Frankl suggests that the full meaning of awful moments in our life might not be manifest for years, until they suddenly take on clarity through the long view of time. In Frankl's view, what may appear to be terrible at one moment can have a completely different meaning later, when the fullness of an experience makes sense to the person. For Frankl, a tragedy may not be tragedy, and misfortune could be fortune in disguise.

Frankl's ideas again forced me to reexamine my life with my adoptive family. Finding my biological families when I was twenty-four years old and the quarter century of hoping one day to meet my oldest half-sister from my biological father collided in my head. Sitting in a room with my half-sister, it seemed like time had suddenly stopped. What the hell was happening?

I already knew that morning my half-sister was the oldest of two daughters born to our shared father. He was born in a small city in a Midwest state and later moved to another small city where his father found a good position. His father, my biological grandfather, was a small-town veterinarian. They lived in a home at the center of this small rural community. With his wife, my biological grandmother, they raised three other girls with my father. My birth father was the youngest. I visited their house in 2007, where it is now a historic site. I got a tour from two women who ran the local historical society.

My two paternal biological grandparents were married for more than fifty years. My biological grandmother died in July 1981, when I was just sixteen, and my biological grandfather—known mainly as "Doc"—passed away near his son in San Diego, in June 1982, when I was seventeen. I never met either. Neither ever knew of my existence.

My birth father was born at the end of the Great Depression in 1939. He graduated from his small-town high school in 1957. In 2007, when I visited the high school, his picture was still hanging in the school hallway, where class pictures of past graduates line the walls. He attended his state university, not that far from his boyhood home. He became a member of the ROTC program (Reserve Officer Training Corps) and a fraternity brother with the Delta Sigma Delta Dental fraternity. He proved to be a very smart and capable student, earning his professional degree in dentistry and a doctorate in dental surgery from the state university in 1964.

During his medical training he completed a one-year residency at Detroit General Hospital, at a time when Detroit was in its heyday with 1.8 million residents. It was a pivotal year for him in the bustling Motor City. He met his future wife whom he married in Detroit, and also slept with another woman—both of them later bore his children. His two daughters were "legitimate," from his wife. The son was "illegitimate," from another woman. I was that bastard. To this day, I am still the bastard. I embodied an alternate universe he tried to hide from his family and himself for decades. In the end he failed because I had other plans than the ones written for me by the social engineers who created the nation's adoption system.

He met that attractive other woman, my birth mother, at a party they both attended. She was an attractive twenty-four-year-old woman with blond hair. She worked as a lab tech at Wayne County General Hospital, in her hometown of Detroit.

Soon after they met in the early summer of 1964, the woman learned she was pregnant after they slept together. He denied it. He was married to his first and only wife in December of that year, almost four months before I was even born.

It is likely that his marital status weighed heavily on his mind, as it did for millions of young men eligible for the draft with a war in Vietnam that was heating up. My birth father had two ways that would enable him to avoid military service. One was student enrollment, which was coming to an end for this young ROTC member and dentist, and the other was by marriage. It was widely reported during the 1960s and later that the most common means for deferment were university studies and getting married.

President John F. Kennedy's Executive Order 11119, from September 1963, changed Selective Service System regulations for all draft-eligible men.[5] Married men without children were placed one step lower in the draft pool order of call than single men. After this order was implemented, local draft boards were required to select men for induction in the following order: delinquents, volunteers, and 1-A single men (ages nineteen to twenty-six, oldest first). Next in line was the group who became known as "Kennedy husbands." My birth father was a Kennedy husband. Being married put my birth father at the end of that line for the military draft.

My birth father, the man who denied he was my father and who had become a distinguished dentist, also joined the group of many men who ultimately avoided the nation's call to arms in the jungles and rice paddies of Vietnam. I do not know if the growing conflict influenced his marriage decisions. But many other young men who were draft eligible could not avoid the draft and the fate that came with it. I am certain that he avoided another duty: his paternity for a developing child in my mother's uterus. He steadfastly denied his role in fathering me for decades, all the way to his grave in 2004.

My birth parents' sexual relationship was never meant to be anything more for my birth father, and the pregnancy was unwanted by my birth mother. Abortion was illegal in the United States in 1964 and 1965, when my birth mother carried me to term. She likely had few other choices because of her lower-income status, the societal shame that accompanied pregnancy for single white women, and possibly pressure from her mother and father—my maternal biological grandparents. I cannot say for sure because no one ever explained this decision to me, even after all these years that I have known my birth mother and our family.

She went to a maternity home for "fallen" young women like herself in suburban Detroit to hide her pregnancy. There were hundreds of such homes in the United States at the time. On April 16, 1965, a young boy was born in Crittenton General Hospital on Tuxedo Street, about three miles northwest of downtown.

My half-sister knew nothing of the place where I was born. I likely will never know how much she knew about her father's life-changing year in Detroit. Did she have even a vague understanding of how her father met my birth mother, slept with her in circumstances that still are murky to me, and then denied he was my father?

While facing my half-sister, I did not know how much to tell her. Should I tell her I already had pictures of her father's marriage to her mother in December 1964, given to me in May 2007 by her aunt, who by blood was also my biological aunt? The pictures I have show a dapper young man, smoking a cigarette, with his very attractive and stylish auburn-haired wife.

What do you say to someone who you have been hoping to meet for decades? What if you have an uncertain amount of time to share a life history about who you are, why you wanted to meet them, and what this means to someone who was denied basic identity information most of his life. How do two half-siblings, separated for nearly five decades, talk about their family background? Can one speak honestly in that situation, when one of those sibling's very existence poses an almost existential threat to a family narrative of a happy, upper-middle-class family in upscale San Diego, complete with a husband, wife, two kids, and a dog?

Our unplanned half-hour meeting in her living room unfolded as a whirlwind of family stories and odd confessions. She said for the last twenty-five years her family told her not to trust me, after I had found my birth father in San Diego on May 27, 1989, and had exactly one conversation with him lasting less than several minutes. It was the only time I even met him face-to-face before he died in 2004.

She said her mother even told her that I wanted to commit a terrible crime against her and her family. I sat stunned and almost speechless by this suggestion—that I might actually plan a violent offense. Prior to my half-sister's revelation, I had no idea how anyone could have told such an over-the-top story. After the meeting, I then found similar stories from court cases from the 1960s through the 1990s, where adoptees' rights to birth records were denied. Lawyers at some court proceedings introduced bastard stereotypes of adoptees, claiming they wanted to kill their biological parents. Attorneys seeking to keep state adoption records closed have used this urban legend, without ever showing any evidence anywhere that adoptees seeking their past ever sought any revenge or harm.[6]

I told my half-sister that I could not control what her mother, father, or other family members may have said about me. I said I always wanted to know who I was and where my family came from, without any ulterior motive. She told me her aunt and our mutual cousin, the aunt's daughter, never told her about my visit with them in 2007 at our aunt's home in a Midwest state. During that visit, my biological half-cousin and biological aunt had shared stories and pictures with me about my birth father and our shared family.

I learned that my half-sister only met her grandma just once and that my biological grandmother may have been anorexic. I had learned from other residents of the Midwestern state where my biological grandparents lived and who knew the family, that my birth grandmother may have had some mental health issues. She reportedly once hit her husband with a hammer and hung on to the car screaming as he tried to drive away from home. Neighbors reportedly saw and spoke about that incident in the small town. My half-sister said she really did not know her grandfather, even though he had moved to a community next to San Diego in his last years and died at a nursing home there in 1982. My half-sister was old enough to know him and have visited him. I suspect she was not being fully honest. She was a teenager living at her parents' home at the time her—or more precisely our—grandfather died of cancer.

She shared her high school and college picture books with me. She asked if I was gay—something that made me laugh. It embarrassed her. She used the words "our father" and "my brother" at least once each. She looked at my face and said I had her father's eyes and eyebrows.

Her comments surprised me. They validated a reality she may never have fully accepted, or tried to ignore, until the person forcing the issue sat across from her, in the comfort of her home and holding her dog in his lap. Did she momentarily let down her guard, or did she have a similar feeling I have had when meeting biological relatives? I still feel wonderment at the similarity in appearances I share with another human. That sensation always forces me to accept that there is a genetic closeness that is deeply rooted in our evolutionary psychology.

I suggested to my half-sister that the purpose and meaning of things as complicated as family and kinship may not be clear until the end of the journey. So our meeting that morning, I said, might be a chapter that had more to come.

I tried to talk openly about health and mental health in our family backgrounds. I told her the stories about our grandmother's alleged displays of erratic behavior. I talked about not having a great adoptive father and not being a Christian. She asked about my faith, but I never inquired about hers. I told her about my adopted mother's emotional aloofness and also her growing dementia. I discussed work, my moves, and how I found my birth family in 1989. I gave her my version of reaching out to her and her father over the years. These stories likely conflicted with what she had heard from her mom, dad, and relatives. She had a lot to process, without any warning.

Mostly, she wanted me to know that her family was far from perfect and that I should feel blessed because I was not living her family experience. Her parents had divorced, and now she was fighting with her sister, who also was my half-sister. She said she was alone and had no family. It sounded sad. The story sounded similar to the one message she shared with me on the phone in 1998, when I called her. During the five-minute call she mostly said, you don't want to know this family. I had not reached out to her since that time until now, sixteen years later.

My half-sister could not have known what I was thinking. She would not have guessed that I was comparing her upbringing in relative economic wealth as the daughter of a dentist in an upscale neighborhood and beautiful home in San Diego to my own lower-income childhood in a much tougher area outside of St. Louis. She did not know I was thinking about the years of abuse my alcoholic father subjected my family to, sometimes almost killing me and my sister when he drove us blotto drunk. She could not have known about my mother and my family's hard times barely getting by as a single-parent household, with her low salary as a public-school teacher. She did not know that I had to work throughout high school doing grunt jobs, including being a janitor, to earn money to pay for my own clothes—something I once hated but appreciated more when I matured. I sat there, now wondering, was this all good luck up until this point? My accidental conception between a man and woman in uncertain circumstances, my adoption, my fate with less than perfect adoptive parents, my constant quest for information withheld from me by bureaucracies that did not care about my rights to basic identity documents. Was it really as Viktor Frankl had written about so eloquently? Was this about finding meaning in misfortune and rising above it and growing, and by doing that turning a bad experience into something life-affirming?

I did not have time to dwell on these thoughts. After thirty minutes, my half-sister's face suddenly grew serious. She got off the sofa and said I had to go. Before I headed out the door, I handed her the letter I had written on the plane coming down. I originally planned to leave it at her door if she was not home. I said she could still contact me during my short four-day trip. She said OK, but never reached out to me that week or since.

Back in my rental car, I texted my old college friend, who I was going to visit later that day. He had encouraged me to come down and try knocking on her door. When he saw my text that I had just met my half-sister, he responded, "D'Man!" I smiled. Yes, I really was D'Man, again.

At eleven thirty in the morning, an hour after leaving my half-sister's home, I was splashing in the Pacific Ocean at beautiful La Jolla Beach. There were just a few people. The waves were gentle, rolling in with calm sets. I was bodysurfing in the clean, clear blue waters feeling a sense of freedom.

Twenty-five years earlier I had bodysurfed here, on the same day I had met my birth father at his door for the only time we spoke with one another in person. He had told me to get off his property and that I was not his son. Ironically, or by fate, it was my half-sister who had first answered the door, though we did not discuss that long-ago event when we met earlier that morning.

Now I had come back to the beach that had calmed me before. This time it was a different story. Instead of being rejected, I was vindicated and validated by my half-sister who had never acknowledged me until that day.

In the water, I thought about the power of listening to my inner voice. I had never given up on the idea of meeting my half-sister. I knew in my gut that this is one of the most important things I could ever do in my life. I also had taken a leap of faith that this trip was the right thing for me to do. Even with setbacks, rejections by my half-sister in 1998, and little, if no support from any family and friends, I stuck with my plan.

More importantly, I thought about what all of this meant. Chances like this do not occur often in life. Perhaps I was blessed. Maybe I never really knew how fortunate I was, and my narrative had been backward. Maybe, just maybe, my perceived bad luck was actually powerfully good luck in disguise. If true, that would require action on my part, that morning and every day to follow.

A large wave rolled in. I caught it, bodysurfing to the shore. I smiled at how amazing my life felt at that precise moment. I again thought about Frankl's wise words I had read just hours earlier: "So live as if you were living already for the second time and as if you had acted the first time as wrongly as you are about to act now!" It was time to start anew.

Chapter 2

The Most Suitable Plan

The most suitable plan for the unmarried mother has been found, in most instances, to be the relinquishment of the child so that it may be placed in adoption. A child kept by the mother may suffer from lack of support that a father, family, and other relationships provide.

—American Academy of Pediatrics, Committee on Adoptions, 1960

When my birth mother relinquished me for adoption in Detroit in 1965, society took little notice. Tens of thousands of other children that year in the United States joined the club of newly born infants who would be relinquished as adoptees. Nearly all of us shared a common story as illegitimate and out-of-wedlock children. Society, families, churches, and social and medical services, created to address unwanted pregnancies, had determined that having this select group of newborns leave their mothers for new families was best for all of us.

My beginning is also the complicated story of my birth mother's experience giving birth and relinquishing her child. Though a profoundly personal event, her life-changing decisions followed a pattern taking place in every state across the United States and Canada—largely hidden from public view and public debate.

Social historians E. Wayne Carp[1] and Barbara Melosh,[2] as well as adoption legal scholar Elizabeth Samuels,[3] have all documented these major shifts affecting millions of women and their out-of-wedlock children in the decades following World War II. During that time, the practice of adoption underwent a massive transformation. Melosh calls it social engineering, which implies organized efforts to make large-scale changes to society involving groups with influence and political power.[4]

In the pre–*Roe v. Wade* years before 1973, white women comprised the majority of pregnant women who were forced into hiding during their entire pregnancy. They also were burdened by societal stigma that labeled them as having mental health issues for their supposed sexual indiscretions. The impact of these stereotypes is hard to measure, but we know the impact was widespread given the sheer number of adoptions and out-of-wedlock births.

The Child Welfare League of America (CWLA), an influential nonprofit organization that played a key role in shaping US adoption law and policy, published its *Standards for Adoption Service* in 1958. It is a slim book at seventy-eight pages that details prescriptions for agencies, adoptive parents, vital-records keepers, birth mothers, adoption agencies, medical specialists, and all of the participants in adoptions. The medical, social, and legal ground rules it framed would affect the lives of my mother, my adoptive sister, me, and hundreds of thousands of other birth parents and adoptees.

The book's goal was to inform public opinion, influence judges and lawyers, and guide adoption-agency practices nationally. Instead of highlighting the harm of removing biological children from their blood kin—as social welfare professionals had done for decades before—it offered a manual that recommended having illegitimate kids put up for adoption as a beneficial act for their well-being.

The league's manual notes, "Many young women who become pregnant out of wedlock have serious personality disturbances, need help with their emotional problems, and in most social groups encounter serious social disadvantages if they keep their children with them."[5] The guidebook encouraged adoption agencies to accept the surrender of children born out of marriage when birth parents were emotionally ready, not when suitable adoptive parents were available.[6] The manual was skeptical that societal views that harshly judged single white mothers would allow them to have a successful life with their child because of "illegitimacy." The stain of that label, in the agency's view, would cause lasting harm: "Although there has been considerable modification in society's harsh attitude toward her it still remains extremely difficult for the unmarried mother to raise her child successfully in our culture without damage to the child and to herself."[7]

I cannot say if this manual and other publications of the era influenced work practices of the social workers assigned to my birth mother and adoptive parents. Neither side of my family divulged these pre-birth tales to me, but it is very likely this climate of secrecy and stigmatization around unplanned pregnancies prevailed in Detroit, as it did in other major American cities.

In the Motor City and other metropolitan areas, well-established institutions managed the transfer of infants like myself to families with whom they had no genetic relations—in other words, strangers. I doubt my birth mother or adoptive family knew they were part a nationwide approach to address unprecedented numbers of unplanned infants and a desire by tens of thousands of families to raise these children. Half of the adopted infants would end up with families with whom they had no biological connection. The other half were placed with families who shared some biological relation to the adoptees.

Record collection on adoptions has long been imprecise. The most widely quoted data set on US adoptions through the mid-1970s was published in a paper by Penelope Maza for the US Children's Bureau. The study found the United States recorded 2.4 million adoptions from 1944 through 1972—the last year before abortion became legal in the United States.[8] The study made estimates without precise data, because data collecting was voluntary not mandatory.

In 1937, there were an estimated 16,000 to 17,000 adoptions in the country. By 1944, that bumped to 50,000. In 1957, the figure hit 91,000. The year I was born, in 1965, the number reached 142,000. Finally, by the peak year of 1970, there were 175,000.[9] That means 479 kids a day that year, on average, were placed in homes of parents who agreed to take children that mostly single women had agreed to relinquish.

Kin-based adoptions were always common, involving parents related to an adoptee. From the 1940s through 1971, adoption petitioners related to adoptees made up half of all adoptions. By 1975, the rate jumped to six in ten.[10] Even in an era when adoption was a widely accepted practice, promoted nationally by social service systems, stranger adoption was never preeminent. Most of these transfers of a young person from a biological parent to adoptive parents were done legally. Black-market operations also operated. They were not approved or monitored by any regulated government agency or religious charity.

Social workers found themselves at the front lines of these demographic changes, ushering in the new American institution of modern adoption. When social workers and maternity-home professionals gathered at a Washington, D.C. conference in 1958 organized by the US Children's Bureau, they brainstormed how adoption could address the demographic challenge of illegitimacy they saw nationwide. The number of "white infants" was far exceeding their availability for placement. They ominously surmised, "No accurate count of the number of couples seeking a baby to adopt exists but a ratio of ten couples to one child is frequently quoted by agencies."[11]

In 1975, the federal government stopped collecting adoption statistics, creating a demographic black hole that still prevents adoptee-rights advocates from knowing their true numbers in the US population. Official counting resumed in 2000, when the US Census Bureau began asking questions in its survey of American households: if children in the household were biological, stepchildren, or adopted. In 2010, the bureau recorded more than 1.5 million adopted children under eighteen years of age living with an adopted parent, and also fewer than 2.8 million step-kids. This compares to a total US estimated population of adopted children, including those eighteen and older still living in households with their parents, at slightly more than two million persons.[12] The tally does not count the likely millions of adult adoptees who are no longer living with their adoptive parents.

Estimates of the total number of adoptees in the United States have been pegged at five million or higher.[13] Though the population is large, the Census Bureau is still not tracking the larger number of post–World War II adoptees, undermining those adoptees' efforts to be counted, and thus count in policymaking at the state and national levels.

I was just one of the nonrelated, stranger adoptions. When I was born, my existence was kept hidden, except as part of the imprecise data collection. Those who knew about me included the medical staff who delivered me, the social service workers who placed me in a foster home before I was settled, and eventually the couple who adopted me. In fact, I was one of likely thousands of babies born in a hospital with a wing that cared for children of unwed mothers. I arrived in the world unplanned, and almost certainly unwanted. I would soon have my family history wiped clean.

Not every child adopted was born out of marriage, nor was every "illegitimate" child given up to the system. But out-of-wedlock sexual activity by men and women without access to family planning helped to drive this societal change. My birth mother belonged to this group of women who had to confront such difficult choices once she learned of her pregnancy. She could raise a child as a single mother without a great career, maybe have her parents care for her child, have an illegal abortion—if she could find one and potentially harm her health—or put her child up for adoption.

Data from the National Center for Health Statistics show a dramatic rise in "illegitimate births" during the twenty-five-year period from 1940 to 1965. The end result of cultural transformation captured in these numbers is adoptee adults like me. The number of births outside of marriage more than tripled from an estimated 89,500 in 1940 to 291,200 in 1965—when I arrived into this world. Five years later, in 1970, these out-of-wedlock births reached 398,700, during the same year when annual adoptions peaked in the United States. More than half were by women fifteen to nineteen years of age. My birth mother was not a teenager like this group. The number of out-of-wedlock births kept rising steadily through the 1990s, but women were less and less likely to give their children up for adoption.[14]

The Centers for Disease Control and Prevention (CDC) published a major study in 1995 on factors leading to fewer adoptions. It showed dramatic behavior changes, particularly among white women. The report to Congress on out-of-wedlock births in the United States made little reference to the complex system of adoption, except in comparison to abortion as a parental choice. Adoption laws, social stigma, and state rules restricting rights to birth records for birth mothers and adoptees were ignored in the study, as if these factors had no bearing on choices made by women. The CDC overlooked how these systems played major roles in the way medical professionals and social services encouraged outcomes, especially for white mothers like my birth mom.

Between the 1960s when I was born and the 1980s, more women of all races were deciding to parent their children as unmarried mothers. In short, there was no longer the societal stigma that once shamed them into hiding or having a child out of wedlock. In the early 1960s, 61 percent of white women who gave birth were married by the time the baby was born. This includes the so-called "shotgun marriages." By the 1980s, that proportion fell in half to 34 percent. The same pattern held for African American women in the same time frame (31 to 8 percent) and also among Hispanic women (33 to 23 percent).[15] From the 1950s onward, African American mothers and their families expressed greater tolerance of out-of-wedlock pregnancies, visible in the statistics showing fewer relinquishments of children born to single mothers. African American single mothers also faced outright segregation and lack of access to adoption services provided to white pregnant women.

The CDC found that before 1973, when the *Roe v. Wade* decision legalized abortion, about one in five premarital births to white women resulted in a child being placed for adoption for the years 1955 to 1972. I was one of those children. These were the peak years for adoption, particularly of white babies like myself. This ratio had shrunk to less than one in ten for the years 1973 to 1981. From 1982 through 1988, the figure dropped to one in thirty. Overall by 1993, a full third of births in the United States were taking place outside of marriage.[16] The out-of-wedlock child, like myself, was no longer a pariah who needed a "rebirth" through adoption. That child had become socially normal.[17] However, stigma for being born out of marriage never really went away, for adoptee and non-adoptee children.

Adoptees' place in the national consciousness remained constant over these decades of major societal change. Adoptees still make up a large and mostly silent minority in the US population. Adoption historian E. Wayne Carp rightly calls adoption a "ubiquitous institution in American society, creating invisible relationships, with biological and adoptive kin that touch far more people than we imagine."[18]

My place in the larger US adoption story arc occurred when the adoption social experiment attempted to address the many new children born outside of marriage. It occurred on the timeline when birth records for birth parents and adoptees were slowly being sealed by legislatures and when pregnancy outside of marriage remained mostly taboo for white mothers.

The mostly powerless groups of adoptees and birth mothers, who had no meaningful advocates in any political setting, were expected to play a proper and compliant role for life. The systems managing these outcomes used laws and unfounded psychological theories to keep birth mothers and their relinquished children from developing bonds later in life through access to original birth records—even long after those actions were found to have harmed adoptees and their birth mothers.

To cope with the explosion of children born outside of the institution of marriage, adoption was sold to society. It was also advertised to the parents—birth mothers and adopting parents—and to the professionals. The intermediaries marketed the delivery, care, and placement as the "best solution" for all. Social service, religious, legal, and medical groups collaborated in this effort. The Child Welfare League of America's national adoption standards from 1958 framed adoption as a healthy option. It also diminished and ignored the impacts on mostly single birth mothers, who the league believed were incapable of healthy motherhood. The guidelines stated: "Adoption is a way of providing family life for children whose natural parents are unable to perform the parental role."[19]

In 1960, the American Academy of Pediatrics published a detailed manual on the role medical professionals should play in assisting with adoptions, providing medical care, and partnering lockstep with social services, legal professionals, mental health specialists, religious organizations, and other stakeholders. The manual notes, "Adoption is intimately connected with the problem of the unmarried mother." It further recommends, "the best solution for the unmarried mother is to place her child for adoption. . . ." The growing number of children also troubled the nation's pediatric professionals, who cited with alarm that "the number of children born out of wedlock seems to be increasing ever more rapidly than the total birth rate of the United States."[20]

Through the institution of adoption, a child would be given emotional stability and, as Melosh calls it, "improved life chances afforded by growing up in a two-parent family." This also allowed the adoptive parents to recoup the losses of their infertility. The social workers who promoted the nation's flourishing adoption practices prescribed it to adoptive mothers and especially to single pregnant women, helping to strengthen postwar morality, sexual mores, and conformity.

Social workers were the institution's strongest supporters, who saw themselves as the professionals who safeguarded the interest of the children and the interest of the single pregnant women. Many adoptee-rights and birth mother advocates have criticized social workers' controversial role promoting adoption and the methods and tactics they used in the decades following World War II. Examples of how these hundreds of thousands of negotiations took place can be found in Melosh's summary of adoption in the state of Delaware in her book *Strangers and Kin*.

Melosh is mostly sympathetic to social workers, unlike the more critical adoptee-rights advocate Jean Paton, who herself was a social worker but who often found their actions over decades harmful to adoptees. As Melosh describes one case, "This social worker intervened forcefully. . . . She used her position to exert considerable pressure on a client who was rendered vulnerable by her youth, her troubled family situation, and her pregnancy." The answer suggested to a generation of single, and mostly white, pregnant women was to relinquish one's infant for adoption, supposedly in the interest of both the mother and the child. Melosh concludes the "best solution" that emerged had the widest public support from the late 1940s through 1970.[21]

Social workers, as a newly emerged professional class, embraced views that illicit sex represented a form of mental pathology, particularly among white women.[22] Increasingly after World War II, social workers observed the rise of pregnancy out of marriage for "the nice girl next door," as one 1940s maternity-home social worker called them. Social workers that decade began turning to psychiatry to explain the rise of middle-class teenage girls and young women who turned to help at maternity homes for single mothers. Rather than viewing these expecting mothers as "'delinquents, moral defectives, or prostitutes,' social workers diagnosed them as neurotic." Increasingly, the solution to these alleged neuroses was promoting adoption to pregnant, young women.[23]

The medical establishment staunchly supported the social workers as well. The American Academy of Pediatrics outlined in 1960 that adoption should be recommended to the single mother and her out-of-wedlock child. The group candidly agreed with its peers that adoption provided the best choice. "The most suitable plan for the unmarried mother has been found, in most instances, to be the relinquishment of the child so that it may be placed in adoption," the group opined. "A child kept by the mother may suffer from lack of support that a father, family, and other relationships provide."[24]

The impact of the pressure from medical and social work professionals, as well as from society, family, churches, and peers was profound. For example, in 1965, the year of my birth, the Illinois Department of Public Health counted 205,904 live births. The same year, vital-records keepers in Illinois recorded 8,046 adoptions—a jump from the 7,791 in 1964. The figure is a staggering number of relinquished children relative to all live births. That means of all recorded births in Illinois the same year I was born, one in every twenty-six children born was officially an adoptee, or nearly 4 percent of all new infants. A year later, in 1966, the state would record 8,552 adoptions among all newborn children in its vital-records registry.[25]

Melosh also highlights how stereotypes from society and the mental health field in postwar America unfairly labeled women who had out-of-wedlock kids. They were "deemed neurotic—as manifesting a disordered femininity." They were "bad women, their sexual transgressions exposed by pregnancy." In the postwar decades, medical practices and societal attitudes also restricted women's access to safe and reliable birth control. In the 1950s and 1960s, the limited promotion of sex education to young people and their ensuing guilt about sexual activity also inhibited many young people from using contraception.[26]

One of the most famous women who has publicly shared her story as a birth mother, Joni Mitchell, described the harsh world she faced the same year I was born in Detroit. She experienced a similar situation to my birth mother in Canada, just 230 miles away in Toronto. In a 2013 interview with the CBC, she described her experience as an impoverished twenty-one-year-old artist, relinquishing her daughter, Joan Anderson, at Toronto General Hospital. She called the facility a prison. With no easy access to birth control like the pill and no parental support, she said society offered almost no promise to her raising her daughter alone. "It was the dark ages then for women," said Mitchell. "I was a criminal. I was a fallen woman. It was a very difficult situation."[27]

The writer Ann Fessler profiles the stigma of the years before the early 1970s in her 2006 oral and social history called *The Girls Who*

Went Away: The Hidden History of Women Who Surrendered Children for Adoption in the Decades Before Roe v. Wade. It examines the decisions and circumstances of women, before the *Roe v. Wade* decision, who gave up children for adoption. "Caught in the middle, single pregnant women were shunned by family and friends, evicted from schools, sent away to maternity homes to have their children alone, and often treated with cold contempt by doctors, nurses, and clergy," she writes.

According to Fessler, from the late 1940s through the early 1970s, it was common knowledge that a young woman—a white woman—in high school or college would disappear for many months and then return. "If she returned, she most likely did not come back with her baby but with a story of a sick aunt or an illness that had kept her out of school." People did not question these accounts, and they put emotional distance between themselves and the disappearing women. Fessler argues that women were made to feel they had to preserve their reputation and save themselves and their offspring from a life of shame. According to one mother of this era interviewed by Fessler: "This was in that period of time when there wasn't much worse that a girl could do. They almost treated you like you had committed murder or something."[28]

Fessler also shows the profound inequity of the prevailing attitudes for mothers, not the many nameless fathers. "According to the prevailing double standard, the young man who was equally responsible for the pregnancy was not condemned for his actions," she writes. "It was her fault, not their fault that she got pregnant."[29]

The men who impregnated birth mothers, like my respected ROTC and dentist birth father, escaped societal scorn. Women had to accept the brand of mental illness and change. According to this view, reforming the mentally ill mother could occur with the lifelong separation from her birth child, which would give the woman a chance to fulfill her desired identity as a woman by raising her legitimate children and by raising a family. The burgeoning adoption market provided the "system" through which this idea was sustained—a two-part solution to a problem of societal change.

Social workers during these decades viewed these unplanned pregnancies as symptomatic of social or psychological pathology. According to Melosh, social work professionals during the boom years of adoption believed that illegitimacy posed huge burdens on children and limited their chances in life. They also rejected the idea that out-of-wedlock births ruined a young woman's chances in life.

This marked a radical transformation to how social workers conceived of their work supporting young pregnant women. Melosh notes that in the 1920s and 1930s, social workers strongly believed that keeping a child together with his or her parent provided the greatest benefit to the child. One prominent report on adoption from the Welfare Council of New York in 1948 still saw adoption as an ultimate last resort, not a recommended practice. The group noted, "No child should be given up by his natural parent hastily under press of circumstances, without thoughtful scrutiny of these circumstances by responsible and experienced authorities to make sure that there is no other solution offering equal or better possibilities for his future."[30]

That viewpoint switched dramatically by the 1950s and 1960s, in response to demography and growing demands to find homes for the hundreds of thousands of babies born out of marriage—toddlers just like me. My cohort of hundreds of thousands of fellow adoptees came into the world as unplanned infants, with a father who denied paternity, and a mother unable to, or strongly urged not to, raise us. Though babies like me were not called bastards in any of the literature of the era, they were treated with the stain and stigma still associated with the name.

The Child Welfare League of America's 1960 guidelines for assisting unmarried parents characterized US society as unable to accept parenthood out of marriage. It represented "a specific form of social dysfunctioning" that would harm the parent and child. Illegitimate children were perceived as lacking "protection of his status in society," and single mothers would be denied social acceptance, economic opportunities, and familial support.[31] Adoption theoretically could remove this stigma by placing the child with new parents.

For social workers from the 1950s through the 1970s, adoption also offered the means to redeem the mothers. It let them erase the "mistake" and gave them a second chance to succeed within the accepted boundaries of the American dream that limited sex and parenting to the bonds of marriage. They played a key role in facilitating the adoptions that transferred the children from the birth mother to the expecting adoptive parents. My life history, as the so-called mistake, set me on a life trajectory determined by these national practices impacting millions of mothers and children. It was my fate, but one where my birth mother's role was largely shaped by societal, professional, familial, and religious pressures.

An adoption policy planning meeting of social workers, convened by the US Children's Bureau in 1958, highlighted the vulnerable nature of single, pregnant women and how their profession could best help them. The group mostly framed that support as guiding the expecting mothers through the relinquishment of their infants for adoption. "It is essential that the social worker protect the parent rights of the natural parents and make known to them the implications within surrender of their child," the panel wrote. "The child welfare worker deals with the severance of emotionally-laden ties. Through deep understanding and skillful handling, the parent and child are less likely to be damaged."[32]

The stories of how young women brought their children to term and then said goodbye are not happy ones. Having a child, under extremely stressful situations and being forced to hide a pregnancy, is a traumatic event. Run DMC rapper Darryl McDaniels, an adoptee born a year before me in May 1964, only learned when he was thirty-six years old that he was adopted. In response to that discovery, he created one of the few multimedia narratives of a birth mother's painful experience of having her child in a maternity ward, and then having the baby taken for adoption. "She was just a young girl in her youth, and her parents tried real hard to hide the truth," sings McDaniels.

The 2006 song and video, covering Harry Chapin's *Just Like Me*, with fellow adoptee and singer-songwriter Sarah McLachlan, presents one of the few dramatized portrayals of how such an event leaves a lasting and lifelong impression on a birth mother. When I saw the video for the first time in 2016, I felt a visceral connection to McDaniels's and his birth mother's story. She was just like my birth mother, and he was just like me. I smiled and thought: at last, someone had finally shown to a wider audience how hundreds of thousands of these births took place. Finally, someone had the courage to show what this meant for these women and children, who were separated because of the widely accepted view that relinquishing an illegitimate child would be the "most suitable plan."

Chapter 3

A Place for Unwed Mothers

Once remove the stigma from unmarried motherhood and the necessity for such "rescue" work would, of course, quite vanish away. The problem would become one purely of morals and religion, with no social implications at all aside from the support of the child involved. Such a state of affairs will hardly come about in the United States in our lifetime, if ever.

—Otto Wilson, Robert South Barrett, and the
National Florence Crittenton Mission, 1933

My birth mother never told me where she had to live in a self-imposed exile in a Detroit suburb, in a home that would house pregnant, single white women. I later learned the location of my birth mother's maternity home through my records I finally received from Michigan, decades after I first asked for the information. The home was located in the suburbs. From the outside, nothing could have been more middle-class and suburban. Inside lived a single pregnant woman, and likely others before and after, who made life-changing decisions. Her pregnancy ended when she delivered me at Crittenton General Hospital. The facility served as a hospital and a temporary home for single women like her, where dozens of pregnant women lived before delivering their children.

My birthplace, Crittenton General Hospital, was one of the flagship facilities created by the National Florence Crittenton Mission, a philanthropic organization that eventually played one of the most important roles in the country's bold new experiment in expanding adoption. Founded by a wealthy New York druggist, Charles N. Crittenton, the mission quickly grew from its street-ministry grassroots serving prostitutes in New York in 1883. It was incorporated by Congress in 1898, and by 1909 it had established seventy homes across the country, just twenty-six years after its founding by the millionaire businessman.

In addition to helping prostitutes, the mission served vulnerable and victimized women as well as women who were pregnant out of marriage. It gave them shelter and medical care. In the cities where it sprang up, Crittenton homes provided safe places for single mothers to raise their infants and receive vocational education in remedial women's occupations to help rebuild their lives. By the early 1900s, it was providing training to the new profession of social workers and working to destigmatize single motherhood to the public. The mission and its homes would soon play much larger roles.

In the 1920s, Crittenton's official policy opposed separating a mother and child for adoption. The organization strongly believed that children should be kept with their birth mothers as the best possible outcome for both.[1] Many other Christian charities serving the same population shared this view. They offered employment and life skills for single mothers and supported keeping mothers and their children together. During the 1920s, the Crittenton mission matured into a modern social service organization that minimized its evangelical activities while promoting professional standards.

In 1943, the national organization began to break from its long-cherished original mission of keeping mothers and children together. It adopted standards for case-planning for each resident and started working with local adoption agencies.[2] This coincided with larger national trends, where homes came under the control of professional social workers.

Historian Regina Kunzel, in her study of the rise of social workers and maternity homes in the first half of the twentieth century, writes that the National Florence Crittenton Mission faced "enormous pressure from social workers" and from individual Crittenton homes to end their long policy of keeping mothers and children together. Some Crittenton officers complained that the placing of babies for adoption was "no longer doing Florence Crittenton work." But by the 1940s, "supported by the commitment of social workers to adoption, most homes were routinely arranging for the adoption of babies."[3] In 1947, the national mission finally surrendered its policy of keeping mother and child together, marking a new era: the victory of the professional ethos of social workers over the founding ideals of the organization's original evangelical women reformers.

With its original mission abandoned by the late 1950s and early 1960s, the organization became a major American institution in the promotion of adoption for mostly single, white mothers. Young women who stayed at these facilities were strongly encouraged to relinquish their children to adoption agencies rather than keep their infants, at the urging of social workers, family members, faith-based groups, and churches. The mission had transformed into an adoption-placement service from a service group dedicated to the union of single mothers and their kids.

Starting in 1950, the National Florence Crittenton Mission organization also created the Florence Crittenton Home Association, to serve as a clearinghouse for the dozens of homes nationwide. In 1956, the organization launched the Florence Crittenton League, which offered casework and adoption services—continuing the break from the agency's original mission. In 1960, the home's association changed its name to Florence Crittenton Association of America and its homes were staffed by professionally trained social workers. Many of those social workers strongly encouraged adoption as the best possible choice for single women boarders.

"Maternity homes of the 1950s and 1960s were, to a great extent, a place to sequester pregnant girls until they could give birth and surrender their child for adoption," writes author Anne Fessler of Florence Crittenton and other maternity homes of the era. "Though maternity homes were the only place a girl in trouble could turn for help outside of her family, by the 1950s they best served her interest if her interest was in giving her child up for adoption at the end of her stay."[4]

A 1952 Crittenton brochure states, "The mother is under no compulsion, either to leave her baby with us, or to take him with her. There is no priority for either." But the pamphlet also states, "although the mother should perhaps make the choice, not always is she well qualified to make this last decision."[5] Those who were qualified to make the decisions were social workers and maternity staff at the homes.

In her book *The Girls Who Went Away*, Fessler has meticulously profiled many of the tens of thousands of single women who lived in maternity homes, including in the Crittenton facilities in dozens of cities across the country. They gave up their children during the period often called the "Baby Scoop Era." The term is commonly used today by those familiar with adoption history. However, it means little to the general public, and it does not accurately describe a nationwide system organized by the country's medical and social work professionals to separate millions of children from their natural families through legal adoption over three decades.

From her interviews, Fessler concludes maternity home staff used tactics "that sometimes crossed the line from persuasion to outright coercion."[6] Some young women took assumed names during their weeks and months away. Some boarders only used first names and were encouraged by staff to not communicate with each other after they were discharged. In many homes, the attending staff strictly limited access from the outside. All mail, visitors, and calls were controlled and monitored by the staff.[7] Women were denied visitation with boyfriends, personal friends, and family. In some cases, birth mothers were deliberately misled about their rights to keep their infants and services available to them.

Aside from the Crittenton run facilities, the Salvation Army and the National Conference of Catholic Charities also ran similar homes. Writer Kathryn Joyce, who has profiled the role of US evangelical Christians in the global adoption industry, called the coercion from the Baby Scoop Era "brutal and unapologetic."[8] She compares the hundreds of dormitory-like facilities to "wage homes," where outcast women were required to do domestic labor to pay for their keep. These closely resembled the often brutal and, at-times, lethal Magdalene Laundry asylums in Ireland for so-called "fallen women," which ran from the late 1700s to 1996.[9]

"They wanted to keep us scared to death," said birth mother Karen Wilson-Buterbaugh, a former seventeen-year-old mother who stayed in a Florence Crittenton maternity home in Silver Springs, Maryland. Wilson-Buterbaugh founded the Baby Scoop Era Initiative to document adoptions from the late 1940s through 1973. Summarizing that era of adoption promotion, she writes, "It was so traumatizing that many mothers didn't remember the births."[10]

The hospital of my birth, Crittenton General Hospital in Detroit, succeeded two earlier Crittenton hospitals and homes. Its history closely tracked the national changes in the parent organization. The first Crittenton home in Detroit opened in 1897 over a store on what is now Broadway Avenue, to serve vulnerable single and pregnant women. The operation expanded and moved to a Victorian mansion on Brush Street, also in downtown Detroit. In six years, it had already outgrown its capacity. The organization then opened the Florence Crittenton Hospital on East Elizabeth Street in Detroit, which could hold up to thirty women at any time. The new hospital exemplified Crittenton's changing mission as a combined hospital and maternity home.[11] Like its predecessor, it too could not keep pace with demand for its service. By

1927, the hospital had outgrown its capacity to meet the need to serve vulnerable women.

The local mission bought new property and raised funds to open an even larger facility. The new Florence Crittenton Home and Hospital opened in 1929 at 1554 Tuxedo Avenue, about three miles from downtown Detroit. It was the largest Crittenton home and hospital in the country when it opened its doors. Two of the facility's wings were devoted to the care of the single, pregnant women and their infants. By the early 1930s, those two wings already had 115 dormitory beds, 100 cribs, 40 bassinets, and a nursery that served this revolving population.[12]

According to the mission's records, the hospital supplemented its operational costs with a third wing. It offered medical care mostly to lower-income women and children. The third wing was separated from the two wings for the unwed women, such as patients like my birth mother. The public wing also focused on maternal care and general surgery.[13]

By 1950, the hospital made plans to change again, to have many of the single boarding mothers stay in a separate maternity facility called the Florence Crittenton Maternity Home, located at 11850 Woodrow Wilson. That facility was built and opened in 1954. It was less than half a block from the hospital, which by that year called itself Crittenton General Hospital. The hospital and maternity home also were connected by a little-known service tunnel that has achieved urban legend status among some Crittenton adoptees of Detroit. The home itself could accommodate up to sixty young women, who had semi-private rooms. The home offered them class instruction, an auditorium, a dining facility, and even a beauty shop, according to the mission's records.

"Every effort was made to maintain a homelike atmosphere for the patient," according to the official records.[14] In reality, the young women were cut off from family and friends, and were faced with one of the most momentous decisions of their lives without any social networks to support them. In many cases, they would be pressured by social workers, maternity staff, and medical professionals to relinquish their infant children to adoption. Many mothers during this era reported being forced to sign their relinquishment documents while still under the influence of drugs following their birth or during post-labor recovery.[15] In my case, my birth mother signed the relinquishment papers nearly three weeks after my birth, after I had experienced more intensive care at Detroit's Children's Hospital because of health complications.

Crittenton General Hospital was the largest of all Crittenton facilities in the country by the early 1950s. In some cities like Boston, Crittenton homes and hospitals also shared the same roof. By that time, Crittenton maternity homes and hospitals had become way stations. Pregnant women from their teens to their early to mid-twenties stayed out the last days, weeks, or months of their pregnancy.

By the 1950s and 1960s, many Crittenton homes and other similar maternity facilities were transformed from being homes to "wayward young mothers" to being secret shelters where embarrassed middle-class parents could hide their daughters during their pregnancy. In those homes, young expecting mothers were strongly pressured into placing their children for adoption. Adoption historian Barbara Melosh describes how facilities that once promoted supporting and rehabilitating young expecting mothers began pushing adoption as a means to reform the mother and their children.[16] More than 80 percent of young women who were served at these homes surrendered their children to the adoption agencies, which placed the infants with adoptive families like my own.[17]

After Detroit's Crittenton Home opened in 1954, Crittenton General Hospital used only one of its three wings for "unwed mothers," like my birth mother. Many but not all of the single women temporarily stayed at the maternity home next door. I was born in that wing dedicated to single women, most of whom would never see their children again. There was also a nursery to care for babies. The rest of the hospital's 194 beds provided private hospital care, including obstetrics, surgery, and pediatric services.

The year I was born, in 1965, the median length of stay for mothers at all Crittenton hospitals and homes was eighty-seven days, according to a national study conducted by the parent organization. More than eight in ten women stayed in maternity homes, and the remaining groups were served by other types of shelter, like group and foster homes.[18] In my birth mother's case, she likely spent most of her pregnancy away from the hospital, even though the facility had living facilities for similar pregnant women.

Crittenton General Hospital also served as a training facility for residents, in addition to being a maternity home and hospital that supported the adoption of relinquished babies. It had provided medical training since its founding in 1929. In my case, the obstetrician who delivered me was completing his first obstetrics residency in the United States. He came from overseas, like many other doctors who arrived in the United States and were employed to serve low-income and high-needs patients in inner-urban and rural hospitals.

The hospital itself moved to the Detroit suburbs in 1967, where a new facility was built. This was the same year as the deadly Detroit race riots that left forty-three dead and one thousand buildings burned and when white flight helped fuel the city's dramatic decline in white residents, like my birth grandparents in 1968. The new facility became known as Crittenton Hospital Rochester. The hospital formally severed ties with the parent Crittenton organization in 1971.

By that time, the Crittenton General Hospital in Detroit was too expensive to operate, due to the city's declining population and mounting expenditures. Occupancy dropped in half by 1973. The Detroit hospital permanently shuttered its doors on March 22, 1974. At the time, I was still a young boy in the St. Louis area. I was oblivious to my origins as a Detroit adoptee, who was born and then surrendered into the status of foster child at one of the nation's preeminent maternal care facilities that promoted adoption.

The original hospital in Detroit is now torn down, erased from memory—except by the thousands who were born there or who gave birth there. The former location today looks more like a war zone due to Detroit's severe economic distress and poverty.

The remaining suburban hospital in Rochester was called Crittenton Hospital Medical Center until changing its name again, in August 2017, to Ascension Crittenton Hospital.[19] The facility's current website shows no record of how the former and original Detroit facility once provided health and social services to vulnerable women and children. It offers no background on how the Detroit hospital primarily served as a maternity facility and hospital for unwed mothers and their illegitimate babies. The hospital's minimal historic communications do not acknowledge how the original Crittenton facilities in the Motor City played a pivotal role facilitating adoption in one of the country's largest cities.

The hospital's administration, as seen through its public communications, has omitted six and a half decades of its past in the hospital's official timeline through the year of my birth.[20] A short video it published linked the hospital to the original Florence Crittenton Home that opened in Detroit in 1900 for unwed pregnant women.[21] The video does not mention adoptees, illegitimate children, or pregnant single women. Through historic omission, the hospital has erased its tainted and shameful past. Unless a person knew the history of the Crittenton organization, they would never know the facility provided an important institutional response to unwanted pregnancies for the birth mothers and their relinquished children.

Today, it is as if I were never born out of wedlock and relinquished by my birth mother to an adoption agency, like thousands of other Crittenton hospital adoptees. Bastards and fallen unwed mothers, it appears, still cast shame and stigma on some medical facilities that once specialized in maternal childcare services for both stigmatized groups.

The hospital did not reply to my repeated phone and email requests for possible information on the older hospital's records concerning the number of women it served in Detroit or the number of babies like myself it may have delivered who were later adopted. It also did not answer my question why it did not mention the hospital's true origins with the Crittenton mission. In one curt email reply, the hospital staff wrote, "Unfortunately we have no historian on staff, however, the website does have a brief description of our history. . . . Good luck with your endeavor." A hospital librarian eventually sent me two photocopied stories on the hospitals dating from the 1960s and 1970s, without any information about the number of adoptees born at the Detroit facility or the number of women it served.

The exact number of adopted children born at Detroit's Crittenton hospitals and homes is not available from any other Detroit sources, including archives at the Detroit Public Library. Service and birth records may no longer be available at the Rochester hospital bearing the Crittenton name. Ultimately the hospital's new owners, Ascension Health, a Catholic-run care system, have minimized how one of its facilities had dedicated decades of service to those who became pregnant out of marriage. The shame and stigma of illegitimacy that the original founders of the Crittenton mission sought so hard to overcome for decades throughout the United States had not gone away at all in 2017, even at a hospital that still bore the Crittenton name. Illegitimacy is still, as one expert on the history of illegitimacy and bastardy, notes "the paradigmatic skeleton in the cupboard, a secret far more shameful than bankruptcy, insanity, or any crime."[22]

Unlike Detroit, some Crittenton maternity hospitals have published their records, without covering up their official history serving single pregnant women. The Crittenton Mission built the Florence Crittenton Home for unwed mothers in Peoria, Illinois, in 1937, twenty-one years after the first home was opened in the city. That medical facility resembled a mansion, like many of the Crittenton homes and hospitals in more than seventy cities. It included a full hospital wing for birthing with pre- and post-delivery rooms. Like the original Crittenton General Hospital in Detroit, it was also a facility that provided living facilities that kept pregnant women outside of public view.

The Peoria facility included nine dormitories, shower rooms, four nurseries, a sewing room, classroom, kitchen, dining room, recreation room, sick ward, laundry facilities, and more. The Peoria facility, between 1938 and April of 1965, counted more than four thousand deliveries.[23] Given the size of metro Detroit, as the fifth largest city in the United States by the late 1950s, it is safe to assume thousands more infants would have been delivered in Detroit's Crittenton hospitals and homes from 1900 through 1973.

The year I was born, the Florence Crittenton Association of America was gathering national data with the Salvation Army and the National Conference of Catholic Charities for a project funded by the US Children's Bureau. The data from the three agencies profiled the women served in their maternity homes. The findings were reported in a series of annual reports called *Unwed Mothers*. The detailed information provides a composite picture of the unwed women they served, the circumstances of their pregnancies, and their family backgrounds. The reports also reveal the overwhelming majority of women staying at Crittenton and other maternity homes chose adoption instead of keeping their kids in their family or rearing them as single mothers.[24]

Of the 1,509 women served by the Florence Crittenton Homes in 1965, 1,151 of the mothers chose adoption for their children, or 76 percent, compared to 70 percent of all three entities combined. Only thirty women staying at Crittenton homes said they would care for their child independently.[25] Of the Florence Crittenton mothers, nonwhite mothers agreed to raise their children at a rate more than three times higher than their white peers. What's more, only 5 percent of the families of white girls planned to care for their children, compared to 22 percent for nonwhites—revealing a high level of shame that illegitimate children posed to white families. My birth family clearly was among the majority that shunned having an illegitimate baby raised in its midst.[26]

The vast majority of the mothers served by Crittenton facilities were single—95 percent were unmarried. Many were also young and had limited post-secondary education. As a group, more than four in ten of all mothers served in 1965 had not finished high school. My birth mother was among the 36 percent who had a high school diploma. Just 3 percent of women served had completed college, indicating the problem of illegitimacy was less prevalent in more affluent households. Half of these mothers were students. The overwhelming majority served by all maternal care agencies in the study were young—about seven in ten were twenty-one years of age and younger. My birth mother was among the 19 percent who were between twenty-one and twenty-nine years of age.[27]

This was also a financially vulnerable group. Only 33 percent of the mothers had jobs, while 62 percent relied on their parents financially. Their financial dependence on their parents was likely a major factor in the decision to relinquish their infants. The data from all of the birth homes show that most of the mothers did not come from broken homes. Of those interviewed, two-thirds said their parents were still living together, signaling they came from two-parent households.[28] My birth mother matched that national trend.

In one key way, my experience stood out from the typical mother served by Crittenton and other agencies. Of the alleged fathers, a third were students and one-fifth were unemployed. Only 4 percent were reportedly professional, like my dentist-resident birth father. This fact, combined with my birth mother being older than most of the young mothers—twenty-four years of age—made my birth circumstances more of an outlier experience.

Today adoptees, who are now adults like me, are seeking answers to their life stories that began at the Crittenton homes and hospitals. There are thousands of adoptees like me who have, over recent years, posted information on online adoptee-search websites, referencing their birth at this hospital, all seeking the same information about their lineage, biological parents, and medical history.

I read many of these postings on a website called the Florence Crittenton Home Reunion Registry. (It was still functional in 2016.) It is dedicated to Crittenton babies, written by adoptees born in the years just before and after me.[29] All are still searching for their birth parents because they are denied access to records by the State of Michigan. A man born in 1963 at Detroit Crittenton Hospital wrote one post I found in 2015. His mother was from Scotland, and his father backed out of marrying the mother—similar to my own story. "Looking for birth parents, siblings, or other family," he wrote. "Interested in obtaining medical info, heritage."

The Crittenton homes and hospitals and other maternity homes that served single pregnant women have even greater meaning for the hundreds of thousands of women who passed through their doors. Stories of what happened at the nation's maternity homes and hospitals can be found in personal narratives of birth mothers and in the oral histories that Fessler captured in her 2006 book. Some women who relinquished their children have published their own stories online. One personal narrative I found by Karen Wilson-Buterbaugh describes her pregnancy and giving up her daughter on July 1, 1966, a little more than a year after I was placed for adoption.[30]

My birth mother was twenty-four years old when I was conceived and born. She was more mature than Wilson-Buterbaugh. However, Wilson-Buterbaugh's account as a pregnant seventeen-year-old has many similarities to the maternity home experiences of my birth mother and thousands of other single mothers.

After she learned of her pregnancy, Wilson-Buterbaugh left her family and went into hiding in Silver Springs, Maryland, at a maternity house she describes as a "shame-filled prison." That Florence Crittenton home was among dozens throughout the country offering a similar sanctuary and service. From what I have heard, my birth mother's home in suburban Detroit, was a happier place, with kids and a nice couple. Though not a Crittenton maternity home, it filled the same role.

Wilson-Buterbaugh writes that most women her age did not know what a home for unwed mothers was until they were left at their door, suitcase in hand. She calls the experience a form of "thought reform" and "brainwashing." She describes burdens of parental pressure and coercion by social workers, who would communicate that the expecting mothers would have to pay for their hospital bills, doctor's fees, and foster-care costs. The eventual delivery of her daughter proved especially lonely and alienating:

> I was taken to George Washington University Hospital by cab and told to walk in and give my name and tell them I was from the maternity home. . . . I was admitted and prepared to give birth. I was given so many drugs I remember very little of labor and nothing at all of the delivery. My daughter, Michelle Renee, was born the next morning at 2:30 a.m. . . . That same morning she and I rode together back to the maternity home in a taxi. We stayed together in the post partum ward for ten days. My baby girl was brought to me for each daytime feeding and then was returned to the 'nursery' to be cared for by the nurses over night along with the other babies. At any given time, there were about ten to twelve new moms in the ward.[31]

I have no records that illustrate how I was cared for during the first weeks of my life. My birth mother has not shared any stories about precisely how long I remained in her care when I was born. I know it was less than three weeks. To this day, I do not know if I received the needed maternal health benefit of drinking breast milk and the immediate physical affection of being held in my birth mother's arms. Both are proven conclusively as having lasting, lifetime health benefits for the infant and his or her healthy development.[32]

In 2016, I found the gynecologist who delivered me at Crittenton General Hospital. He agreed to speak with me after I sent him copies of my records that showed his name in my medical records, including my original birth certificate. I think this unusual request from a former baby he once delivered brought back memories. It is not often former infants reach out to the doctors and nurses who brought them from the womb into the world—particularly adopted ones.

When we spoke, he was experiencing medical issues but still eager to share a story about his residency in obstetrics. He provided a brief history of the hospital and its namesake. He described the passion of the founder, Charles Crittenton, to help single pregnant women. When we conversed, he described that many single, pregnant women stayed at the adjacent Florence Crittenton Home.

The now-retired doctor said the hospital employed residents from the University of Michigan Medical School and Wayne County General Hospital. Both institutions had first-rate medical experts, he said. He indicated that two attending physicians were always available for consultation at the hospital. Experts in diabetes, heart disease, and problem pregnancies also were always available for consultation and case management.

Data collected in 1965, the year of my birth, indicate the Crittenton facilities provided quality prenatal and maternal care. Credit should be given to specialists like the gynecologist who delivered me and treated my birth mother. The Florence Crittenton Association of America reported for 1965 that their facilities had fewer birth complications and loss of life than children nationally, which the group credited to its prenatal care services. Crittenton facilities counted fourteen infant deaths, or nine per one thousand.[33] For the same year in the United States, infant mortality was nearly twenty-five per one thousand births,[34] indicating that the women served by the homes received additional health benefits that helped the new children.

My birth doctor also said up to twenty-five pregnant women boarded at the maternity house—the number according to the records is up to sixty—and that other women had limited stays at the hospital. The doctor said when I was born, federal systems like Medicaid and Medicare were not available to provide financial support for the birth of children. The two federal entitlement programs that provide health-care assistance were created by legislation after my birth and signed into law in July 1965.

The former Crittenton medical resident said many young, pregnant women who gave birth in the hospital also had worked in the hospital kitchen. He remembered that many of the pregnant women lived next door at the Florence Crittenton Home. He was not sure how the mostly older teenage women paid for the costs of their hospital stays. He suggested the parents covered the costs or the women themselves paid their bills by working as part of their hidden, maternal stays. Data collected by the Florence Crittenton Association of America in my birth year, 1965, found that 73 percent of the 1,108 mothers surveyed had their maternity stay and services paid by their families, compared to 18 percent receiving public assistance. Their lack of financial independence likely played a major role in their decisions for relinquishment.[35]

Wilson-Buterbaugh's experience and the service environment at Detroit's Florence Crittenton Home and Crittenton General Hospital, where I was born, highlight similarities found in Australia and Ireland. In both countries, the Catholic Church played a major and, at times, coercive role in these nation's adoption practices. The controversial role of the Catholic Church in Ireland's recent national adoption practices is more well-known in the United States largely because of the acclaimed 2013 film *Philomena*.

The movie stars Dame Judi Dench as Philomena Lee, a former young, unwed mother now in her later years looking for her adopted son, and Steve Coogan as Martin Sixsmith, the author of the original book of the same name who helped her in her journey. In brutally painful terms, the film portrays how a Catholic-run adoption system in Ireland forced young pregnant girls, usually orphans or wards of Catholic homes, to give up their kids, who were sold to wealthy American parents. The film also alludes to young mothers who died in childbirth, along with their babies, at these places—a national scandal in Ireland to this day. In this true story, the mother who surrendered her child eventually discovers he was raised in the United States as Michael Hess, and died of HIV/AIDS before she could reunite with him more than fifty years after his birth.

Australia experienced a similar story that involved some of the nearly 150,000 babies who were adopted between 1951 and 1975.[36] The Catholic Church in Australia even issued a formal apology for its role in strong-arming young women to relinquish their children for adoption.[37] A number of these children, pegged in the thousands, reportedly were coercively taken from unmarried, mostly teenage mothers and given to childless married couples as adoptees.

The government of Australia released a detailed 2010 report that focused on abusive practices that led young women to surrendering kids out of marriage. The report notes: "Contrary to the popular myth that 'time heals all wounds,' one theme that was fairly consistent across the different studies and methodologies reviewed here was the notion that the pain and distress of their experience of adoption did not just 'go away' with the passage of time." All but one of Australia's governments and territories have issued public apologies for adoptions that occurred in the three decades after World War II.

Australian Prime Minister Julia Gillard, in 2013, acknowledged the problems and the new research that found flaws in past adoptive practices—similar to those in the United States. She apologized to the thousands of birth mothers who gave up their children unwillingly. The Australian leader called it a "shameful" policy that had created "a legacy of pain."

Dan Rather, in an investigate report broadcast in May 2012 called "Adopted or Abducted," found a detailed pattern of coercive tactics by US Catholic charities that were integral to the placement of adoptees.[38] Rather notes: "Go back and read the literature from the time and you'll see pamphlets like this one titled, 'When you've made a mistake: advice for unwed mothers.' Inside there are quotes like, 'If a couple is waiting for your baby to come along, don't stand in the baby's way. Give him up to a normal family life.' The booklet, from 1968, also lists page after page of maternity homes across the country. Many, but not all publications from the time are courtesy of groups associated with the Catholic Church."

My birth mother and her family were not Catholic or even regular churchgoing people. My birth mother never told me how her parents—my now-deceased biological grandparents—reacted to her pregnancy. Evidence from research of this era shows there was tremendous stigmatization and sexism. I have heard some stories from sources—whose identity I will not share—that my birth grandparents likely supported the decision to have me given up for adoption. If true, this means they supported the system that hid my mother and turned the experience for her into a taboo topic. This means they were willing to allow their own grandchild to disappear from their family network and never be seen again. It is hard for anyone who is adopted to know that one's own family would allow you to be given away to government agencies and unknown strangers, never to be seen again.

The oral-history interviews Fessler assembled with women who gave up children reveals that parental shame played a dominant role in the system that allowed for the placement of out-of-wedlock babies with adoption intermediaries. Parents feared being ruined in the public's eyes more than they cared about the well-being of their daughters and their own future grandchildren in the hands of complete strangers.

Fessler writes, "The parents' fears of being ostracized from their community or church ultimately led them to treat their daughters in precisely the same manner that they feared the neighbors would treat them."[39] Both of my biological grandparents on my birth mother's side of the family are dead. I will never know how strongly they supported my adoption placement, or how they may have been ashamed of being parents of a young woman who had sex out of marriage.

However, my grandfather intervened in his own way and confronted my birth father in person before my birth father was married to his future wife in late November 1964. This took place while my birth mother was pregnant, and I was developing in her womb. It was not a pleasant exchange, and my grandfather told me my birth father adamantly denied his paternity during the brief dust up.

I can understand from my own story why my birth mother never wanted to discuss this gut-wrenching story with me. She never volunteered the details, and I never pressed her for these intensely personal memories. The record of this event eventually will go with her to her final resting place. Only she will ever know what happened with the social workers who met with her. Only she knows the tales of the other young mothers where she stayed and how she was treated by doctors and nurses who were present at my delivery.

After I was born and then given away as a foster child to an adoption agency, my birth mother had to move on with her life. She never knew what happened to me until that fateful early spring day in April 1989 when she found a note under her door from a young man that said, "I am your son. I would like to meet you."

Chapter 4

How Scott Became Martin: A Life Told in Records

It is felt that Martin feels quite secure with his adoptive family and that they in return are quite pleased with him. . . . We are recommending that final order be entered on this child and that his name become legally Martin Rudolf Brueggemann.

—Caseworker Notes, Adoption Records of Rudy Owens, 1966

Everyone who has been involved in the American adoption system has been aware of the underlying issues of secrecy that has shrouded it from the 1940s to the present. The list of parties is far-reaching. Those most intimately aware of secrecy have been adoptive families, adoptees, and birth parents. Beyond the families, participants also included the state agencies and workers managing adoptions and records. Other participants were public health agencies, probate courts, the lawmakers who passed legislation restricting records for adoptees and birth parents, the homes for pregnant birth mothers, and the hospitals and health professionals who delivered and cared for hundreds of thousands of young children.

This is the eight-hundred-pound gorilla in the room that to this day is largely ignored, except by those trying to reform regressive state adoption laws. Adoption historian E. Wayne Carp describes how secrecy creates tensions in every stage of adoption. "Everyone involved in adoption must confront at one time or another questions about secrecy and disclosure," he writes.[1]

The story of how I was changed from one person with a past, to one without legal access to any records of my family origins, begins in a specific location. In my case, as with many other adoptees, my birthplace represents an important piece in the story of how American adoption created a new person, wiped clean of one's history.

I was born in Detroit's Crittenton General Hospital, the successor to the first two Florence Crittenton Homes that opened in the Motor City starting in 1900. The hospital first opened its doors to single pregnant mothers in 1929, when the organization's mission intended to keep mothers and children together. When I was born, it still served single, pregnant women in the Detroit area like my birth mother. Up to sixty young pregnant mothers at any given time stayed at the adjacent Florence Crittenton Home. In 1965, one of the hospital's three wings was dedicated to serving those patients. By the 1960s, the facility was the largest National Florence Crittenton Mission hospital and home complex in the country, serving the needs of single mothers. By this time, the hospital and home had become one of dozens of maternal care institutions that facilitated the adoption for infants born by the single and vulnerable women the mission served.

Health facilities like Crittenton General Hospital, and its affiliated Florence Crittenton Home, served as an official crossroads where different players in the expanding adoption system intersected. These forces made out-of-wedlock births medically safe for birth mothers and their children. It was also where mothers often said farewell to their relinquished sons and daughters, in some cases forever, and the state and its proxies assumed control of each child's destiny.

In 2016 I interviewed the long-retired doctor who delivered me at this one-of-a-kind hospital. The former obstetrician told me all of the pregnant women he cared for and who passed through the hospital's doors received excellent medical care from competent doctors and nurses, social service supports, and the best possible treatment available. He said he and his fellow residents, along with attending nurses and other birth care specialists, were well-trained and well-supervised by physicians who managed the care of single pregnant women like my birth mother. A birth mother's status as a shamed woman, he added, had no influence on that medical care.

The growing national adoption system could not have worked without the quiet but critical involvement of the US medical establishment. They delivered the babies, cared for the women giving birth, and approved adoption placements of children who were "relinquished" to the adoption agencies by birth mothers with states' formal legal blessings. Though the medical staff did not manage the adoption cases or set state policies for records once a child was relinquished, national medical groups like the American Academy of Pediatrics promoted adoption as the "best solution" for single white women and played a central role in nearly every safe and legal adoption placement. In hospitals and clinics, they did their jobs as competent professionals, like my delivering obstetrician. In my adoption, multiple doctors delivered me, provided medical checks before I was placed for adoption, and did follow-up medical screening—all meticulously documented in my adoption file records.

At Crittenton General Hospital and other medical facilities that handled deliveries, the medical and social service professionals also played complementary roles in a widely expanding national system to address a perceived social problem of rising rates of children born by single women. My review of the research on adoption, and its legal and medical history, did not unearth any reported peer-reviewed study or memoirs of such practitioners ever discussing their personal views on the women they served or the adoption system they supported for decades. These professionals have provided no individual insights into their central role in promoting adoption as the preferred option for single mothers or in creating critical vital and medical records for infants who were about to have their identities changed. What is clear is that without the specialists in both fields performing their roles daily, the adoption system could not have worked.

Professionally the pediatricians and social workers in the late 1950s and early 1960s described a near harmonious and symbiotic partnership of their professions in the rapidly expanding enterprise of American adoption. They each recommended close collaboration to promote the health of the mother and child, but also the preferred outcome, notably the "best solution" of having a single white mother relinquish her child to address the surging demand of families seeking white infants.[2]

A panel of social welfare and adoption experts convened by the US Children's Bureau in 1958 noted, "Doctors and attorneys in addition to giving direct services should be used as consultants to the [adoption] agency and members of agency boards and special committees." The bureau's panel of experts wrote, "Prompt service should be given to the unmarried mother and a good working relationship established with doctors, nurses, hospital administrators, teachers, ministers, and other individuals who are in a key position to refer her to the [adoption] agency for service."[3]

The American Academy of Pediatrics in 1960 outlined the central role of medical professionals in all legal adoptions. The group described physicians as "a necessary participant in the total evaluation of the child," before an adoption could be completed. This included gathering the mother's family medical and genetic history, keeping a record of the mother's health during pregnancy, tracking the child's health history after birth, and providing physical exams and lab tests. The group claimed doctors were the "only professional worker who can assess the child's condition."[4] In its recommendations on the successful placement of relinquished infants to prospective adoptive families, the national group noted that physicians should play a central role in the final decision-making, in partnership with adoption-agency staff, psychologists, and psychiatrists.[5]

The Children's Bureau also summarized the central role of doctors in the institution of adoption by the late 1950s, when tens of thousands of single women already were being urged and pressured into relinquishing their newborn children. "For the child whose good start in life depends on the physician, he provides or arranges for periodic diagnostic appraisal and continuous medical supervision," the agency noted. "The physician's appraisal of the child is one of the key services in the adoption process."[6] In the eyes of the agency that set national standards for adoption care and administration, medical specialists also played essential roles as consultants to determine a child's suitability for placement with prospective adoptive couples. The agency noted the medical personnel played equally critical roles maintaining accurate medical records of the child and ensuring the accurate record of vital records and birth registration. The bureau also saw the medical community as fellow advocates in promoting recommended adoption practices.

In addition to their intimate roles in all facets of adoption and the care of adoptees and mothers, physicians closely collaborated with social service agencies in creating the detailed records that ensured an adoptee's complicated dual identity in vital records. The child's reports, medical histories, and more became permanent records in the parallel identity documents that were created before and after the relinquished infants were adopted. The records were ultimately managed by the records keepers in the probate courts and state vital-records agencies. The legacy of this birth-records and original-identity-records system lingers today for millions.

These documents are spoken of as highly classified state secrets by defenders of what has become an outdated closed-records system. Civil-rights-minded advocates for open birth records consider them to be essential and basic identity documents that are the legal entitlement of all citizens by birthright. In researching my adoption history and the records handlers who interacted with me during my birth family search in the late 1980s, I found only one surviving and retired official who physically handled my actual adoption files.

I contacted Wayne Avery, the former manager of the Wayne County Probate Court, in early 2016. For several years, he supervised all adoption records and records requests in the 1980s. This included my formal written requests for original birth records that were repeatedly denied. His signature is on all of the letters I still have from the court concerning my file. He told me during our phone interview that adoption records were stored in a secure area in the Wayne County courthouse building. He and his staff considered records to be closely guarded personal information, accessed by designated staff. His employer nurtured the larger national culture of secrecy, and for Avery and his staff, that meant adoptees' sealed records were never to be shared except under direct orders from his superiors.

Starting in the 1930s, states began issuing what are called amended or revised birth certificates for finalized adoptions. These documents list the adoptive parents as a child's parents, not the biological mother or father. The original record of birth, known today as the original birth certificate, is stored by the state in most circumstances. Through World War II, these original documents were available to adoptees and both sets of parents, until changes in states laws began to shut down access to them for birth parents and adoptees.

By 1941, thirty-five states had passed legislation that allowed vital statistics registrars to legally replace the names on adoptees' original birth certificates with the names of adoptive parents and the new and second name they gave the adoptee. Nearly every state had such provisions by 1948. Adoption historian Carp emphasizes child welfare or public health officials never intended for the newly created birth certificates that were created by state public health departments to block adoptees' access to their original documents. On the contrary, they recommended that the original records should only be seen by adoptees when they came of age or through a court order.[7]

The amended birth certificates issued by states after an adoption were all certified by public health records keepers as a legal, vital-records document. They remain the most important piece of paper needed for all aspects of modern life: enrolling in school, getting a Social Security number, obtaining a driver's license, and more. They also erased blood kinship ties and made identity changes legal and permanent.

In my case, my amended birth certificate, issued by the Michigan Department of Public Health on May 13, 1965, nearly four weeks after my birth, formally changed my name. It signaled my previous identity was now a secret—documented and stored like all vital records, but hidden and considered taboo. Public health officials literally placed my birth certificate into secure storage. They intended to keep it from me my entire natural life. That was the consensus when I was born and remains that way in 2017, in Michigan.

As of December 2017, only nine states—Hawaii, Alabama, Alaska, Colorado, Kansas, Minnesota, New Hampshire, Oregon, and Rhode Island—allow unconditional access to original birth certificates without restrictions, up from just three states in 1991. Alaska and Kansas never changed their laws—having always allowed adoptees to access their records—while South Dakota changed its law that now allows restricted access to a birth certificate by an adoptee, with a court order.[8] In June 2016, Hawaii became the latest state to open its birth records, when Governor David Ige signed legislation giving all adult adoptees "unfettered access" to "sealed adoption records," essentially duplicating England's successful national adoption statute from 1975 that grants all adoptee adults eighteen years or older to have unblocked access to all of their original birth documents.

The openness of these nine states contrasts sharply with Michigan, my birth state. Therein lies a major policy problem. The United States has no national adoption-records law. One effort called the Model State Adoption Act emerged in Congress in 1980 that would have opened all records for all adoptees. But in the face of opposition by secrecy supporters, it failed, and its open-records provisions were rewritten by 1981 to do the opposite and protect the privacy of birth parents. In that form, the proposal died to the dismay of the second generation of adoption-rights activists.

Another national effort to codify state adoption laws, called the Uniform Adoption Act (1994), drew a firestorm of criticism from adoptees, adoptee advocates, and even adoption advocates. The act proposed provisions that would have sealed all adoption records for ninety-nine years and created a passive adoption registry system that is considered ineffective in connecting birth family members by many adoptees and adoption law researchers. The act even would have criminalized the searching for birth records. It was accepted as a uniform proposal for states to embrace as legislation by the group charged with codifying state laws—the National Conference of Commissioners on Uniform State Laws. To date, no state has adopted it as a model statute.

Throughout the debates over access to birth records, medical personnel continued to play active roles. They ensured the well-being of children and also the medical legitimacy of what became a discriminatory vital-records-keeping system that treats most adoptees differently than non-adoptees. Today much is known about the roles of social workers in the history of adoption. Much less is publicly known of the doctors' and nurses' roles in adoptees' birth and final placement with new families.

The doctors' legal role is clearly visible through doctors' required legal signatures on health records. The legal framework for the records helped state governments normalize these hundreds of thousands of adoptions following World War II, while eliminating the illegal black market that still existed through the 1950s.[9] With the exception of witness protection programs and some covert government intelligence services, there is no other class of persons in the United States with dual identity documents and states of personhood—a fact not lost on adoptees without access to their records.

Evidence of the highly intricate records-keeping system that created two realities for adoptees became very clear to me in May 1989, the first time I received and reviewed copies of most of my original birth records from the Wayne County Probate Court. My birth mother had agreed to sign a consent letter required by the Michigan Central Adoption Registry acknowledging she was my mother and that she granted the court permission to give me copies of my own original identity documents. At that point, the court had to release my original records. A quarter century into my life, I finally could read about who I was, in the simplest medical language. It became immediately clear physicians and nurses played disproportionately important roles in my first weeks of life.

The records include detailed "children's medical record" forms, six pages long. One set of the forms provided my weight, height, vaccination history, abnormalities, and the dates of discharge. The record also showed the outcome of a medical exam, the length of the labor of my birth mother, my gender, my race, my pre-birth religion, and how my main body functions and parts were performing. The only doctor's name I can read on my birth records is one typed out, the attending doctor at my delivery in the spring of 1965. He is the same doctor I interviewed in 2016.

Overall, medical personnel found that I was normal, except for projectile vomiting. Three days after my birth, I was transferred from Detroit Crittenton Hospital and moved to Detroit Children's Hospital for an eight-day stay. The records show it was a "work-up," but I was losing weight and getting chest X-rays, and it is likely my health was failing, requiring this intensive care.

At that time, the Lutheran Children's Friend Society, the adoption placement agency, used my original birth name, Scott Douglas Owens.

The examining physician for the foster family who cared for me the next five weeks and who signed the discharge gave me the final seal of approval as fit for adoption. He wrote, "From a medical standpoint the child is recommended for adoptive placement." The doctor played out his role precisely as the American Academy of Pediatrics recommended. This physician provided one of the most essential services in the adoption system. He cared for a child surrendered to a state-sanctioned adoption agency, and he was doing his job to ensure my well-being.

The signature on that form is impossible to discern. It was one of three doctors' signatures in my initial health review, highlighting the great care the medical professionals paid to ensure my good health, as attested by their signed names. It demonstrates a level of state involvement in the process, and also care and compassion for children who became wards of both the state and placement agencies, as I was.

The thoroughness of my records attests to reforms that improved adoption health services in the first half of the twentieth century. Progressive-era children's advocates had developed health clinics and immunization programs for children. The US Children's Bureau, established by Congress in 1912, educated the public on medical issues. Attention to children's medical care and records had spilled over into child-placing institutions during this time as well, including developing cognitive tests for children ready for adoption to see about birth defects.[10]

Adoption reformers, like Dr. Arnold Gessell (1880–1961), worked to develop a broad range of motor, language, and mental tests to prevent the adoption of "defective children," but also make it more humane for adopting parents and children. There were legitimate fears unhealthy infants with serious impairments were being adopted in unregulated adoption black markets that attracted widespread media attention. In 1926, Gessell noted, "Clinical safeguards can not solve all the problems of child adoption but they can steadily improve its methods to make them both more scientific and humane."[11] In the end I was deemed non-defective with a battery of tests that can be traced directly back to these innovations.

For its part, the Children's Bureau promoted reforms of state adoption laws and research, and it organized conferences on child placement issues for adoptees. Scandals exposed so-called baby farms and black-market adoptions. In response, Children's Bureau field agents showcased abysmal conditions in maternity homes and orphanages, and investigated the placing-out and interstate traffic of infants from the 1910s all the way to the decade of my birth, the 1960s. Overall, the Children's Bureau helped to inform the public about why adoptions required regulation. This included prior placement investigations, post-placement supervision, and long probations. All were considered minimal standards to protect adoptees and adults, and ensure that adoptive families turned out well.[12]

In my case, however, these well-established practices worked for the short term but not the long term. Though there were established procedures when I moved into the final custody of my adoptive family, these did not reveal that the father of that family was an alcoholic. No system is perfect. My adoptive family proved that point, perhaps too well.

Almost five weeks to the day after my birth in 1965, my identity was changed, legally, through a state-sanctioned adoption decree. My past identity was sealed in a box, in a storage room, in a Michigan government office building. The line for my birth mother on the decree was marked "unknown to petitioners," followed by "whose rights in said child have been released to Lutheran Children's Friend Society of Michigan." The decree further states, "That said child is not related to the petitioners," to indicate that my relation to my adoptive parents was not one involving a biological relative. It was a stranger adoption.

The decree also provides a key legal statement that granted full parental rights to my adoptive parents. It records that I had been transformed into a new person. I was now legally and permanently severed from my former families and the original name I was given when I arrived as a screaming infant five weeks earlier in Detroit: "That [adoptive parents] desire to adopt said minor child and to bestow upon said child their family name with the intent to make the child their heir, and to stand in all response as the lawful parents of said child. That after said adoption the petitioners desire the said child's name to be Martin Rudolf Brueggemann."

Medical professionals reviewed my health, again with great care in late September 1965, when I had grown and then weighed nearly eighteen pounds. They gave me a full exam, signed by a doctor whose name is impossible to read. This time my records used a new name, "Martin Brueggemann." A final record entry tracked by my adoption agency and kept with my permanent file was made in late January 1966. That record noted my DTP, polio, and smallpox vaccines—again signed by another doctor, with illegible script.

The set of adoption records that I later received from my placement agency after I had found my birth family also contained a summary of the last recorded entry made by the agency. A social worker added a report in mid-July 1966. It is a remarkable record of how adoption placement worked, as a records-tracking system involving the network of medical, social work, and vital statistics stakeholders nationwide.

By that time my family had left Detroit and had moved to Boston. A caseworker had been contacted in Boston to check on me. The caseworker reported I was suffering from ear infections and colds—likely related to my parents smoking in the home, which at the time was not considered a serious risk to children's health that we know it is today. The doctor who was contacted reported I was in "extremely good health except for having low resistance." For the first ten years of my life I remained a very sickly kid, more prone to viral infections and fevers than my peers.

According to the caseworker's notes typed into my permanent file, she wrote, "It is felt that Martin feels quite secure with his adoptive family and that they in return are quite pleased with him. . . . We are recommending that final order be entered on this child and that his name become legally Martin Rudolf Brueggemann."

On August 8, 1966, the Wayne County Probate Court made its final determination of adoption. For a reason I cannot explain, the court document still listed my name as "Scott." My old self had snuck into the sheet, perhaps as a clerical error. Even on paper after I was adopted, the residue of my former infant identity followed me into the future. My file number was marked 32019.

To this day, that is the number by which the State of Michigan defines me, as a case, with records showing I was a child with two names. More than a half century after my adoption, when I was forced to petition the Third Circuit Court of Michigan to obtain my original birth certificate from the state's vital-records officials, the state still used the same tracking system. That number assigned to my case fifty-one years earlier followed me to the present.

Being a number to the courts and to Michigan's public health records keepers also meant I was not a real person. That felt unsettling. They still saw me as a case, not a baby or later as an adult. They never saw me as a human being entitled to full legal rights. When I tried to pierce this bureaucratic wall in 2016 by demanding that the records keepers treat me as a person, and consider the underlying facts of my case, they stayed securely in their fortress and never acknowledged my humanity. In fact, they refused to talk to me about my case or my rights. To them I was always just a number and case, whose treatment would be determined by the strictest interpretation of law as possible. In my case, that also meant possibly breaking the state law they were sworn to uphold.

Chapter 5

Knowing You Are Adopted: Just Look in the Mirror

The adoptive parents must have good health, a stable marriage, exhibit a degree of maturity, and must have evidenced some ability to adjust to the reality of their childlessness. . . . While the adoptive parents will get great satisfaction from nurturing, stimulating, and encouraging the child, the primary goal in their care of the child is to help and love him for his own sake. They should be people who are warm, flexible, understanding, and with a desire to help a child develop his capacities.

— Ursula M. Gallagher, *Social Workers Look at Adoption*,
US Department of Health, Education, and Welfare, 1958

Fewer than one hundred photos exist that document my childhood through my adolescence. Looking at them now, they confirm beyond any doubt I never resembled my birth mother, my adoptive sister, or my adoptive father. Nor did I look like their extended families. Even as a young boy I could tell that grandparents, parents, children, and even cousins shared a clear physical resemblance in the families all around me. I was different and would always be different from all of them because my family members looked nothing like me. I also knew in my bones that I would never share my life's journey with my "blood" kin.

Despite the volumes of advice given to parents about bonding among nonrelated members of adoptive families, those ties can never erase an adoptee's self-knowledge of being genetically different. In my case, I always knew I was adopted. There is not a single "aha" point in time I can recall like those found in so many autobiographies. I never had a cathartic moment, with sudden awareness of an important and life-changing fact. That is what happens in fiction or dramatized biographies that stretch the truth and tell people what they want to believe. My life was not make believe, even if the journey to self-discovery remains mythical at its core.

The way most of us first know we belong to each other as kin is through our shared facial features. I could immediately tell I did not have the eyes, eyebrows, nose, ears, mouth, chin, or even body types of my adoptive parents. When I gazed into the mirror when I was younger, I saw a young boy and then a scrawny teenager with dishwater blond hair, ears that prominently stood out, a very large nose, thick lips, blue-green eyes, and a boxy head. I was a late bloomer and mostly very skinny through my early twenties. Even today I weigh just above 150 pounds and stand a hair under six feet.

When I looked at my adoptive mother and father as a young boy, I saw no physical similarities. My long-deceased adoptive father stood at six feet three. He wore dark glasses and did not have my facial features, with his square German jaw and the flattop on his balding head. He was much larger than me, physically. His temperament changed like the wind. He was highly volatile, mostly because of his alcoholism. I was quiet and private. My much shorter, five feet six mother, with her brown, curly hair, has a much darker complexion than mine. She always has been more outgoing than me, and our outward behaviors never had much in common. Even until I was eighteen and older, people who did not know my adoption story continued to say I resembled my adoptive mother, when neither of us believed that. Those were forever awkward moments for both of us, particularly after I had found my biological mother.

My adoptive sister was born in Saginaw in 1963. She was placed with my family two years before me. Physically she was heavier than me as we entered adolescence, and she grew heavier as she aged. I have barely gained a pound since I was twenty-two, thanks to my diet and love of intense physical exercise.

This clear morphological difference provides the most striking visual proof we hail from different biological families. She also has dark brown hair, a big smile, and wide brown eyes. We bore and still bear no physical similarity at all. Growing up, no one seeing us together in a crowd would ever guess we're brother and sister. As we both got older into our thirties, and my sister's health began to deteriorate because of weight and lifestyle choices, I began to notice how she resembled many Native American women I had seen who had experienced hard lives. To this day, I believe my sister is likely part Native American from Michigan, perhaps a member of the Chippewa nation.

When I was placed for adoption in 1965, social service agencies that brokered adoption placements embraced a prevailing practice to place children with families that they believed resembled the child. Theoretically, the matching of races of parent and child served everyone's best interest. According to one social worker, speaking for her field in the 1940s, careful matching would ensure that "no one will ever say" to an adoptive parent, "This cannot be your natural child."[1]

By the mid-1960s, the use of matching across the country had subsided, but not in my case. By this time, the experts in the field were more focused on early placement of relinquished children with new families. They wanted to promote the "best solution," by putting illegitimate kids such as myself into a family where we could flourish, while at the same time addressing the need to help reform the women who had out-of-wedlock births, like my birth mother.[2]

Before I would have been placed, one or more social workers—likely from the religious social service agency that brokered my placement—would have conducted a home study of my future parents. This would have involved one or more home visits and data collection on my adoptive parents' education, religion, and community connections. Adoptive parents were expected to have the financial resources to raise a family and housing in neighborhoods that promoted the "health, safety, well-being and self-respect of the family."[3] While the guidelines published by the US Children's Bureau in the late 1950s did not propose a rigid faith test for adoptive parents to meet, they recommended that adoptees have the "opportunity for religious and spiritual development."[4] Having a religion improved those parents' standing to adopt a child.

Social workers also would have attempted to determine my birth parents' true motives for adoption. Social workers were, according to one account, "playing God." This was mostly driven by their moral and professional responsibility to ensure a "child's right to have an emotionally secure family life."[5]

Agencies, like the one that placed me, also looked for happy marriages, a couple's healthy ties to family and friends, the prospective parents' ability to love a child, and also grief over their own childlessness.[6] The guidelines promoted by the US Children's Bureau in the late 1950s outlined the traits social workers looked for among prospective adopting families. "The adoptive parents must have good health, a stable marriage, exhibit a degree of maturity, and must have evidenced some ability to adjust to the reality of their childlessness," the bureau's expert panel concluded. "While the adoptive parents will get great satisfaction from nurturing, stimulating, and encouraging the child, the primary goal in their care of the child is to help and love him for his own sake. They should be people who are warm, flexible, understanding, and with a desire to help a child develop his capacities."[7] The adopting parents had to prove themselves both worthy, but open to being inspected for pathology.[8]

The clear pathology manifest in my father's alcoholism was completely missed by those who met my future family in 1964 and 1965. To this day, I am still baffled how wrong things went and how my adoptive father so completely fooled the agency that was entrusted to place me in a mostly stable household.

Social workers would have visited the two-story brick home where my adoptive parents lived since 1958, on the 14000 block of Glastonbury Street in Detroit. They would have seen a prosperous, tree-lined suburb on the west side of the then still vital industrial city, when Detroit was still at its apex. Nothing could have appeared more normal and secure than this area, with its solidly middle-class, single-family brick houses. The neighborhood alone provided proof I likely would have a happy upbringing.

My birth mother was blonde, and of Finnish, Welsh, and mixed English ancestry. So, the social workers likely determined that would be a close match to my adoptive parents, who were both German-American. But I did not look like them at all, mainly because we had no genetic relationship.

From the early 1900s onward, so-called religious matching also was widely practiced by adoption placement agencies. There were heated debates among religious leaders, including from the Catholic Church, who opposed having children from Catholic mothers adopted out to Protestant families. By the late 1950s, the controversy of placing adoptees with families to match the religion of a child's biological kin with the religion of the adoptive family dragged on.

The Child Welfare League of America, one of the nation's most important private national groups that promoted child welfare, issued national guidelines for adoption in 1958 that offered two views. One was by the Catholic adoption services, which recommended keeping Catholic adoptees with Catholic families, and the other by mostly nonsectarian, Jewish, and Protestant agencies that suggested religious views should not be imposed on all adoption agencies. The statement by the latter group, however, claimed the "religious and spiritual development of the child" was essential in an adoptive home. These agencies strongly recommended that "a child should ordinarily be placed in a home where the religion of adoptive parents is the same as that of the child, unless the parents have specified that the child should or may be placed with a family of another religion."[9]

Adoption historian Barbara Melosh notes that "matching" of children—by intellect, race, ethnicity, and even religion—dramatically declined nationally by the 1960s, as the idea of cross-racial adoption and adopting other than "healthy white babies" became more widespread.[10] However in post–World War II America through the mid-1960s, religion was still common in the matching of children with parents. It was thought that adoptive parents who demonstrated religious practice also demonstrated good citizenship, and religious matching happened through a form of self-segregation. Protestant families could be served by Protestant social welfare agencies, and Catholics in a similar way.

I fell into the orbit of the Lutherans. Both of my adoptive parents were practicing Lutherans. My birth mother ultimately surrendered me to the Lutheran Children's Friend Society, later to become the Lutheran Child and Family Services of Michigan. Founded in 1899 in Bay City, Michigan, the parent organization was among many Christian child welfare groups in the state dedicated to helping abused, neglected, and foster children. It was rooted in the church's mission to demonstrate what church officials called "Gods' love," through actions helping the needy. It had transformed by the 1960s to an agency that also brokered adoptions, with religion as a factor in my placement with a Lutheran family.

A relative told me later that my birth mother's father, my maternal grandfather, had reached out to the Lutheran group on my birth mother's behalf. Neither he nor my birth mother were practicing Christians or Lutherans, based on what they shared with me over the years.

In the end, my adoptive family met this important religious litmus test. My adoptive father was an ordained Lutheran minister serving students at Wayne State University, in Detroit, when I was adopted. Born in 1924, he was already forty when he legally became my father. He was the oldest of four sons. The third oldest one died because of an infection from appendicitis when he was a teenager. His father, a well-to-do and stern German-American businessman, ran a successful paint contracting company in Cleveland, Ohio. His mother raised the kids and was a dutiful housewife.

My adoptive father and his next youngest brother were sent as teenagers to Concordia College, in Fort Wayne, Indiana, an American version of the German gymnasium. It was meant to prepare students for the Lutheran seminary, whether they wanted a life in the clergy or not. My adoptive father enrolled there in 1938, during the Depression. Three decades after my adoptive father's death, my adoptive uncle described him as a social person and a loner, as someone whose addictive traits were beginning to show with drinking. He was apparently "brilliant," according to my adoptive uncle. My adoptive father wrote in and edited student publications. He then went to the preeminent Lutheran seminary in the country, Concordia Seminary in St. Louis, from 1946 to 1949. By then, according to my adoptive uncle, he had already begun drinking alone: "At the seminary [he] displayed outstanding talent in writing and editing the student opinion magazine and yearbook. He immersed himself in [Soren] Kierkegaard and Pogo. At the seminary he lived in a single room. He would read and write into the wee hours and probably nursed several bottles of beer as well."

After finishing at Concordia in 1949, he took a post leading a congregation in Bridgeport Township, a small rural community just south of dark and dreary Saginaw, Michigan. If a minister even then were to rate that placement, it would have been considered a second- or third-tier church. The shining stars from the seminary would never go there. Life in that rural town was likely culturally isolated and bleak. My adoptive father never once spoke of his time in that church. He spent nine long years there, until 1958. That is where he met my adoptive mother, where she had just moved as a young teacher fresh from Bronxville College. She was young and beautiful—and very alone. They were married in Hawthorne, New Jersey, in July 1958.

Raised in a conservative, German-American home in New Jersey, she was the oldest of three siblings, with two brothers who later moved to Indiana. They grew up in a working-class neighborhood in Paterson, New Jersey. Her family struggled, and she passed some of her life's hard lessons to me in unhealthy ways. She transmitted her brand of parenting that she learned from her parents. Her father was an unhappy alcoholic, like the man she married. He died when I was very young. Her mother, an immigrant from Germany, was sent penniless to America as a teenager because her family could not afford to support her during Germany's terrible depression. Though likely a heartless act at the time, it spared her from living through Hitler's Nazi dictatorship and World War II. My adoptive grandmother chain-smoked and never once said anything nice to anyone as long as I knew her, until she died when I was in college. I can understand why she became that way, and why my adoptive mother became a lot like her.

As a young woman on her own, with no friends in a small Michigan city, I also can see why my adoptive mother would have accepted the proposal of my adoptive father. He came from a proper family that had more means than hers, so he seemed like a good match. They were separated by twelve years. As an omen of bad days to come, the couple took a honeymoon in Nova Scotia. According to a news story published right after the nearly fatal accident, their car crashed through a guardrail and rolled two hundred feet into a ravine near the town of Sydney. My adoptive father may even have been drinking before the wreck, or maybe my mother was driving. I will never know the truth. A photo from a news story shows my adoptive mother on crutches. She told me once that she was nearly unconscious and had to climb up the cliff, bleeding with a badly damaged leg, to flag down a passing car. That accident was a terrifying moment that ended quickly. Their marriage proved far worse. It became a long-unfolding disaster that finally ended in divorce sixteen years later.

Religion proved central to my adoptive family's identity. My adoptive father chose my name, "Martin Rudolf Brueggemann." My first name honored the German, an early sixteenth-century Protestant reformer Martin Luther. My middle name, "Rudolf," was intended to honor his own domineering father also named "Rudolf." The name was meant to create a new identity, as a German and Lutheran child, who would carry on the family patriarchal traditions of my adoptive kin.

Ultimately the adoption system had imposed religion in my life. Lutheranism—good and bad—became a permanent part of my childhood experience and my worldview into adulthood. From a nurturing and cultural perspective, I dutifully became both Lutheran and German-American. At the same time, my identity as a German-American Lutheran is also completely fabricated. I never became a believer. I attended church until I was eighteen, at my mother's hard insistence. Later in life I appreciated that church a lot more than I did as a kid. Tribally, I feel a strong attachment to Lutherans, and I consider some Lutheran ministers I met and befriended among the most inspiring leaders I personally know.

As an adoptee you are forced to own the name of the family who raises you, even when you always know you had another one that was taken from you and hidden. Family inheritance and kinship are intimately tied to family names. Asking an adoptee to accept the identity of this group of people with ties going back centuries means he or she must accept the fiction that they were born anew through social engineering. This never made any sense to me, ever.

As long as I can remember, I never liked or wanted the Brueggemann family name. Everyone who met me thought I was German, even when I was not. Having people think I was ethnically and historically part of one group of people with whom I had no kinship ties always felt like a scab. It never quite healed and felt picked when a stranger made wrong assumptions about me that did not acknowledge my true identity. I especially disliked having that name when I visited Germany, a land where I had almost no ethnic ties except distally from my biological father many generations back.

Banks, schools, educators, records keepers, credit agencies—you name it—constantly misspelled my family name as long as I had it. Mostly I disliked the name because I inherited it from a man who failed the most important challenges of life. He was a terrible husband and worse as a father. He bears responsibility for all of his actions as an adult, husband, and father. However, *his* family name was not my real name. For me, it was *that* name *that* asshole gave me.

Shel Silverstein's classic song "A Boy Named Sue" captures this sentiment best, as sung by Johnny Cash in one of the greatest live recordings ever. I know its lyrics by heart, and I always sing them: "Now, I don't blame him cause he run and hid, but the meanest thing that he ever did, was before he left, he went and named me 'Sue.'" Unlike Sue, I did change my "awful name" later in life. I never had a fistfight with my violent, alcoholic, adoptive father. I chose a path of forgiveness.

The records of my early pre-childhood and early childhood are murky, mostly because my adoptive mother never talked about our time in Detroit or our next home, Boston, Massachusetts. My adoptive father also said nothing while he was alive. My family's decisions to adopt a boy and girl remain the murkiest details of all.

Neither of my adoptive parents or any of their extended kin ever talked about infertility and why they could not have their own children. The topic is still taboo with family members alive today. In 2015, I reached out to an adoptive cousin for possible answers. He told me he had heard my adoptive father contracted mumps in 1961 or 1962, in his late thirties. If true, my adoptive father likely had testosterone deficiency, or hypogonadism. This affects nearly one out of three men between the ages of forty and seventy-nine, according to research. One common cause for the condition is mumps, which can lead to long-term testicular damage. That in turn has an impact on testicular function and testosterone production.

My adoptive parents also faced tremendous pressure from both of their families to conform to societal expectations of raising a nuclear family. The burden was particularly heavy for a Lutheran minister's family, who had to project being a model Christian family. According to the Child Welfare League of America's adoption service standards dating from the late 1950s, "Great value is placed on children, and a family without children is considered incomplete. For children who cannot have the care of their natural parents . . . adoption is considered the most desirable means of ensuring family life."[11]

With society and social workers eager to place the glut of "illegitimate children" like me in proper Christian homes, adoption made sense for my family. Everything was supposed to turn out right. What could go wrong with a Lutheran minister and his lovely wife on a *Leave It to Beaver* street in one of America's most prosperous cities? Except, things went very, very sidewise, just like things went terribly wrong for my birth city, Detroit. In my case, the faith of my adoptive parents may have blinded my Lutheran adoption agency from seeing problems that should have been visible but likely were glossed over because my adoptive father was a respected Lutheran community leader.

Before the end of 1965, my adoptive father left his job as a campus minister at Wayne State University in Detroit and accepted a post in Boston through a Lutheran organization called the Wheat Ridge Foundation. That group funded experimental ministries. My adoptive father was recruited to serve young people near Northeastern University. We moved to a flat near the school on Gainsborough Street, an area then plagued by frequent crime.

My family arrived in Boston before the end of 1965. We left not long after in October 1967. No one ever told me why, and I have no memories of my time there. I suspect my adoptive father's drinking problem played a role.

This time we moved to Clayton, Missouri, a neighboring city next to St. Louis. Our modest home was a block from Concordia Seminary, my adoptive father's alma mater. The seminary owned our house, but it appeared we were normal middle-class homeowners and practicing Christians. My adoptive mother took care of the two kids. My adoptive father ran yet another campus ministry position, this time at the prestigious Washington University, located a half-mile from our home. The Lutheran Church of the Missouri Synod (LCMS) sponsored him. The LCMS is the more conservative arm of the two main Lutheran churches in the United States.

I remember little of this time or my father's work. He was based at a student center, located in a converted old brick house, near the university. No one has ever told me what he actually did to make a living. I heard only from one person, an old classmate of my stepfather, who told me in 2016 that my adoptive father had a very prominent role on the Washington University campus, which must have made his fall from grace that much harder.

Until he was removed from the ministry six years later, my father's alcoholism spun wildly out of control. Before I was even adopted, according to my adoptive uncle, my adoptive father already had sought an alcoholic-treatment program in the Chicago area. He continued to be a problem drinker and worse. He often erupted in violence. On occasions, he beat my mother, and more than once we had to leave the house in the middle of the night after he attacked her. Decades later in 2016, my adoptive mother, whose memory was slipping, told me the thing she remembers the most from her time with her husband and my father was how he hit her.

My adoptive parents finally separated in 1973 and divorced in 1974. He would stay in the St. Louis area until 1974, when he received a last-final-call offer to run an LCMS church in Huntington, West Virginia. He moved. Up until the time I was thirteen, I would visit him several times a year with my adoptive sister. These are some of my darkest memories.

My adoptive father eventually lost his last job as a minister during this time. He moved twice, and each ratty, dirty home and apartment became progressively worse, as did his health. During those years, the Huntington area suffered high unemployment and poverty. It remains an impoverished area today.

I can think of few bleaker places to be alone with a dysfunctional parent. My adoptive father stayed drunk almost twenty-four hours a day, except on the first days when he would greet us at the airport shaking from withdrawal. He did things I will never put in print and never share with another person. I did my best to keep away from him, often wandering the city alone as a young kid. My adoptive sister and I are very lucky we are alive today, given the dozens of times the he drove us completely blotto drunk. I can still remember how I thought he would crash us off a bridge crossing the Ohio River and kill us all. When I revisited Huntington in September 2015 and looked at that bridge, it brought back dark memories of that night. To this day I still think I used up all my nine lives with some of our close calls.

My adoption experience during these turbulent years does not include a dramatic page-turning moment that makes for great literature. Until I left for college when I was eighteen, my self-identity as an adopted person never seemed that important. I was far too busy being a wild, rebellious teenager who dabbled in drugs, and even pointless small crime. Luckily, I reformed and then spent all my energy trying to maintain good grades, holding down low-paying jobs, and saving as much money as I could for college. Thinking thoughts about my distant kin and biological family was a middle-class luxury I could not afford.

I recall knowing I was adopted when I was four or five years old. My adoptive parents must have told me. I cannot recall how I reacted. I talked about it with some friends, and I knew they were different because they looked like their families when I did not. I also did not find any secret documents in the house, that some adoptees claim to have discovered, which revealed a dark family secret. There was no mysterious hidden family story or being switched at birth at the hospital. It simply was all I knew. A more dramatic moment of discovery probably would make for a more compelling story, but that is not mine.

I also did not have any of the supposed childhood fantasies of having "other" parents, which psychologists frequently claim occur as children progress through their cognitive and psychological development. There is still an abundance of what I consider to be sometimes comical psychological gibberish published in peer-reviewed articles. The psychology field continues to be obsessed with Freud's Oedipal theory and variations of this topic. This pseudoscience also remains a popular subject that the therapy community analyzes endlessly in adoption literature.

There are even kid's books for adoptive families on this theme, like one 2004 title imaginatively named *You're Not My Real Mother.* That topic is also frequently discussed in adoption blogs, in which parents complain about their adoptive kids, who in turn are complaining about their parents. Reading these entries, I think, so when did modern American kids not complain about parents and when did parents not complain about their kids? How can parents and their teenage kids complaining about one another be considered anything but normal?

In my case, my sister and I never once said such things to our adoptive mother, or even to our self-destructive adoptive father. We probably knew that complaining about anything, real or imaginary, was not going to change our reality. We had to muddle along together, however imperfect things were most of the time. As tense as things were for my adoptive mother and me—and they are downright awful at times—I knew I had to support her internalized fiction. She needed to believe that our family was normal and healthy, even when it was fraying wildly at the seams. In some senses, we were strangers banded together by fate. I have always accepted that, now more than ever.

When I was growing up, my adoptive mother was always Mom, good and bad. My adoptive father was Dad, but also the monster to watch like a hawk when I was sent to stay with him. I had nothing to do with him after I was thirteen, except once when I visited him at eighteen, just before I started college. I drove to Cleveland to see him as his health was failing. I let him know that I forgave him for how he treated our family. No apologies ever came my way—he had not really changed. He died in 1985 of cirrhosis and other complications that followed decades of smoking and drinking.

My sister and I never bonded in a way I see with siblings connected in other biological families. To this day I am jealous of the connection I see in other families. My sister and I were cool at best. For me, that distance remains. There are many reasons. Mostly, we are very different people, and we have made very different life choices. Our relationship is as good as it will get.

I also bore no resemblance to my cousins in either of my adoptive families. All told, my adoptive families included two uncles on either side and nine cousins, of which two are younger than me. I have always known we looked different. Not until I was in my teens did I begin questioning our relations as true family.

For me, true family members are people with whom you feel connected and who support you and communicate with you. People who may send a friendly note just because, rather than the obligatory, annual holiday letter. In my mind, those connections should be a cousin who might invite you to a wedding, or reach out during a trip to your part of the country. That was never my story. I never received any wedding invitations, or announcements of children being born, or children graduating from high school. I count only a handful of gatherings over the decades with a few of my adoptive cousins since I became an adult. I believe this is intentional silence from them as a group. I expect nothing will change until we die.

After my family experienced a very rough divorce, which ended our short-lived experiment as a normal, middle-class American family, my mother and my sister and I did our best to get by as a single-parent household in the St. Louis suburb city called University City. It sits just north of our former home in Clayton. Our circumstances were probably not the scenario the social workers in Detroit had ever envisioned for an adopted child when they placed me with my family in 1965.

These were not easy times. This equally white and black suburb posed plenty of personal safety challenges for me. We first lived in an apartment on a street that had rough edges and rough characters. I was mugged several times and never felt safe on our street from third to fifth grade. Finally, my adoptive mother purchased a modest house a few blocks away, which we called home until I graduated from high school in 1983. I poured years of sweat equity into caring for and improving that home and felt it was as much my home as my mother's. We barely made it with my mom's salary as a single mother working as a teacher.

I was a skinny white kid. In the 1970s and early 1980s, there were real racial tensions in my city's schools, where 70 percent of all students were African American and most of the remaining kids were white. Being skinny and small is never a good bargaining position for a young man in the proverbial school mosh pit. Taunting and raw physical violence in the schools was a real and daily occurrence. I was once hospitalized in a racially motivated assault in junior high school that nearly blinded me in my left eye. Adoption was the last thing on my mind most of the time. Plotting to get as far away as possible from St. Louis occupied a lot of my creative energy before I left for college.

During this stage of my life I knew nothing about my past except trivial details. I knew I was born in Detroit, which made me remotely care about the Detroit Red Wings and the Detroit Lions. To get my Social Security card and satisfy other documentation needs, I had to order my amended birth certificate. That piece of paper claimed it was "the true and correct reproduction of the certificate on file in the Michigan Department of Public Health, Lansing, Michigan." But that statement amounted to fiction. It ignored my original certificate I knew nothing about then. The amended document lists my full adoptive name and birth date, my adoptive mother's full name, my adoptive father's full name, the place of birth, and the date the amended document was filed, on May 13, 1965. I had no other record of my life and ancestral family history until I was twenty-three.

My adoptive mother worked in low-paying public school systems as a teacher during that time, struggling to keep us in a home while having a meaningful life as a single mom. From the time she divorced my alcoholic and abusive adoptive father in 1974, until the time I graduated high school in 1983, our family was completely on its own. We had no fiscal or emotional support from our extended "family." I started working as young as I could—babysitting, mowing lawns, working underage in fast-food restaurants—because my mom could not provide any support beyond a home, simple food, and a few frills.

That period of our lives taught me most about what family means and did not mean. These experiences were good teachers. They were honest. I always knew exactly where I stood in relation to my larger adoptive family. We were, and remain, mostly strangers. We were connected by a system that tried to convince those who were adopted that we would be the same as biological kin. I always knew this story was false. I believe my adopted external family thought the same as well. In this family circle, where my sister and I were the odd couple, no one had the guts to be honest about the underlying truth. We were tongue-tied, because adoption was and still is a taboo topic for families.

I have always suspected that my two uncles and six older cousins on my adoptive father's side of the family never once reached out to help or even lend emotional support because they had no ties to any of us biologically. Not a single family member on my adoptive father's side intervened and demonstrated concern about the well-being of my adoptive sister and me, even when we were young children in the care of a well-known alcoholic and were visiting one of the uncles in Cleveland and my adoptive grandmother. Not once did they ask us, "Are you safe with your adoptive father?" None of them really cared about our family after the divorce. My adoptive mother was not their kin. Because my sister and I came from two separate families unrelated to their clan, there was no genetic relation, and thus they had no imperative to really give a damn.

For a few winters, my family made a once-a-year trip to Indianapolis to see the older of my adoptive mother's two younger brothers, who had two sons older than me and one younger. They also came down on a handful of occasions to see my aunt's relatives in the St. Louis area, but not really to see us. We also visited and stayed with my adoptive father's brother—the middle of the three surviving brothers—in Denver for a week. All four of his kids were older than me by two to more than fifteen years. I never saw my two older cousins in Cleveland after I was twelve, except one of them on a very brief visit in 2015. They were the kids from my dad's youngest brother. They were both ten years older than me. As a family, we stopped all visits to any of my adoptive father's kin after 1978. No one shed any tears during the decades of continued silence.

Once I left the St. Louis area for good in 1983, I never had any meaningful connection to my uncles, aunts, or cousins except on just a few occasions spread over thirty years. Occasionally I still send Christmas cards to some of them, and I still receive some in return from a couple of aunts and uncles. For all of us, the cards feel obligatory, not genuine. We never called each other. Only recently have I tried to rekindle a connection with a cousin on my adoptive mom's side of the family through our shared love of surfing. We are friendly, but we do not feel like family.

With my adoptive cousins, we are strangers forced together because of a legal process not rooted in genetic kinship. I have accepted this, decades ago. None of us will be going out of our way to connect as family the rest of our lives. It is hard to stay close to people who you do not connect with on a regular basis. It is even harder trying to pretend you care for people who have no genuine connection to you. In my "family," relations on all sides know we can never change the underlying truth that we will never be kin.

As for my adoptive mother, the person I have and always will call Mom, she was far more supportive of my adoptive status, and eventually my biologically family, than I expected. Yet to this day, I never really talk about my birth kin with her. When I spent my time doing my adoption search from the time I was twenty-two until I was twenty-four, I reached out to her in a way that forced us to finally discuss what we never had or wanted to confront. I asked her in 1988 to sign a statement to support me if I needed to litigate in the courts.

It was one of five such statements I planned to submit to a court if I could no longer find my birth family with the few clues I had. The idea of going to a court seemed crazy, since I barely earned enough money to get by. I planned to petition a Michigan court to ask the state to release my identifying information it kept from me. I know my request caused my adoptive mother a lot of pain. Years later I learned from my stepfather that he thought I had been cruel by asking her to sign the statement, and later by finding my birth families and maintaining relationships with them. He always said my actions as an adoptee searching for this caused her unnecessary pain.

In a personal statement that I wrote on my adoptive mother's behalf that she signed, likely with many regrets, she said:

> Based upon our discussions and my own personal knowledge of my son, I truly believe that the resolution of this matter—namely his access to 'identifying' information—would be a tremendous psychological and emotional relief for him. Although his search for his birth parentage raises issues between us, I, as his mother, feel his ultimate well-being is at stake in regards to this matter. Therefore, I fully endorse this for him. I request that all parties who review this statement allow my son to receive access to his 'identifying' information, to which I believe he is entitled as an adult adoptee.

Her signature is still on the document I keep in my adoption records. I believe she would not have agreed to sign this statement if she did not believe in the words too. They accurately captured the complexity of an adoptive mother–adoptive son relationship, tested by many challenges and the needs of the adoptive child to one day learn for himself where he came from. Nearly three decades later, we have stood that test of time just fine.

Chapter 6

Blood Is Thicker Than Water

'Who am I?' 'Where do I come from?' 'How much of my present reality is controlled by heredity and how much is controlled by my environment?'

—Rudy Owens's Statement, 1988

The urge to know one's kin and ancestry is not just a basic human desire. Seeking our identity lies at the root of self-awareness and our meaning in life. For those who have been brought into the world as adoptees, by circumstances they did not control, this desire is the incessant drumbeat. It bangs inside one's head, loudly and softly, but always audible so long as the question is unanswered.

Those who deny that "blood is thicker than water" know nothing of this siren song. For an adult adoptee or a birth mother who have their biological kinship severed by the institution of adoption, this old phrase has sharper meaning. Unfortunately, the American adoption system's denial of records to most US adoptees forces them to defend these natural feelings to those who have never felt such cravings—and never will. Justifying such deep feelings can be thankless, and adoptees are asked by the country's largely pro-adoption culture to be thankful for having been robbed of core connections that define their humanity.

The yearning for knowledge of one's past helps to fuel the modern-day genealogy industry supported by websites like *Family Search*, run by the Church of Jesus Christ of Latter-day Saints (Mormons), and *Ancestry.com*, the successful Utah-based genealogy search firm that was started by two Mormons. The yearning was also transformed into a national cultural experience for Americans with the first screening of the 1977 television miniseries *Roots*, which adapted Alex Haley's historical family history, *Roots: The Saga of An American Family*. Haley achieved international fame for documenting his long and successful family search that stretched back to his ancestral villages in Gambia, West Africa.

Haley eloquently describes why his own search mattered, particularly for many African Americans whose histories and families were cruelly severed by slavery. It was an institution that separated them from their homeland and then children from their families in the Americas. "In all of us there is a hunger, marrow-deep, to know our heritage—to know who we are and where we have come from," writes Haley. "Without this enriching knowledge, there is a hollow yearning. No matter what our attainments in life, there is still a vacuum, an emptiness, and the most disquieting loneliness."[1] Haley's story became a cultural event, and the story resonated widely in the United States, especially for adoptees who did not know their family ancestry and kin.

During my adoption search, in 1988, I wrote several different detailed summaries that I meant to share with either a court to petition for my records or with my birth family when I would find them. The document I wrote for the courts, but never used, was clinical and confessional. Today it gives me insight into what motivated me so strongly in my early twenties. As I look back with more mature eyes, I believe more than ever that deep desire to know one's kin drove me to search for my birth families and my birth records.

I wrote: "I do not know when I have not spent much of my free time lost in thought about my genetic identity. I have been obsessed with the questions of my very existence. 'Who am I?' 'Where do I come from?' 'How much of my present reality is controlled by heredity and how much is controlled by my environment?' These questions, for me, an adoptee, have more prescience than they do for non-adopted persons."

I then described how the search was sidetracking my professional life:

When I came to Seattle, I turned this quest into a full-time occupation concurrent to my other business and personal affairs. This has been a rewarding, but even more, an incredibly frustrating experience. . . . The toll of this search has been an enormous mental and emotional strain, on top of the time and money that I continue to pour into this endeavor. I have had to put my future professional and education goals on hold while I conduct my search. . . . I believe that I am entitled to know who I am and where I come from. Unfortunately, the present legal system separates these fundamental human questions from my present reality, which I believe is both unfair and unnecessary. I feel like a victim by a bureaucracy that is unable to understand the emotional realities of the persons involved in the adoptive experience like myself and my birth mother, whoever she may be.

For adoptees, kinship means having genetic kin they can call their very own, not what government agencies, social service providers, and the host of groups and individuals tied to the issue called "family." Adoptee Betty Jean Lifton, the author and psychologist who passed away in 2010, wrote three books about adoptees and their search for identity. She called the adoptee's search for knowledge an archetypal, Jungian yearning, with profound life-changing impacts for an adoptee. "What importance is there to the blood tie? . . . What happens to people when they are cut off from their blood connections?"[2]

The coauthors of the study called *Being Adopted*—including a psychologist and a psychiatrist who worked in the field of adoption and adoptee research—concluded that any adoptee's search for their ancestry was both inevitable and normal: "We are often asked, 'What percent of adoptees search for their birth parents?' And our answer surprises people: 'One hundred percent.' In our experience, all adoptees engage in a search process."[3]

For adoptees, kinship has a completely different meaning than it does to the many promoters of, what I call, an adoption industrial complex. Reporters such as Dan Rather have called that confluence of these interest groups the institutionalized adoption system,[4] which overlooks biological science in the promotion of a now-beloved institution. The kinship of the modern era is a manufactured one, though constantly changing in the last 160 years. The nation's leading child welfare agencies promoted a hopeful idea that there would be no differences between adoptive and non-adoptive families. They optimistically hoped that blood-based kinship was not necessary to create families, so long as adoption was available. These founding principles of American adoption practices lasted throughout the twentieth century and carry on to the present day.[5]

The pivotal importance of kinship, in its genetic and evolutionary sense, is not welcomed in the adoption placement and advocacy world. Even adoption advocacy groups that promote evidence-based research, such as open access to birth records for all adoptees, promote agendas that also defend an all-powerful myth and central idea of modern American adoption that strangers can be the equivalent of blood relatives. These are conflicting ideas. They represent a form of advocacy hypocrisy that has been criticized by the earliest adoptee-rights advocates such as Jean Paton, to contemporary birth parent and adoptee-rights defender Claudia Corrigan D'Arcy.[6]

One of the most prominent adoption research and advocacy groups of the last twenty years, called the Donaldson Adoption Institute, closed because of financial pressures in early 2018. It embodied this advocacy tension best. It was pro-adoptee on some issue papers it published on the pros and cons of open birth records. In 2007, it advocated "to restore unrestricted access for adult adopted persons to their original birth certificates."[7] In 2017 it began calling adoptees' legal right to those records a human-rights issue. Yet the group avoided the underlying issue of kinship and how this intrinsically related to the adoption experience for adoptees every day of their lives. The institute's website used ambiguous language that provided no clarity on the underlying evolutionary-psychology issue: why adoptee and birth parents' identity records should never have been closed, for decades now.

One of the largest organizations that promotes adoption and the profitable transglobal adoption industry, the National Council for Adoption (NCFA), claims it "is committed to the belief that every child deserves to thrive in a nurturing, permanent family."[8] The group remains one of the leading and vocal opponents of open-records laws that would allow adoptees to learn their genetic and blood ancestry, as is practiced in countries like England, Norway, and France by federal law. The pro-open-records group Bastard Nation claims the NCFA has a "long history of coming into states that are contemplating legislative change such as making the adoptee's original birth certificate available to the adoptee and persuading legislators, through bogus and unfounded arguments, that open adoption records will cause more abortions and fewer adoptions."[9]

For adoptees, silence on the issue of family kinship and genetic relations by pro-adoption organizations is telling. It tells adoptees these groups still support an invented notion that family bonding can occur in ways that mirror or mimic bonding that occurs among genetic kin. Research in evolutionary biology has shown that is not the case.

The concept of kin selection, also known as inclusive fitness theory, is more than fifty years old. Today it is widely accepted as a predictably strong evolutionary-biology model that explains why people make sacrifices for others who have their genes.[10] Called Hamilton's rule, after its creator W. D. Hamilton, it explains that a person will take altruistic action like running into a burning building on behalf of close relatives, such as offspring. But that same person will take fewer risks for more distant relatives, such as cousins, and will be willing to sacrifice more toward distant relatives than toward genetic strangers. The investment means one would trade two brothers for eight cousins, because of the relationships that are measured in total genetic similarity.

Research on family and kin relations has shown that kin relationships have higher levels of emotional closeness than non-kin relations. Overall, genetic kinship is one of the most powerful predictors of emotional closeness in any human relationship.[11] In general, kin selection theory predicts that parents will provide less beneficial behaviors to their unrelated children—which can include step and adopted children—relative to their biologically related children.

So long as pro-adoption advocacy groups avoid kinship research and its underlying science, they will never fully embrace the underlying rationale for openness in birth records. They will eschew research that indicates adoptees and birth mothers have distinct yearnings that only birth relatives have. They will discount a reality for adoptees that some family relationships cannot be fully duplicated in adopted families. Accepting this research means some of the main messages promoting adoption have to be questioned, calling into question the practice itself as a social, economic, business, and cultural institution.

Relevant research on the importance of blood kinship and kinship theory for non-biologically related family members has been published, but it is not discussed by most groups who promote the business of adoption. The strong evidence pointing to different health outcomes and the way humans nurture their offspring differently depending on biological relations, likely will not be fully acknowledged by supporters of the adoption status quo in the United States. Supporters of the adoption and also the foster-care system argue adoptive and stepparents have the same imperative to love and care for their biological and non-biological offspring. However, research in foster-parent care shows there is strong bias against nonbiological kin.

Research by Canadians Martin Daly and Margaret Wilson on bias against nonbiological children by stepparents, called "the Cinderella Effect," shows that "non-violent discrimination against stepchildren is substantial and ubiquitous" globally, according to their 2002 paper, "The Cinderella Effect: Parental Discrimination Against Stepchildren."[12] This is a taboo topic mainly because it challenges the idea that stepparents—and maybe also adoptive parents—are hardwired to nurture children who are not related to them by blood differently. This is a white-hot idea that divides child-psychiatry experts and nonexperts, foster and adoptive parents, and the large online adoption community.

At the heart of this premise is how humans, the most socially advanced species, express Darwinian selection through selective care of the closest relatives. According to Daly and Wilson, "there is nothing magical about parental discrimination: preferential treatment of one's own young exists only where a species' ecology demands it."[13] The two see no reason why the evolution of the human psyche would be excluded from this logic.

Daly and Wilson's research uses epidemiological evidence, including the use of an archive of 87,789 validated reports of child maltreatment in the United States. They support their findings with dozens of peer-reviewed studies of stepparenting abuse across cultures that also find similar patterns of abuse and stress. Daly and Wilson's research also went well beyond lethal and abusive treatment of children by their non-genetic parents. The outcomes they list show how medical care is restricted, education funding is withheld later in life, and other forms of nonphysical abuse and favoritism prevail.

Research Daly and Wilson cited shows that in several countries, including Canada and the United States, stepparents beat very young children to death at per capita rates that are more than one hundred times higher than the corresponding rates for genetic parents. Children under three years of age who lived with one genetic parent and one stepparent were estimated to be seven times as likely to be the victims of validated physical abuse as those living with both their genetic parents. Numerous other studies have also demonstrated that children living with stepmothers do not receive the same regular medical and dental care as children living with their genetic parents, and less money is spent on food in stepmother households.[14]

The two researchers do not mean to say stepparents are terrible people. They propose the opposite. Daly and Wilson argue that our understanding of stepparenting should not "suffer from the misconception that a 'biological' explanation for stepparental violence is a claim of its inevitability and imperviousness to social controls, which, if accepted, will excuse the violence." They claim that these misunderstandings block progress in understanding and helping kids. The greatest harm, they argue, is done by "those who adhere to the implausible notion that stepparenthood is psychologically equivalent to genetic parenthood and that 'bonding' experience is sufficient to evoke the full depth of parental feeling."[15]

Daly and Wilson did not address data on adoptive parents and adoptees, perhaps intentionally. Many critics say their model focuses on violence that occurs when a new male enters into a relationship with a female with existing children, and thus are perceived as competition. This is different from adoption, which is more voluntary, though fraught with unspoken stress. Overall, the experiences are different for all parties, but alike in many ways too, because one or more parents is not genetically related to the child.

I also have experienced life in a "blended" family, with a stepfather and three stepsisters. I have now concluded that the lack of kinship I share with my stepfamily is an underlying source of friction for our very imperfect relationship over more than three decades. There simply is no bond that joins us, much the way I feel about my adoptive cousins, uncles, and aunts. For me, there is no blood that ties us, nor DNA to bind us. We are not true kin, both as I perceive it and as I have experienced this relation for decades now.

Other researchers have also supported the evolutionary-biology model that individuals care more for their biological offspring than children with no blood relations. A 2011 study by German demographers Sebastian Schnettler and Anja Steinbach used long-term data on US adolescents that could compare different information on many child relations: biological siblings, half-siblings, and nonrelated stepsiblings. They found in every respect, stepchildren provide lower assessments of their relationships with their parents than biological children do. They also conclude differences in the assessments increased proportionally to the differences in genetic similarities among siblings. In short, biological parenthood matters.[16]

At its heart this evolutionary model is nature at its most basic core, particularly from the gene's point of view. In this selfish gene model, the only thing that matters is maximizing fitness and survival for the gene. Chances for spreading one's gene in a population happen through reproduction of a gene in the gene pool. Survival odds are increased through reproduction of a gene's own carrier, as well as supporting the reproduction of others who likely share the same genes as the carrier. In other words, one should favor one's close genetic kin, and not socialized relationships that do not share genetic kinship, such as nonrelated adoptees and some stepchildren.

A few in the evolutionary-psychology field challenge this model as it applies to modern adoption. Researcher Kyle Gibson, in 2009, attempted to disprove the Cinderella Effect as it applies to adoptive families. Gibson claims that adoptive parents in households with an adopted and biological kid invest more resources in adopted children than in genetically related ones—in terms of money and tutoring, for instance. He does not address emotional measurements, and he does not quantify the act of parental love or its impacts. He also acknowledges that adoptees statistically experience more negative outcomes: "They were more likely to have been arrested, to have been on public assistance and to require treatment for drug, alcohol or mental health issues. They also completed fewer years of schooling and were more likely to divorce." The rationale for parents favoring adopted kids, he determines, is simply "the squeaky wheel gets the grease," and "they are more likely than genetic children to need the help."[17]

However, Gibson's research lacks statistical validity, and thus his findings cannot be applied to the wider group of Americans who are adopted. The sample size totaled 126 surveys, which is vastly too small to yield results that have any application to a wider population,[18] let alone the millions of US families with adoptees. Nor did his study ensure randomness of a sample—a critical technique for scientific and polling research. Gibson's study drew from only one adoption agency in a state he did not mention. So while some pro-adoption advocates have embraced his findings in popular magazines as if the findings were fact, they also ignore the fundamental research flaws that invalidate the applicability of his conclusions for a small sample group.[19]

It is noteworthy that some of the earliest child welfare advocates for pregnant women and homeless children in the United States, from the late 1800s to the early 1900s, did not view adoption as a suitable replacement for parenting by natural parents. Adoption historian Barbara Melosh writes that these reformers "were skeptical that permanent homes for children could be found among strangers."[20] What's more, before World War II, professional social workers regularly collected and provided adoption-case record information about adoptees and shared it with adoptive parents, adoptees, and to a lesser extent birth mothers, because of the importance they assigned to biological kinship and their own professional social work standards.[21]

While debates occur in journals in the evolutionary-psychology field, the research does not filter into the marketplace eager to serve the millions of parents raising offspring who are not the same biological kin. A long list of adoption guidance books can be found online or at public libraries for the parents who have to confront the issue of bonding, whether they are adoptive or foster parents. Many books will not touch on the topic that an evolutionary role for kinship and blood affects parenting behavior. For instance, Deborah Gray's *Attaching in Adoption*, re-published in 2012,[22] altogether avoids the issues of biological kinship and adoptees' desire to know their ancestry. Instead, it offers guidance on "normal and healthy attachment" and barriers that prevent it.

Some authors wade into the debate online. One 2013 online article in *Adoption Voices Magazine*, by author and adoptive parent Sally Bacchetta, notes, "Adoptive parents don't love their children the same way biological parents do. That's an uncomfortable notion for a lot of people, but it's true. We don't love our children the same way. We can't. That's not who our children are. Our children come to us from someone else. . . . Our children carry someone else with them into our hearts, and we love them differently because of it."[23] While this view was hotly contested by many adoptive parents, the critics there and elsewhere do not cite evidence about clear differences in outcomes between adoptive and biological children, due to the reality that they do not share true genetic kinship.

Studies have shown differences in health outcomes for adoptive children compared with biological children at the population level. As utterly cruel as this sounds, this means I likely will not be as healthy or live as long as someone my age in my economic and racial group, simply because I was not reared by a biological parent. As someone trained in public health and with an adopted sister who has demonstrated unhealthy behaviors with a high risk of many chronic diseases, I am extremely mindful of the implications of the research. I have seen these outcomes play out over decades in my family.

In 2010, four Danish researchers—Liselotte Petersen, Thorkild I. A. Sørensen, Erik Lykke Mortensen, and Per Kragh Andersen—published a paper comparing the health outcomes of more than 12,700 adult adoptees born between 1924 and 1947 with the rest of their countrymen. They wanted to see how well the adoptees fared for illnesses and mortality against the entire population. The researchers concluded that adoptees have higher levels of early death than everyone else in the population. Specifically, the excess in mortality before the age of sixty-five in adoptees was 1.3 times higher, a statistically significant finding. Also adoptees were statistically more likely, before the age of sixty-five, to die of infections, vascular complications, cancer, alcohol-related problems, and suicide. And for adoptees who died after the age of sixty-five, they had higher rates of cancer, alcohol-related deaths, and suicides than their countrymen overall.[24] In short, Danish adoptees were sicker and were likely to die earlier than their non-adopted countrymen.

From this statistically strong population study, one cannot draw a conclusion about why the adoptees fared worse overall. Issues surrounding openness about an adoptee's family-blood ties and the ability to access information creates well-acknowledged and clearly documented psychological harm. This has been reported now for more than a half century. For adoptees, not knowing one's family health histories also creates well-understood health risks. Adoptees lack their family and genetic-health information to help them manage their health care throughout their life. There can be combined and cumulative impacts. In the end, these were measured at the population level, where it matters.

Professor Ellen Herman, an adoption-history scholar who also runs a University of Oregon website called the Adoption History Project, has studied the history of how the United States responded to the evolving nature of adoption involving the government, child welfare policymakers, social scientists, and the millions of participants in adoption. Adoption was the identified social problem, and the solution was as she calls its "designated kinship by design." It has been a large-scale experiment from the beginning, testing, as Herman calls it, "enduring beliefs in the power of blood, and widespread doubts about whether families could thrive without it."[25]

From ancient civilizations to the present, kinship has played a central role in how humans have dealt with the concept of adoption. In the past, blood relations were considered elemental to the practice. The pivotal importance of kinship, and blood relations, still connects the past to the present.

Adoption, as a means to create a structure that ties parents and children who are not biologically related, has been around as long as humans have been keeping records. It can be found in most cultures, with and without written records. The Code of Hammurabi, of the Babylonian Kingdom from 2285 BCE provides, "if a man has taken up a young child 'from his waters' to sonship and has reared him up no one has any claim against the nurseling."[26] In ancient Rome, adoption was widely used by the "best families" of the empire, mainly to ensure the integrity of the important houses. The adoptees were often adults, not children, and confined to wealthy families and not the poor. Most adoptions involved extended kin. In post–Confucian China, adoption practices were common, mainly to bring a male relative—again biological kin—into the family for inheritance and maintaining family-ritual memorial obligations. Like the Romans, the practice was related to preserving family names and property. Adopted sons were eligible to inherit property.[27]

Blood and family kinship continues to play an absolutely central role in adoption globally. Today, up to one half of all adoptions in the United States and globally involve bringing together members of related children, such as nieces and nephews.[28] From a historic perspective, adoption was always designed to serve the needs of the adults and families for kinship, religious, community, or basic economic reasons—not to promote the welfare of the child.[29] The wider idea of allowing adoptions of nonrelated persons into a family for the child's benefit is still a new idea in the United States—the country that became a pioneer in the idea that turned into the larger system we know today. The first state law recognizing adoption was passed in the United States in 1851, in Massachusetts. Other countries followed much later with modern adoption laws: England in 1926, West Germany in 1977.

The United States stands apart from its mother country, England, by breaking with the centuries-long English legal tradition of primogeniture. English society codified its preference for blood ties, and only the eldest natural and legitimate son could inherit property. Nonlegitimate children were not eligible, making adoption a forbidden act for centuries, leading in part to the start of orphanages, homeless houses, and the placing of children into apprenticeships in its colonies in the seventeenth century.

Ironically, today it is England, not the United States, that allows all adopted adults to have access to their birth records upon their eighteenth birthday under a national law.[30] The message for all English adult adoptees is elegantly simple and unambiguous: "You can access your birth records if you don't have them because you were adopted. You need to be 18 or over to do this. Everyone adopted before 12 November 1975 will need to attend a counseling [*sic*] session with an approved adoption advisor first." That is it. By contrast, the United States' patchwork system of state laws continues to discriminate openly and legally against adult adoptees who seek their original birth records without any intermediaries or state obstruction.

One of the brightest developments in recent years was when Governor David Ige of Hawaii signed legislation that replicates England's national law and gives all adoptees eighteen years of age and older unrestricted access to their birth records. This model state legislative reform, which got almost no national coverage from any media, found fault with past legislation that prevented adoptees from knowing their history, and especially their ancestral kin.

The final bill signed by Governor Ige in June 2016 is also significant because it acknowledges evidence for openness as a best public health practice and that adoption is no longer a shamed-based child-placement and social practice. "Furthermore, cultural changes have largely diminished the stigma surrounding adoption, and recent genetics research has highlighted the importance of genetic history to an individual's medical care," the signed bill notes. "This measure eases the restrictions on access to sealed court adoption records in the interest of transparency and access to family medical history and ethnic background."[31]

Chapter 7

Legalized Discrimination Against Adoptees: The Demon Behind the Problem

All are equal before the law and are entitled without any discrimination to equal protection of the law.

—Article 7, *Universal Declaration of Human Rights*

For more than six decades, millions of adopted Americans have faced legalized discrimination. No one set out to do intentional harm to adoptees. Yet the institution of adoption that grew after World War II singled out adoptees for differential treatment. Persons surrendered at birth inherited this system as a birthright with no meaningful role in the national dialogue deciding their fate.

Today, the policies, laws, and culture that have grown over the last sixty years collectively deny adoptees equal status under the law. For adoptees, this outcome is particularly ironic. The movement to make adoption records more secretive from adoptees, depriving them of basic rights, came when social movements at all levels of society were demanding change and succeeding in expanding legal rights for all Americans from the 1950s onward.

In the United States, adoptee-rights groups have unsuccessfully challenged laws that discriminate against classes of people as unconstitutional under the Fourteenth Amendment of the US Constitution. The amendment, interpreted by the courts to end discrimination against African Americans and other minorities by states in civil rights court challenges up through the 1960s, states, "No state shall make or enforce any law which shall abridge the privileges or immunities of citizens of the United States; nor shall any state deprive any person of life, liberty, or property, without due process of law; nor deny to any person within its jurisdiction the equal protection of the laws."

Arguments for a constitutional right to equal treatment under that law for adoptees have been kicking around for half a century. The debate began when the national Adoption Rights Movement (ARM) gained steam after the 1960s. Adoptees began demanding equal rights once states started restricting access to their birth records, when less than twenty years earlier they could review those documents. By the 1970s, hundreds of groups had started in North America and the United Kingdom to help adoptees connect with birth mothers. While the United Kingdom opened adoption records to adoptees with a national law called the Children's Act in 1975, the door closed further in the United States. During this time, numerous adoptees filed lawsuits to open records.

The most influential US group that captured the public imagination and inflamed defenders of closed records was the Adoptees' Liberty Movement Association (ALMA), led by adoptee and author Florence Fisher. She articulated a clear stand for "free access to our original birth certificates and the records of our adoption."[1] ALMA took the state of New York to court in 1977 with a federal class action lawsuit.

The ALMA suit hoped to pry open the Empire State's adoption-records laws to adult adoptees. ALMA claimed adoptees had a constitutional right under the First, Thirteenth, and Fourteenth Amendments to their personal information contained in sealed adoption records. In a highly creative argument, the ALMA demanded records access under the Thirteenth Amendment, which prohibits slavery, claiming adult adoptees who were prevented from finding their birth parents was the equivalent of antebellum slave children being sold before they were old enough to know their parents. But the courts, including the United States Court of Appeals for the Second Circuit, ruled adoptees had no such "fundamental" right to learn the identities of their birth parents in any of the cited amendments.[2] In stark contrast to the actual history of US adoption practices, the court found that sealed records had no relation to illegitimacy, and as such adoptees had no social stigma associated with illegitimacy that would provide them greater scrutiny of those records.[3] Since that defeat, the ALMA retreated from its former advocacy focus and dedicated itself to connecting adoptees and birth parents through a participant-funded registry system.

In a much broader human rights framework beyond the US Constitution, treating adoptees differently by state laws—as practiced throughout the United States—should also be seen as a denial of basic human rights. One of humanity's most basic rights bestowed on all persons at birth allows everyone to know who they are, to know their kin, and to know where they come from. These are eternal human questions. They exist outside the boundaries of race, income, religion, or nationality. Article 7 of the *Universal Declaration of Human Rights*, by the United Nations, states, "All are equal before the law and are entitled without any discrimination to equal protection of the law."[4] As of 2017, all but nine states are partially or outright violating this principle of international law, not to mention the Fourteenth Amendment, through laws singling out classes of citizens for unequal legal treatment regarding their legal identity documents.

Unfortunately, these "rights" positions are not shared in the halls of state government. They are not covered by the media, who mostly cover adoption issues with occasional feel-good reunion stories or with legislative stories on bills attempting to reform closed records. In 2017, the media periodically picked up news of legislative debates of proposed changes to laws governing adoptee birth records in Florida, Massachusetts, Connecticut, New York, Texas, and a few other states. The media that year also put the spotlight on the implementation of a law passed in 2014 in New Jersey that opened birth records in 2017 for thousands of New Jersey-born adoptees, but also created problematic birth parent vetoes that deny about 550 adoptees their claims to legal rights to their birth certificate.[4] This also set a legal precedent some adoptee-rights advocates say harms all future advocacy for adoptee equal rights—that of universal legal rights for all adoptees to their birth records.

The stories rarely provide the deeper context that focuses on foundational legal and human rights. What's more, human rights arguments for identity documents are mostly shunned by even so-called "adoption advocates"—who masquerade to support adoptees but also promote the global and growing "business of adoption."

My lifelong efforts for equality have shown me that the general disinterest in the basic rights of adoptees can be traced to the deep, archetypal fears of bastards and illegitimate children. It is also a byproduct of how those involved in adoption have been widely stigmatized by society, the mental health profession, and political-interest groups vested in maintaining the status quo of closed records.

The only national adoptee-rights advocacy groups calling for universal open records do not have deep enough pockets or an organization that matches the Human Rights Campaign's capacity to promote gay and transgender rights. The lack of a clear national campaign for adoptees' legal equality and the broader public ignorance of how adoption laws deny equal rights to adoptees is likely the reason why adoptees have few allies among interest groups who also experience discrimination.

According to a 2015 national survey commissioned by the now-closed Donaldson Adoption Institute, adoptees are seen as a group that experience less stigma than other members of society. The institute's survey of nearly two thousand persons nationwide found that only 25 percent of those contacted found adoptees faced stigma. Adoptees ranked near the bottom of other groups who were thought to face greater social stigma, including transgender people, the poor, gays, the obese, ethnic minorities, the elderly, veterans, and more.[6]

The Adoptee Rights Coalition promotes open records for all, but in recent years has not been actively involved in national advocacy, according to its published materials. The most well-known and quoted group remains Bastard Nation. It frequently is labeled as "extreme" by supporters of closed records and groups who participate in the transglobal adoption industry. Even ardent and longtime supporters of open birth records have called it "a radical adoptee rights organization."[7]

Bastard Nation's main policy plank, if it were implemented nationally, would be a national adoption law similar to what was implemented in Scotland in 1930 and England in 1975. In the more than eight decades since birth records were opened in Scotland and later in England and Wales, more than half of those adopted have sought their genealogical information from their records and/or made contact with a birth relative, often the mother. This happened without any negative consequences for society.[8] The solution proposed by Bastard Nation is a system that has already worked for decades helping adoptees and society at the population level and in a country very similar culturally to the United States.

The group's mission statement unequivocally states:

> Bastard Nation is dedicated to the recognition of the full human and civil rights of adult adoptees. Toward that end, we advocate the opening to adoptees, upon request at age of majority, of those government documents which pertain to the adoptee's historical, genetic, and legal identity, including the unaltered original birth certificate and adoption decree. Bastard Nation asserts that it is the right of people everywhere to have their official original birth records unaltered and free from falsification, and that

the adoptive status of any person should not prohibit him or her from choosing to exercise that right.[9]

The group played an instrumental role in the successful and historic voter initiative in Oregon in 1998, known as Ballot Measure 58. The measure drew national attention. Opponents outspent proponents 20–1, and Bastard Nation members and their supporters eschewed past arguments that withholding records is somehow psychologically damaging—a controversial claim that is still used to stigmatize adoptees.[10] The measure states "any adopted person 21 years of age and older born in the state of Oregon shall be issued a certified copy of his/her unaltered, original and unamended certificate of birth."[11] Bastard Nation mobilized support through the internet. The group also tapped into messages used during Fisher's legal advocacy two decades earlier. Bastard Nation framed their message around traditional American ideas of equality and civil rights, the harm of discrimination against minorities, and also mistrust of government that overreaches its authority.[12]

Gregory Luce, an influential Minnesota-based lawyer, who advocates on behalf of adoptees seeking their equal rights and unrestricted access to their original birth records, argues that Bastard Nation is the only national group since that time that has stood true to its mission to defend adoptees' rights to their birth records as an inherent human right, compared to other national groups like the American Adoption Congress. That group has supported legislation that denied this right to all adoptees in birth records bills debates in state capitols during the last ten years. "One thing that Bastard Nation does—and is relentless in doing so—is refuse to give in to compromised legislation, at the beginning, at the end, at any point. Bastard Nation has been crystal clear about this position for more than two decades, and yet people go apoplectic when Bastard Nation actually holds fast to its compass and works hard to defeat compromised legislation," writes Luce. "Bastard Nation has been the only national advocacy group to do this."[13]

US adoption laws that openly discriminate against adoptees are particularly noteworthy because the movement to make adoption records harder to access by adoptees came at a time when voting rights, civil rights, gay rights, disability rights, and women's rights were being secured for all Americans from the 1950s onward. The loss of rights for adoptees and birth parents even came as adoptee advocates began to organize for more openness. Yet today, after the US Supreme Court has legalized gay marriage in all fifty states and all US territories, scant mention is made of the legal double standard for adoptees and birth parents. In addition to basic archetypal fears of illegitimately born people and cultural biases against bastards, adoption issues are still cloaked in shame associated with out-of-wedlock childbirth that the nation collectively tried to hide for decades when sexual mores changed following World War II.

As of December 2017, only nine states provided adult adoptees unfettered and full legal access to their original birth records. Another sixteen states have what some adoptee-rights advocates called "compromised laws," which limit the rights of adult adoptees to access their original birth certificate. These restrictions are in the form of birth parent disclosure vetoes, the redaction of an adoptees' information found in birth records or a birth certificate, or restrictions that are placed on access to an original birth certificate because of an adoptees' birth year—as I experienced in Michigan because of when I was born. Those states include: Washington, Montana, South Dakota, Nebraska, Oklahoma, Minnesota, Wisconsin, Michigan, Illinois, Missouri, Tennessee, Ohio, Delaware, New Jersey, Connecticut, and Massachusetts. The remaining twenty-six states, including the District of Columbia, have laws that provide no true access rights to adoptees to their original birth certificates, except by court orders.[14]

As with many movements that fought for basic rights, the adoptee-rights advocacy had early and visionary leaders who identified concerns and worked for change long before society acknowledged a national problem. Though she is mostly unknown today, Jean Paton became the first true intellectual and moral voice of the nascent political movement advocating for rights of adoptees and birth parents.

Born in Detroit in 1908, Paton studied social work and became a social crusader and equal rights champion two decades ahead of her time on behalf of adoptees, a group that had never found a public voice for themselves. She saw adoptees in the context of larger social movements. In a comparison Paton made in 1962, in the midst of the national civil rights struggle, growing women's movement, and even international conflicts for self-determination, she did not see a similar promise for her cause: "Just because we live in the midst of talk about human rights, and the emancipation of submerged populations, and the freedom of minority groups—do not be confident that the problems of adopted people are about to be solved. They are the final minority, the enduring colonials, the silent folk who upon rare occasion speak."[15] As with so many issues surrounding adoption, Paton proved prophetic.

In 1954, she published her first book on adoption, *The Adopted Break Silence*.[16] It provided a narrative of the adoption experience that cast light where there was secrecy, stigma, and societal shame. It allowed adoptees to frame their own story in their own voice and honestly describe issues widely accepted today as healthy and normal: ambivalent feelings about one's origins, the need to search for genetic kin, and a desire to connect with those who have a physical resemblance.

Paton's path-breaking work was published years before any organized adoptee or birth parent advocacy group had emerged. In it she also highlighted the many undesirable aspects in adoption policy. Paton advocated for openness and honesty with adoptees—all more than six decades ago, and all central issues to the legal debates in states with closed birth records that were once open to adoptees. Based on data and interviews from forty adopted men and women, she put forth ideas that have resonated intimately among adoptees since. "Tell them," she wrote, "and tell them from the beginning that they are adopted. And tell them something of whence they came and why."[17]

She published a second book called *Orphan Voyage* in 1968. In addition to her writings advocating for adoptees' rights, she helped to launch the first national organization for birth parents, Concerned United Birthparents, and was a leading force in the founding of the national organization for adult adoptees called the American Adoption Congress. Both emerged in the 1970s, serving the needs of those impacted by the nation's adoption policies and laws. These groups were driven by adoptees like Paton or birth mothers, who challenged the dominant social narrative that condemned illegitimacy, promoted secrecy, and challenged the idea that adoption was the "best solution."

Paton suggested the creation of a mutual consent registry as early as 1949, for example, and embraced the term "bastard" in the 1970s as a term of pride, long before the emergence of the advocacy group Bastard Nation in the 1990s. She was also among many who followed to suggest that searching for one's kin and records was a psychological necessity for individuals as well as collective social action that might lead to overdue reform. She suggested "that the desire to know the natural parents can be the deepest and most compelling factor in an adopted child's life. . . . Unless this desire resolves into reality it may be obscured in a long diversion, and in many cases this will be accompanied by years of unproductive behavior."[18]

She was mostly concerned with, as her biographer E. Wayne Carp called it, "the growth of secrecy in adoption records, the failure to recognize the existence of adult adoptees, and the erasure of the birth parents from the memory of the adoptive family." Paton had, according to Carp, brought to light the many recurring themes that those advocating for adoption reform are still addressing today.[19]

I also am struck how relevant Paton's critique of American adoption remains to this day. She correctly held accountable states, courts, bureaucratic institutions like offices of vital statistics, and professional groups like social workers for preventing adoptees from finding their roots and moving on with their lives. She wisely understood the way "therapeuticians" working on so-called "adult adoptee issues" had co-opted adoptee politics by the 1990s while sidestepping the underlying political problem of opening adoption records. The divide remains front and center today that distinguishes groups like Bastard Nation from other so-called adoption advocacy organizations who ignore or downplay the root political problem. As Paton noted, what good was therapy to an adopted person who desired to search for his first family if the law were not changed. The "prohibition itself that [was] the demon behind the problem."[20]

Most importantly, Paton's wisdom was also based on her life experiences, when records were accessible to adoptees before the end of World War II. She wrote: "In 1942 I had gone to the Probate Court . . . and looked up my first adoption paper, and saw my mother's full name signed by her own hand. There was no rigmarole; you were allowed to see your own paper in a kindly procedure."[21] That openness was about to change to a culture of secrecy, which she was able to observe throughout her long life. Unlike Paton, I and millions of other adoptees born after 1950 encountered a different reality than she did that is based on secrecy and rigidly enforced state laws denying adoptees access to their birth records and biological family histories.

Elizabeth Samuels, a University of Baltimore law professor and adoption law expert, has written extensively about the "demon behind the problem" and has provided expert testimony to states where advocates have worked to reform adoption laws that deny adoptees equal rights. Samuels has shown how states changed adoption laws from the 1930s to the present, incrementally restricting access to adoption records between the 1960s and 1990s. The change was legal, bureaucratic, and cultural. State legislatures, with the approval of governors, passed the laws and became the new champions of birth-record secrecy.

In the first half of the twentieth century, adoption records and birth records were not veiled in secrecy for those most affected by adoption. Carp's study of American adoption found that "there existed among legislators, vital statisticians, and social workers a consensus both in policy and practice of openness in disclosing information to those most intimately connected to adoption."[22] So while court proceeds of adoption and birth certificates were made confidential by state law, Carp notes that the intent of the law was to keep the public from intruding on the privacy and reputation of adoptive and natural parents, who would be shamed by making that information public. Before World War II, adoptive parents, adoptees, and even natural parents could, as Paton did, legally receive information about the adoptions and births from the courts and bureaus of vital statistics.

Prior to the 1950s, adult adoptees had legal access to court records to their adoption proceedings. Adoptees, adoptive parents, and even natural parents could legally obtain information about the adoption and birth from the courts and bureaus of vital statistics. Social workers and advocates for children also believed strongly in having children maintain relations with their kin. The head of the US Children's Bureau said all children had legal and social rights to be protected and, when they grew up, "the right to know about himself."[23]

The Children's Bureau's 1949 legal guidelines for state law and policy governing adoption never mentioned any requirement for states to permanently seal original identity documents from adoptees or birth parents. Rather, the organization recommended state vital records be "complete and accurate" in order "to give the adopted child the information that ties in the details on his original birth record with his new name and status under the adoption decree." What's more, the agency stated that "in later life accurate and complete records will enable him to establish his true identity if occasion arises."[24] The Children's Bureau strongly recommended that states have birth and adoption records be classified as confidential. This would keep a child's status hidden from public knowledge and diminish public stigma, but not hide an adoptee's original identify from oneself.[25]

By the end of World War II, the mostly unregulated practice of adoption in the first part of the century had fallen under state supervision, even though there was no firm consensus how to regulate it. The laws that did emerge, according to Barbara Melosh, arrived through a shared view that adoptive families who were created by adopting a child from a relative or a stranger were considered equal to that of biological kinship. As an outcome, adoption permanently severed bonds of blood kinship and changed them to a legal one.[26]

In the 1940s and 1950s, most state laws still permitted adult adoptees to view birth records. But by 1960, twenty-six states were making both original birth records and adoption records available only by court order. Twenty other states had birth records available on demand. But over the following thirty years, through 1990, all of those states but three—Alaska, Kansas, and South Dakota—closed records to adult adoptees.[27] South Dakota later passed a law restricting access. The intent up through the end of the 1950s was never to prevent adult adoptees from accessing their original birth certificates—the documents bearing an adoptee's original name prior to adoption.

Several arguments emerged in the 1950s and 1960s promoting secrecy. The nation's then-most influential private group promoting children's welfare, the Child Welfare League of America, proposed in 1958 that closing access to original birth certificates, except by court order, would protect adoptees from knowing they were born out of wedlock.[28] It encouraged social service agencies to tell adoptive parents that the natural parents would not know with whom their child was placed. The League's only stated rationale for records secrecy was to ensure adoptive and birth parents did not know each other and to protect adoptees and adoptive parents from social stigma if such personal information was known publicly.[29] In 1969, an American Bar Association committee chair argued that secrecy in adoption protected adopted children and their adoptive parents from potential harassment by a birth parent.[30]

The transition to a culture and legal system enveloped in secrecy required policy and changes at the national level. Samuels notes that the Model Vital Statistics Act issued by the US Public Health Service in 1959 deleted past references in earlier acts that allowed adult adoptees to access their birth records. A 1969 revision to the Uniform Adoption Act omitted altogether earlier adoption act provisions spelling out adoptees' ability to access their records. No references were made throughout the 1960s why original birth records were slowly being closed to adult adoptees.[31]

The new culture of secrecy surrounding adoption records, and the laws passed by state lawmakers, reflected the social attitudes of that day. These ideas surrounding the nature of adoption emerged at the same time the number of unplanned pregnancies was growing nationally, requiring a solution to address the moral stain of out-of-wedlock sexual activity and single parenthood. Adoption was increasingly being regarded as a "complete and perfect" substitute for creating families. A prevailing myth also gained credibility that once adoption was legalized, the newly configured family could become the "real family" and the child would be the same and feel the same as if he or she were born into that family. This model wrongly assumed, as Samuels writes, an adoptee "would never be interested in learning about any other family."[32]

From the 1940s through the 1960s, child development theories emphasized nurture over nature and suggested that a birth parent's purported immorality would not be transmitted in a child's development or future actions. These views coincided with larger societal views that shamed unmarried women. The institutionalizing of this shame can be seen in the changing missions of the Florence Crittenton Homes and other places that spirited away unwed, and mostly white, women until they gave birth to their kids.

According to a view printed in a 1955 publication by the US Children's Bureau—the leading government agency influencing adoption policy—society had a role in helping unwed mothers and changing them, so they could later create families through marriage. "Most of them are in their child-bearing period," the bureau wrote. "Most of them will have other children, hopefully in wedlock. The community has a real stake in helping these girls become stable wives and mothers."[33]

The mental health profession had broadly framed out-of-wedlock pregnancies in the 1940s and 1950s as a psychopathology of the mothers. Reforming a mentally ill mother who had a child out of wedlock could occur with the lifelong separation from her relinquished child, which would enable the woman a chance to fulfill her desired identity as a woman by raising her own children. The growing adoption market, during the postwar baby boom, provided the "system" to implement this ideal.

As a historic event, my adoption in 1965 occurred because of quite natural and normal sexual relations and the unplanned pregnancy between my birth mother and my birth father—a man who never admitted paternity. In the larger historic context, it played out within this untested national experiment to address societal issues, and my life is a byproduct of this experiment.

Theoretically, my relinquishment to another family should have transformed me and my birth mother. The social engineering emphasis of this era is almost never discussed publicly when lawmakers or the media talk about adoption—an almost revered practice in the public's eye. Unfortunately, widespread ignorance of US adoption also prevents honest discussions about policy and legal reform.

During the years surrounding my birth, most adoptions were taking place though a partnership of public or private agencies, all under the aegis of social workers. Social workers served as the primary, but not only, intermediaries who made adoptees' identity change possible from one name and family to another. The Lutheran Children's Friend Society of Michigan played the lead role in my relinquishment and placement. From the 1950s through the 1970s, confidential adoptions were the norm, and no contact was made between the birth parents once they relinquished their children.[34] During this period, the records-keeping system completed the child's identity transformation, both in secret and in accordance with law.

This so-called national consensus as it was practiced also required many other professionals every step of the way. The foot soldiers who carried out the legal mandates and placement services included personnel at the social service bureaucracies and probate courts, along with vital-records keepers, like staff at the Michigan Department of Health and Human Services.

As someone trained in public health and as an adoptee, I can see my historic place in the larger social experiment called adoption, and that experiment troubles me. The transformation to secrecy happened without any major public debate. Policy-makers made decisions without clear evidence proving that records secrecy offered any benefits to mothers and children placed for adoption. I have found almost no documented accounts of any professional group who ran the adoption system questioning this practice or researching whether it provided mothers or their children any lasting benefits. One sociology study from 1965—the year of my birth—on issues that influenced birth mothers' decisions to relinquish their infants, described an almost total absence of research of the national system. The author called it "a large area of almost wholly uncharted territory."[35]

Societal views that stigmatized unwed mothers and particularly adopted children drove the system that changed a child's name and legal identity, while eliminating access to original birth records for birth families and adoptees. That stigma remains to this day. Both of those groups were excluded from the decision-making process to make records secret. Those groups still remain marginalized as political advocates in the eyes of state lawmakers.

Literature during this era contained mixed and sometimes harmful messages for adoptive parents and their adopted children, like me. Some social workers and psychological professionals counseled that any adopted child who sought out their origins was acting out a fantasy. Viola Bernard, an influential psychiatrist whose writings influenced thinking in the field and whose writings on adoption were published by the Child Welfare League of America in the mid-1960s, claimed an adolescent adoptee's need to connect with their past could be satisfied by adoptive parents. She characterized a young adoptee's entirely normal and natural curiosity as tragic, "pathological distortions," calling them "very disturbed young people" who engaged in "fantasy, or even delusion."[36]

Sadly, some of these ideas are still alive today in published literature in the mental health field. I heard this in comments leveled at me when I have explained why I changed my name in 2009. As an adoptee who is used to biased comments about adoption and a quiet, unspoken uneasiness about adoptees, I have ignored ignorant remarks, and I mostly avoid discussing my complicated, legal personal history with people other than those I know well.

Parenting literature from the adoption-boom era also was awash in guidance directed to adoptive parents, telling them how to inform the children they adopted about their origins. Manuals before the mid-1960s told adoptive parents to hide the fact their children were adopted. From the mid-1960s through the mid-1970s, books and manuals told adoptive parents when to share information about adoption.[37]

Adoption advocates, starting in the 1970s and later, claimed that privacy—including confidentiality, surrendering adoptees for adoption, and sealed records—was "a cherished American value under attack by adoption activists."[38] This became what I call the dominant and false history of adoption, without historic evidence to support a political position to defend adoption secrecy and discrimination against adoptees. During the 1970s, legal commentary and court options began discussing sealed records in new language, as a birth parent's "right" to lifelong anonymity.

As late as 1976, the Child Welfare League of America continued to focus on illegitimacy in its national policy proposals on managing birth records. The group's adoption guidelines recommended wiping clean the stain of single-parent childbirth from an adoptee's amended birth records. The CWLA proposed permanent child medical records with a "legitimacy item" for "the protection of the out-of-wedlock child and natural mother, and for the assessment of incidence and trends of the problems of illegitimacy."[39] The agency's proposals to restrict access to birth records did not provide any medical, legal, or other rationale. The league simply stated, "Information should be given to natural parents, adoptive parents or other individuals only when it is authorized by the person concerned or so ordered by the proper court."[40] Adoptees' former legal right to access their identity records had disappeared from accepted practices.

The new direction toward secrecy in adoption radically broke with past norms for access to adoption records and the best practices supported by professionals. As Samuels notes, "Lifelong secrecy had become so entrenched in the 1970s that the rhetoric and reasoning of most judicial opinions and legal periodical articles made it seem as if there had never been a time when a chorus of experts recommended sealing records but allowing adult adoptees access to records."[41] However, the US courts have held that neither state law nor the US Constitution provide guarantees of lifelong anonymity for birth parents from being contacted by their genetic offspring.[42]

Oddly, this legal movement to seal original birth certificates and birth records of adoptees up through the 1990s took place as many adoptees had come of age and began organizing local, state-level, and national movements demanding a universal right to know who they were and where they came from, as found in original identity documents. Advocates that followed Paton included Betty Jean Lifton, author of *Twice Born: Memoirs of an Adopted Daughter* (1975) and Fisher, head of the ALMA and author of *The Search for Anna Fisher* (1973).

Carp's history of US adoption shows that the institution also was changing from within. While the 1940s and 1950s saw huge spikes in illegitimate births that expanded adoption as an institution nationally, medical innovations affecting reproduction, changing cultural mores, and constitutional law also changed the institution of adoption in the 1960s and 1970s. The United States saw a drastic fall in the number of young infants available for adoption domestically, coinciding with the expansion of female reproductive rights and birth control choices for women.[43]

The drop in the number of newborns being relinquished by their mothers also changed the larger story of "illegitimacy." Shifting cultural views toward family planning and pregnancy, particularly for white women like my birth mother, made adoption less necessary as the "best solution" for the child and mother. In 1940, the birth rate for unmarried white women was just under 2 percent, jumping to nearly 11 percent in 1970 and 31 percent in 1993. The rate at which never-married white mothers relinquished their newborns before 1973 was almost 20 percent for those under forty-five years old, compared to less than 2 percent in the early 1990s. As these rates changed for single mothers, experts stopped promoting a view that women could leave their experience of surrendering a child entirely behind them.[44]

Use of the "pill" (female oral contraception) also widely expanded in the late 1960s. In 1973, the US Supreme Court legalized abortion, granting women constitutional protection to use abortion legally. These developments led to a steep drop in unplanned and unwanted pregnancies. Nonrelative adoptions in the United States dropped from a record high of 89,200 in 1970 to 47,500 in 1975, and 50,720 by 1982.[45] By 1975, adoption agencies nationally began to stop taking requests for "healthy, white infants." Social workers were telling prospective parents waiting for such a child that it could take from three to five years.[46]

Many unwed mothers were choosing to raise their children, and shifting public attitudes on illegitimacy laid the groundwork for open adoptions. The promotion of open adoptions arose in the 1970s and 1980s and become a central issue in adoption debates spearheaded by birth mothers, who organized themselves to push for alternatives in adoption practices.

Child welfare professionals, adoptive parents, adoptee-rights groups, and the public since the late 1990s and early 2000s also have gradually pushed for openness to both records and kinship information as the preferred system for infant adoptions. Birth parents are also more open to placing their children for adoption if they know some openness will be present in the adoption arrangement.

In 1996, the critically acclaimed English film by Mike Leigh on adoption, called *Secrets & Lies,* received Oscar buzz and drew international attention to adoption practices and the complications of secrecy in adoption. A few years later, the newly formed Bastard Nation claimed well-funded interest groups were advocating for state legislative changes to permanently seal all records, in order to hide what the group called controversial past practices associated with adoptions—coercion of mothers, fraud, even baby selling.[47] These issues blew up as national scandals in Australia, England, and Ireland later.

Today, most states provide adult adoptees with what is called "non-identifying information." For an adoptee, it is an insultingly tiny amount of information about one's identity. This information usually is a summary or copy of file-records that include the age, physical characteristics, ethnicity, race, religion, some medical information, education levels, and perhaps short life histories of a birth parent or parents. The summaries show the date, time, and place of birth. The information may also list how parental rights were terminated, either voluntarily or court-ordered. Because state, not federal law, has governed adoption practices, these records will vary state by state and also over time.[48]

Adoptees need to make written requests to courts or adoption agencies for these short reports. During my search from 1987 to 1989, I made repeated efforts by mail to find out who could even share this information. My first information batch arrived in 1988 from the Wayne County Probate Court and the Lutheran Child and Family Services—the successor of the agency that placed me. The two-page summary sent to me is written as a narrative, with all of the identifying information whited out on a Xerox copy about my birth mother, her birth parents, and the reported birth father.

The summary describes my physical characteristics, who examined me, the dates of my birthday and placement with a boarding home, and the day my birth mother legally severed her relationship with me forever and entrusted me to the full care and control of the agency that placed me, the Lutheran Children's Friend Society. That one paragraph sums up one of the biggest events of my life and my birth mother's life. A paragraph each describes my birth mother, my maternal grandparents, my birth mother's brother, and the named birth father. The only description of my birth father's parents is based on a single photograph my birth mother saw. The description later proved inaccurate.

The casework supervisor handling my case in 1965 and 1966 prepared a typed summary of my case. I received a more complete copy later, with additional details, after finding my birth mother and after I had the legal right to most of my files. But this was all I had for a year, and it gave just enough for me to conduct a successful private detective-like search on my own. I repeatedly read those sheets of paper looking for clues, trying to read in between the typed lines to learn who I was and where I came from.

As an adoptee, state law only allowed me to access non-identifying information records and nothing more. This forced me to make useless and expensive paper chases for two years with multiple bureaucracies. Adoptee-rights champion Paton concluded in the 1980s that sealed birth and original identity records ultimately did lasting harm to adoptees and turned them into pariahs. "The sealed record almost completely prohibits a person from finding out his real background," she wrote. "He is turned away and feels resentful. As soon as the record is sealed, society has entered into the situation. And the adopted person feels he can't fight society by himself—he becomes an outsider."[49]

Since Paton wrote that statement, the rationales for continuing discrimination against all adoptees from knowing their past and their kin have been shown to be outdated and irrelevant because of the success of open-records laws for adoptees in most developed nations, such as the United Kingdom. In written testimony submitted in 2013 to Ohio state lawmakers on pending adoption record legislation, adoption-law expert Samuels wrote: "With respect to birth parents' current attitudes about adult adoptees' access to original birth certificates, studies and surveys conducted since the 1980s show that overwhelmingly large majorities of birth parents, up to 95 percent and above, are open to contact with their children."[50]

From the 1980s onward, single-parent homes among white families became more widespread, with unmarried motherhood no longer linked to mental illness. Adoptive families were finally seen as having challenges and qualities, grounded in peer-reviewed studies of outcomes of adoptees and their families. Thanks to advocates, many birth parents openly talk about their desire for relinquished adult children to contact them.

However, this is not the consensus in the court of public opinion. Nor is this seen in state statutes. Communications from state and federal agencies continue to frame adoptions as a secretive matter, in which records must be hidden from the most impacted parties. Samuels in her 2013 testimony also noted that closed records remain a serious public policy and basic rights issue for adoptees: "Many birth parents as well as adult adoptees spend years, and considerable sums of money, searching for information about one another. While many are successful in their searches, as countless stories in the media attest, many of the adult adoptees who search for information about their original identities remain unsuccessful and frustrated because they lack access to their original birth certificates."[51]

Legislative reform at the state level to advance adoptees' rights to their records has not kept pace with rights reforms in so many other areas—gay rights, civil rights, disability rights, women's rights. The state legislative environment remains hostile to adoptees who advocate for equality under the law. Christian and conservative lawmakers dominate the legislative agenda in two-thirds of all state legislative chambers. This increased during President Barack Obama's two terms ending in 2016 and expanded again in the fall 2016 election that saw Donald Trump win the presidency.

Before Trump's election, Republican lawmakers in twenty-four states under GOP control planned to launch "aggressive policy initiatives" to limit the federal government and rekindle the culture wars.[52] After the 2016 general election, the Republican Party controlled thirty-three governorships. The GOP at the start of 2017 controlled both legislative chambers in thirty-two states, while Democrats controlled both in thirteen states.[53] The continued GOP takeover in state government, where adoption laws are made, translates to the rise of conservative lawmaking and laws advancing GOP policy views. New abortion regulations, which simultaneously promote adoption, are high on many of the GOP state lawmakers' priorities.[54]

Many Christian-conservative and also Republican lawmakers are sympathetic to adoptions as the "solution" to abortion—a view I do not accept. The Republican Party's 2012 Platform states: "We applaud the Republican legislative initiatives that led to a significant increase in adoptions in recent years, and we call upon the private sector to consider the needs of adoptive families on a par with others." The GOP also makes clear the choice in unwanted pregnancies it prefers: ". . . we affirm our moral obligation to assist, rather than penalize, women challenged by an unplanned pregnancy. We salute those who provide them with counseling and adoption alternatives and empower them to choose life, and we take comfort in the tremendous increase in adoptions that has followed."[55] Such ideas reveal how the party faithful perceive threats to a turnkey issue that motivates their political base. Opening adoption records challenges the model of adoptions as a "solution."

Having worked in the state political environment, in nonpartisan and also partisan Democratic positions, I am worried state legislative environments are more receptive now than even a decade ago to the Christian piety myth. As an adoptee, I have always viewed the Christian myth that being adopted equates to being born again as a marketing strategy to legitimize adoption nationally. This myth may remain the dominant idea in legislative settings, and in the national consciousness, because of the outsized role of evangelical Christians in global adoption and how that influences American thinking.

Law professor David Smolin has examined the growing power of right-leaning evangelical Christians in the highly unregulated and lucrative international adoption market. For the many organized groups supportive of the $14-billion-a-year adoption and child welfare services industry in the United states,[56] adoption is viewed as the ultimate act of redemption. It also demonstrates "God's care for each of His 'children.' The child is transferred into a Christian family and potentially/actually into the family of God."[57] Smolin notes the theology behind this decades-long movement supports state laws that discriminate against adoptees and promote records secrecy.

According to Smolin, the security and legitimacy of the modern American adoptive relationship are "built, legally and psychologically, upon the complete denial of any relationship between the adoptee and their original family." In short, the evangelical Christian view demands continued secrecy that denies adult adoptees their birth records. Smolin writes, "In such a system and viewpoint, it becomes impossible to honor and acknowledge both adoptive and biological relationships. The tendency of the Christian adoption movement has been to uncritically perceive this kind of adoption as supported by scripture and Christian theology."[58]

As a business model, adoption also requires closed records to sustain the organizations who profit from the placement of children, according to open-records advocate and birth mother Claudia Corrigan D'Arcy.[59] Internationally, the trafficking of infants has become a transglobal enterprise that ultimately required US federal intervention in 2014 to reign in what was called "the wild West" in one 2014 investigative story.[60] The raw and amoral logic of supply and demand drives this new global industry. Kathryn Joyce's study of evangelicals' role in this global trade of babies, in her influential 2013 book called, *The Child Catchers: Rescue,*

Trafficking, and the New Gospel of Adoption, notes that demand in the West cannot be filled, "at least not ethically or under current law."

Tens of thousands of poor parents in the developing world now represent the supply in this lucrative international adoption market that is now mostly run by evangelical Christians. Joyce writes this evangelical-Christian and faith-based business sector now is "a multibillion-dollar global industry driven not just by infertility but now also by pulpit commands."[61] The adoption system that separated birth kin in the United States is now separating babies from their families in developing nations.

Joyce shows that these groups now dominate the national discourse on adoption policy. She argues that in the making of adoption and policy in the United States in the 2000s and 2010s, the interests of adoptive parents and their lobbyists have drowned out the priorities and concerns of adoptees, birth parents, and single mothers. Such pro-adoption advocates tend to ignore the unintended consequences of their Christian-based imperatives and the larger "child-rescue industry."[62]

A final barrier preventing legal reform is often overlooked by research and adoptee advocates. As a system, adoption records keeping gives unchecked power to bureaucracies. Once empowered, many, mostly powerless bureaucrats do not wish to relinquish the power they possess over birth parents and adoptees searching for records. In short, a bureaucrat's imperative will always be to say, "No." History shows time and again in a classic Weberian sense how bureaucracies the world over wield power and take on lives of their own.

In April 1989 in Detroit, I met a social worker with the Lutheran Child and Family Services and I asked for my records and birth certificate. She politely refused to help me. She could have tossed me a bone or even a minor clue, but sharing a record would have violated state law that banned the sharing of any identity documents with adoptees without a court order. She wielded incredible power over my life, and she had to know that.

Two days later, after I had found my birth mother with impressive gumshoe detective work, I returned to the same social worker with a signed statement by my birth mother asking to release my information. Three weeks later, she finally released documents about my birth with my original birth name, except my birth certificate. She never expressed remorse for refusing to help me. She was doing her job. She also was emboldened as the gatekeeper holding information sought for years by another person. She alone possessed that power, resting with her simple ability to say, "No." Thankfully she did the right thing. She gave me copies because the law compelled her to send me my records after she received a copy of my birth mother's signed consent to release most of my adoption records.

Adoption historian Melosh describes the secrecy of the American adoption system from the 1940s as being pivotal to the social workers' emerging societal role as baby-broker and family investigator. Their work literally would determine lifelong outcomes for hundreds of thousands of infants and adoptive parents. They also were agents who would manage the records, which became progressively more restricted. "Their access to confidential information was crucial to their professional authority," summarizes Melosh.[63]

That type of life-changing power held by mostly low-paid, lower-level practitioners can be intoxicating, if in the wrong hands. There are countless examples in all areas of government that highlight how persons within a bureaucratic setting seldom relinquish power once they have seized it. The law is the artifice used to justify it.

When I contacted the state of Michigan in March 2016 to receive a copy of my original certificate with documentation that should have released it, I first received a phone call by a mid-level official who did not give her title to me. I later learned she was Tamara Weaver, the deputy state registrar. Weaver conveyed a message that the state would not give me my birth certificate. Weaver defended the position with these exact words: "The law is the law."

Weaver later refused to speak with or reply to me after I left repeated phone and email messages to interview her three months later. I wanted her to explain why she and her department refused to give me my birth certificate, even after I knew my birth families for decades. Her refusal typifies the bureaucratic indifference and treatment experienced by countless other adoptees in the past and present. It demonstrated moral cowardice. She would not answer questions on how her actions provided a public benefit or helped the people of Michigan.

Looking ahead, adoptees seeking legal reform will face continued legal, bureaucratic, and cultural barriers that allow them access to their records. Unfortunately, few adoptees ever speak about duplicating national open-records system found in other developed countries, which give adoptees rights that are denied to US adoptees.

Access to birth records is granted by law for adult adoptees in France, Germany, Denmark, Iceland, Norway, Sweden, Finland, Israel, the Netherlands, New Zealand, and Norway.[64] Moving to a system in the United States that uses evidence like other modern nations is highly unlikely in the United States. The debate is stuck in limbo in states, where adoptees face continued treatment as second-class citizens.

I doubt state lawmakers in forty-one other states that impose full or partial legal barriers for adoptees seeking access to their original birth records will rush to help adoptees anytime soon. Hawaii's leadership and 2016 legislation opening birth records to adoptees may not be replicable in states with more conservative and Republican leadership in the state houses and governor seats. As a result, thousands of adoptees may be harmed because records to family histories will stay sealed. Many adoptees will eventually die from natural causes before they find out their family origins.

This fact is not lost on adoptees and their birth parents. "As a birth parent, unable to send health info to the child I placed in adoption, I want desperately to be able to provide her health information that runs in the family, heart disease and cancer," wrote one birth mother in April 2016 on a failed online petition that asked former President Barack Obama to issue a presidential order to all adoptees full access to their birth records. "She should have the right to attempt to contact me. Not everyone is receptive I know but these laws are outdated and harmful. My mistake should not cost her precious information!"[65]

Chapter 8

Who Am I?

Know thyself.

—Delphic Wisdom

The most basic question all of us will ask is: Who am I? The concept is universal, across nearly all cultures, for as long as humans have been recording their ideas on parchment, papyrus, and clay. Greek philosopher Aristotle famously wrote, "Knowing yourself is the beginning of all wisdom." An older and simpler Greek proverb predates Aristotle. It is known more simply as the Delphic wisdom, referenced by ancient Greek philosophers for centuries as "know thyself."[1]

This wisdom is as relevant today as it was more than two thousand years ago. The 2013 blockbuster film the *Man of Steel* built a film with the most famous superhero of all, Superman, pursuing this knowledge. The rebooted film franchise of the original comic-book character told this hero's tale as a man's—or rather, a Kryptonian's—search for his identity.

The *Man of Steel* relies on one of the oldest mythological stories of human civilization: a hero's search for himself by finding his "true lineage." It is a story arc found in the tales of Moses and King Arthur. In this rebooted myth, the hero is born of one family and sent across the galaxy to be raised by another family in Kansas. He then spends years figuring out who he really is, enduring many hardships from oilrig explosions to planet-saving slugfests.

Minus the over-the-top special effects battles, this film is a traditional tale—a self-discovery journey familiar to all adoptees. The most compelling moments in the film involve conversations the young Clark Kent has with his "adopted" father, Jonathan Kent, played by Kevin Costner. They discuss their ambiguous relations as nonbiological father and adopted son. That tension bursts in a scene where the older Clark tells his father and mother, "You're not my real parents." Right on cue, following that conversation, Costner's character dies in a tornado.

The adult Clark is left adrift not knowing who to call his parents or how to identify with his biological roots or his adoptive roots. So, the journey begins, and he wanders from the Bering Sea to the Canadian Arctic. This cinematic rendering of this rite of passage is nearly identical to what an adopted adult goes through when they have to decide for themselves if they wish to find out their history and biological roots, or accept the decisions institutions and others made for them.

The adult adoptee's decision to undertake a journey of discovery is never easy, and it is often costly. It can be very divisive and unpopular. Such a decision can forever change family relations and be condemned by people who know nothing about this desire to find the truth. It is at its core Superman's tale.

In my case, I literally had to spend years, like Clark, on a pursuit that took me from state to state, bureaucracy to bureaucracy, until I finally solved the case and learned about the identity of my biological parents. I did not find a spaceship buried in the Canadian ice like Clark, and my biological roots are not linked to Krypton. Nor did I meet a loving and benevolent computer-generated father, Jor-El, played by Russell Crowe.

During their conversation, Crowe's Jor-El tells Clark his "real name" is Kal-El. This is identical to what adoptees experience when they learn their "real name"—or the name at birth and on an original birth certificate. That document in most states is treated as a high-level state secret. My birth state of Michigan has laws that make it nearly impossible to find one's past. My efforts to overcome their discrimination took nearly three decades. My birth certificate might as well have been buried in arctic ice, like Clark's spaceship.

In the movie, Clark finds the answers on that space vessel. His original Krypton father is a noble and great leader, just like his adoptive father, in Kansas. But in real life, movie-style fathers may fall far short of the cinematic ideal. My biological father and my adoptive father were not as noble as the fantasy fathers in this film. They would never make it into a screenplay for the masses. I never had a conversation like our film hero did with his biological or adoptive fathers.

In the last act of the film, Superman is exposed as a space alien—the outer-space adoptee. A rogue band of surviving criminals from Krypton chase him down, forcing Superman to choose between his adoptive tribe or his biological tribe.

To validate his adopted life, Superman must first tell his adoptive mother he found his "real parents," watch her sadness, and then he redeems himself for viewers by defeating the rogue Kryptonians. He calls her "my mother" while saving her life. The rescue creates a comforting solution for Superman. He is forgiven for his confusion about his identity, as a man with two pasts. In the end, Superman remains Clark Kent, not Kal-El. He retains his adoptive family loyalty. He hides his biological self, except when needed, though he will never be trusted because he is "different." He has solved his riddle, and the package is neatly tied like most Hollywood movies.

Life does not follow this pattern. There are no heroic battles with invading aliens. Things are messier. But the journey of the real-life hero is no less epic than what the film *Man of Steel* shows. I think the film resonates more deeply, more viscerally with people who have undertaken a similar quest to Clark/Kal-El/Superman. If you have never had to ask the question that confronted our hero, about who you are and where you came from, you may never understand his journey, and also the conflicts and rewards that must inevitably accompany such a quest.

For decades the US mental health field considered this core human question of knowing thyself as a mental health problem for hundreds of thousands of Americans like me, who were born and placed into adoptive families. This harmful misdiagnosis went on for decades, starting in the 1950s. The American mental health profession did not explain this basic archetypal questioning as a universal trait, despite it being well-documented over millennia in our collective human experience and in mankind's greatest myths. Instead, the profession published and promoted egregious and unscientific stereotypes of hundreds of thousands of adoptees, who expressed a very natural desire to find their identity and from whence they came.

Keeping adoptees uninformed has also been a national priority in the political arena from the 1960s through the 1990s, through the power of state laws to seal once open records. In my case, the act of truly knowing myself required being labeled mentally ill or unbalanced and challenging the state's laws as well as the state public health and court systems that controlled my original identity. Those groups were determined to treat me like a child and keep me ignorant about my identity. Not once to this day have they admitted they were wrong or apologized for the harm they caused to me and thousands of other adoptees in Michigan.

For those not adopted, it may be difficult to understand the power and prevalence of adoptee stereotyping. One 1960 published study by psychologist Marshall Schechterof used a statistically insignificant sample size of 120 patients, sixteen who were adopted. Though the unscientific findings have limited validity, he made sweeping conclusions drawn from just a handful of cases. "It would appear that children who have been adopted have potentially a more fertile soil for development of neurotic and psychotic states," Schechterof wrote. "The knowledge of their adoptive status, so often coming in at the time of the Oedipal conflict, can seem to prolong and actually prevent the resolution of this particular area of personality development. There is a lack of boundaries constituting a self; rather, what can be seen is a diffuseness in poorly integrated identifications."[2]

Even after reading this statement many times, I have no idea what he is describing. It could mean I am allegedly at risk of becoming psychotic because I was raised as an adoptee and want to know my past like humans throughout history. Though Schechterof may have meant well, he fed into a dominant view negatively branding all adoptees, and he continues to be quoted today as an expert.

Author Betty Jean Lifton, an adoption-rights advocate and author of the influential adoption autobiography *Twice Born: Memoirs of an Adopted Daughter* (1975), was told by her psychiatrist, who she had consulted about her search in the mid-1950s, "Your need to look for your mother is neurotic. You are rationalizing why you must know who your real 'real' parents, as you call them, are." Such views were commonplace, and their impacts still linger in popular perceptions. The pendulum removing the stigma of labeling adoptees who search for their parents and records as having psychological disorders has somewhat subsided as adoption has become more open to many styles of family configurations.

Today, none of the "experts" who published these theories or practices in the field and used these ideas to diagnose adoptees has issued a public statement or apology that they wrongly labeled curious adoptees as being mentally unhealthy or manifesting what today should be considered natural human curiosity. The American Psychiatric Association (APA), the organization that speaks for the field, has never issued any statement of contrition on behalf of its members and their harmful assessment of millions of adoptees.

In 1973, the APA removed homosexuality from its Diagnostic and Statistical Manual of Mental Disorders (DSM)—something that wins praise today from many left-leaning progressives and supporters of the LGBTQ community. Yet through the 1980s, the APA's *Diagnostic and Statistical Manual of Mental Disorders* continued identifying a problem it labeled "identity disorder," which consisted of "severe subjective distress regarding inability to integrate aspects of the self into a relatively coherent and acceptable sense of self." As adoption historian Carp writes, "No adopted person in the 1970s had imagined that asking the question 'Who am I?' would end up classified as an official psychiatric disorder."[3]

Recent peer-reviewed psychology studies continue to focus on adoptees as overly problematic people, with higher levels of mental health disorders, defined by the APA's disorder guidelines. One 2011 study in *Adoption Quarterly* looking at a statistically irrelevant sample size of seventeen teenagers—thus inapplicable to the wider population—hypothesized that as adopted individuals reach adolescence, "they may become more aware of physical differences between themselves and their adoptive parents, initiating further fantasies regarding birth parents."[4] Again, practitioners rely on words like "fantasies" to reference the human desire to know one's self and kin. The problem to some professionals today remains the adoptee, not the system of hiding identity records from millions of US citizens.

In the field of social work today, adoption is still framed as a mental health disorder, affecting adoptees and even their adoptive parents. The field that so actively promoted adoption as the best choice for hundreds of thousands of birth mothers from the 1950s through the 1970s has invented a so-called specialty called "adoption competency."

In a 2013 article on this newly invented skill set, in the magazine *Social Work Today*, Deborah Siegel writes, "An adoption-competent practitioner understands that everyone, including adoptees, needs human connection and has a basic right to access their biological families, except when direct contact is unsafe." In her view, adoptees are prone to mental health problems and core human rights for adoptees are conditional, not universal. Siegel's social work worldview proposes a therapeutic solution that inserts her profession into an adoptee's private life—not basic equality for adoptees under state law. While Siegel acknowledges adoptees are entitled to knowing who they are, she fails to grasp that meaningful solutions for adoptees are essentially political in nature. Her model is silent about legal solutions and systems change, the way medical and public health professionals have helped to reduce rates of smoking for Americans through law and policy.

Today, schools of social work offer training in adoption, framed as a mental illness. For example, the University of Connecticut's School of Social Work calls its program "Training for Adoption Competency," requiring seventy-eight class hours "to provide quality clinical services to adopted persons, birth families, prospective adoptive parents, adoptive families and kinship families." The program offers no background on the underlying legal barriers that deny equal rights to identity records to adoptees and birth mothers in most US states.[5] Other programs suggest to future social workers that they can pursue careers as "adoption specialists." The very few licensed social workers I communicated with in this field refused to give me my original birth records, including those employed at the social service agency and by Michigan's adoption bureaucracy.

Not all health practitioners embraced views that demeaned adoptees' innate curiosity to know their identity. Some recognized that the search for one's genetic and family history is, at its core, a fundamental human desire, even as they claimed adoptees showed signs of mental health disorders for pursuing their family past.

In 1971, the American Academy of Pediatrics' Committee on Adoptions (AAP) acknowledged the reality that the country's adoption system posed on adoptees, who naturally would be asking one of the most core human identity questions. "The most helpful thing a human being can learn in life is to be conscious of himself as an individual, and to be aware of who and what he is," wrote the committee. "Determining identity is a difficult process for someone brought up by his natural parents; it is more complex for the individual whose ancestry is unknown to him." The organization noted that a "driving need for identity and independence is . . . indigenous to the individual" and "[t]here is ample evidence that the adopted child retains the need for seeking his ancestry for a long time."[6] This marked a fundamental shift in the organization's philosophy from 1960, when it championed adoption as "the most suitable plan" for a pregnant single mother and her child.[7]

However, the group continued to frame adoptees as "conflicted" for seeking information—information that in 1971 was withheld by state law from many adoptees. The group still suggested adoptees were at risk because of their identity confusion. "A recognition of the psychodynamics relating to the adopted child and his family will allow the pediatrician to prevent or modify destructive and harmful behavior."[8] Today, I wonder what members of this group now think of this ominous characterization.

In 2003, the AAP's advice for pediatricians framed an adoptee's search for his or her identity positively, not as a mental abnormality: "As children age into adolescence and adulthood, adoptive children may wish to seek out more information about their biological families . . . it is actually a sign of healthy emotional growth in the search for identity."[9] As of 2015, the AAP notes that the majority of new adoptions are open, allowing adoptees and adoptive families to know the birth parent or parents. The group recommends providing age-appropriate information so adoptive parents can communicate to their adoptive children that they are both adopted and welcome. For adolescents wanting to know their family history, the group states such interest is "normal and appropriate" and that "we all want to know where we came from, and what our roots are."[10]

The group made an enlightened policy decision in 2014 that finally promoted all adoptees' rights for having unfettered access to their birth records, in part to promote their access to their medical history.[11] Yet, the organization a year later remarkably still suggests adoptees should be grateful for their status as adoptees. This embrace of traditional medical paternalism dictates what the former national boosters of adoptions consider to be right and wrong ways for adoptees and birth mothers to think: "Most adopted children and young adults understand that they do not really belong with their biological parents."[12]

To this day, I have yet to meet an adoptee who ever thought of their adoption this way. I know of almost no adoptee who believes so-called experts in white coats with medical degrees, social workers, and mental health therapists—who see adoption as fraught with problems that only they can solve–have any right to tell them how to think or feel about their status. The only ones who should decide the validity of their questioning are adoptees themselves.

Stigma from those in white coats and those who believe adoption is a minefield of psychiatric disorders is hardly surprising. In the United States, few, if anyone—from the doctor, therapist, vital-records manager, nurse, social worker, lawyer, or politician—who created the modern US adoption system, built on the shame of mothers and secrecy of their births, have ever said they made a mistake or were wrong. Many likely thought and still think they were doing adoptees and their mothers a service of kindness and showing Christian compassion. That attitude is visible in pervasive societal attitudes that brand adoptees as ungrateful for not "accepting" their adoptive parents as their true parents. I heard it many times, from strangers and from family members. The view highlights continuing ignorance about adoption as a political and legal system.

Today there is nearly unanimous consensus from medical research of the many benefits in knowing one's medical and family-health history. In comparison to these findings, state adoption laws that deny adoptees access to this information have almost no scientific foundation. From a medical ethics perspective, health professionals in all fields also should be among the strongest advocates for opening all birth records to adoptees, to promote the health of all Americans, especially adoptees. Right now, they are not engaged. No interest group or internal reformers are pressuring these professionals to be involved in what should be framed as a national public health issue requiring immediate action.

The medical and dental professions still have a long way to go in a more national dialogue about adoption. Every adoptee who has ever visited a doctor or dentist's office knows the double standard they confront when asked about their family medical history. I have always left those detailed questions blank, or wrote in bold letters over the boxes, "adopted," or, "information denied by state adoption law." I do that to communicate to the health community that their questionnaires can be insensitive and misguided.

In my decades of dealing with faulty intake forms, I have never had any health form by any health provider have a check box for "adopted" or "don't know, adopted." This is after decades of visiting health facilities all over the nation. By 2018, it is almost unthinkable for nearly all medical providers to be unaware that adoptees are ubiquitous in American society, numbering in the millions. It is one of the more regular insults one endures as an adoptee.

To the medical field, adoptees actually do not exist. I have never met a single person who was asked if they were adopted as a logical and evidence-based risk protocol that should be flagged in a nurse or doctor's preliminary screening of the patient. When I do openly talk about adoption, nearly all medical staff look uneasy, not quite sure how to respond. This could stem from the failure of medical programs to inform doctors of the proven risk factors for adoptees to many long-term medical health issues that are documented in population health studies. It is more likely medical staff are not comfortable addressing the reality an adoptee faces daily of not knowing their past and their medical history.

Since I became an adult, no medical office, once it learned I was adopted, has ever reached out to me and asked, what would you suggest we do to make our intake process respectful of adoptees? What could we do better when we gather the crucial medical baseline that adoptees do not know of their genetic and family health risks? Not one office ever followed up with me after I told their staff that their medical history questions cannot be answered by nearly all adoptees. They did not care, and for them, adoptees' medical health history was never a true priority.

Questions by adoptees challenging the most basic process of obtaining health information on new patients likely embarrass the medical professions. It spotlights their failure to help adoptees and to practice evidence-based health care. Extensive research shows that disease risks are tied specifically to human genomes, and adoptees are not clear what risks they may have because of their heredity. Medical professionals should know better. They do not seem to care that about one in every sixty patients is adopted—a number based on the rough census and other data that counts adoptees.

Today, the interest in family medical history is stronger than ever. Adoptees like all other Americans should by legal right be entitled to this potentially life-saving information. The numbers show how important such information could be, particularly to adoptees who are middle-aged and older. The National Institutes for Health reports that there are more than six thousand genetic and rare diseases. These afflict more than twenty-five million Americans, and about 30 percent of early deaths can be linked to genetic causes.[13]

Genetic mutations play a major role in about 5 to 10 percent of all cancers, the second leading killer of all Americans, topped only by heart disease.[14] Researchers have associated mutations in specific genes with more than fifty hereditary cancer syndromes, which are disorders that may mean some individuals are more likely to develop certain cancers.

For its part, the US Centers for Disease and Control identifies the role of genomes in other health issues, such as birth defects, chronic diseases, and congenital heart defects, and the CDC has created the Office of Public Health Genomics to promote research in the field. The CDC also reports gene-sequencing studies of individuals with some genetic conditions turn up a good number of possible pathogenic variants not found in public databases.[15]

The US Surgeon General in 2004 declared a Family History Health Day, on Thanksgiving, to promote greater awareness on the critical role of family medical history to promoting health. By family history the nation's leading medical advocate means only genetic family history. Family medical histories can identify people with a higher risks of heart disease, high blood pressure, stroke, and diabetes. A family medical history can also provide risks of rarer conditions caused by mutations, such as cystic fibrosis and sickle cell anemia.[16]

Groups like the US Preventive Services Task Force also use family health history information to recommend national screening and preventive services for conditions such as osteoporosis, hyperlipidemia, and breast cancer. The American Cancer Society recommendations for early breast cancer detection recently included changes in mammography recommendations that use family health history in decisions when a woman should begin mammography in persons with a family history where breast cancer is a known risk.[17]

Having access to family health history and information on other relatives—relatives who are genetically related—is considered by the nation's foremost health experts to be necessary and beneficial for individual and population health. But as of 2018, there is no national campaign or policy initiative to promote giving hundreds of thousands of adoptees the ability to learn about their family medical health history.

In my case, I learned only when I was forty-three that my birth father reportedly died of melanoma skin cancer, which was not correctly diagnosed. There is a strong chance his ancestors were at risk of cancer, as heredity plays a major role in the illness. Nearly one in every ten persons diagnosed with the disease has a biological family member with melanoma in their history.[18] So because my father had the disease, and died from it, I am already in a higher-risk and melanoma-prone family.

My biological father's life spent in very sunny San Diego likely contributed to his disease, as did his contraction of hepatitis C from one of his dental patients. That would have severely compromised his immune system. I only learned these facts three years after his death in 2004, from his niece and sister. Since that time, I have taken extra precaution to use sunblock and to be mindful of skin discoloration on my neck from prolonged exposure to direct sun. In my case, I spent years of my early adult life working out of doors without any sun protection, and I should be concerned. I also have made visits to dermatologists when I spot suspicious skin issues—all on the basis of what I learned about my birth father's health history. For me, this information has been extremely important to promoting my long-term health.

State laws ultimately dictate who is restricted from accessing original birth records, and more than half of all states have legal barriers preventing adoptees from knowing who their birth mother and father may be without a court order. The preponderance of proven medical and scientific reasons for openness has not made a tide-turning difference in many states.

Legislative debates, done piecemeal in state legislatures through bills, are attempting to undo regressive laws passed in those states between 1960 and 1990 that closed birth records to adoptees, except in a handful of states. In 2016, an online petition was started. It asked the former Obama administration to issue an executive order to open adoptee birth records as part of a national rally planned in Washington, D.C., in September 2016, even if the action likely would not overturn state laws. The planned rally fizzled and the petition received no media attention. No legal case appears headed for the docket of the Supreme Court that could lead to sweeping changes in all states similar to the historic *Obergefell v. Hodges* case. That decision by the high court, in a 5–4 vote in June 2015, found states could not keep same-sex couples from marrying one another and forced states to legally recognize their unions.

As of December 2017, the Adoptee Rights Law Center—the most thorough resource available on state laws governing birth records for adoptees—reports that only twenty-five states have laws granting adult adoptees eighteen years and older full and true access or restricted, conditional, and partial access to their original birth certificates. In some cases, like Michigan, the conditions are so restrictive for those born between 1945 and 1980, they amount to no access. Of these twenty-five states, just nine allow all adult adoptees unfettered and complete access without any conditional barriers and legal discrimination.[19]

New Jersey, one of the most recent states to reform its restrictions limiting access to original birth records, began to release original birth certificates to adoptees who requested them in 2017. However, the state's law allowed all birth mothers the ability to redact their names—a provision not allowed in Hawaii's law opening adoptees' birth records nor in national adoptee records laws in countries like England. All told, 550 birth mothers, or less than .2 percent from an estimated population of 300,000 birth mothers who relinquished children, chose to hide their names. All told, 1,200 New Jersey-born adoptees asked for their records less than two weeks after the adoption reform law was implemented.[20]

The remaining twenty-six states, including the District of Columbia, restrict access through legal barriers, such as court orders.[21] These also can be rules requiring that signed consent forms from birth parents be provided to the state before adoptees born during certain years could be granted records. Or they could be the much-criticized and poor-performing "confidential intermediary programs" that still prevent adoptees from getting their records directly.[22]

In Michigan, an overwhelming majority of biological kin separated by adoption secrecy laws—birth mothers, relinquished adoptees, siblings connected by blood—have signed consent documents allowing information to be released to fellow family members. According to a Detroit News report from March 2008, 95 percent of more than 26,300 people in the registry indicated they would like identifying information to be released about them.[23]

Excluding recent data from New Jersey, the American Adoption Congress reports overwhelming success for open records in states where restrictive laws have been changed. In six states that implemented access to original birth certificate laws since 2000 (Oregon, Alabama, New Hampshire, Maine, Illinois, and Rhode Island—Hawaii is not counted in this summary), less than .1 percent of birth mothers requested they did not want contact under the laws' provisions. Only one parent of 1,491 requested to be left alone. During the same period from 2000 to

2015, 33,666 adoptees requested their documents from a pool of nearly 830,000 sealed birth certificates.[24]

Every one of those 33,666 adoptees represents a unique story. But all share the common, natural desire to want to know, "Who am I?" So, it was fitting that Rhode Island Governor Lincoln Chafee marked the legal transition in his home state, when the 2011 state law creating access to original birth documents for adoptees was slated to take effect on July 2, 2012. Handing original birth records to four adults who were once adopted, while dozens watched, Chafee remarked, "No matter what people find out, adult adoptees now have the access to the truth, and that is a very important step."[25]

Chapter 9

The Paper Chase

Power concedes nothing without a demand. It never did and it never will. Find out just what any people will quietly submit to and you have found out the exact measure of injustice and wrong which will be imposed upon them, and these will continue till they are resisted with either words or blows, or with both. The limits of tyrants are prescribed by the endurance of those whom they oppress.

—Frederick Douglass, 1857

To this day, the most rewarding act of my life has been finding out who I am. It was the inherently natural and right thing to do, despite the very real costs to my career, resources, and family relations. It made me a better person. It confirmed who I was in the universe. It gave me the grit I needed in so many other moments in my life. It taught me valuable lessons how systems operate and how prejudice works in overt and subtle ways. It taught me never to accept "no" when you pursue the right and just path. It also felt like a mythical journey, complete with setbacks, strong and defiant adversaries, successes, and meaningful personal change. I ended the trip as a different person. I believe I had become a better human being, as well as someone more whole.

On the darkest days, I turned to inspirational stories that gave me the strength I needed to complete my journey. They were two of humanity's greatest myths that stayed with me from childhood. To me, they felt like ancient warriors' tales, told around a campfire to motivate those weary of battle. Those voices from a distant past assured me I had embarked on an epic and mythical adventure, as described by Joseph Campbell's classic treatise *The Hero with a Thousand Faces*. I took these words to heart. I recognized from the start I had undertaken a hero's quest.

From the earliest days I could read, I adored *Le Morte d'Arthur*—the story of King Arthur and his Knights of the Round Table. King Arthur, like millions of American adoptees since the 1950s, never knew his true identity growing up. In truth, he was a bastard king raised as a foster son, not knowing his ancestry. With the help of the wizard Merlin at a gathering of knights, he pulls out the sword Excalibur from a rock and recognizes his royal and true lineage.

Being raised a Christian, I long knew of the tale of Moses, the *Bible*'s most famous adoptee, whose exploits are found in the Book of Exodus. Like many adoptees, Moses realizes late in his life he is not who he believes himself to be. Moses discovers as a man that he is not biologically related to the god-like pharaohs and instead is born of the slaves, the Jews, whom he leads from slavery, to exile, and to freedom.

As I embarked on my own hero's journey of self-discovery, I told myself I would be like them. I naively or optimistically thought I too might have something noble in my past, like Arthur. I would defy stubborn authority and convention and complete the journey out of the wilderness, like Moses. These thoughts I mostly kept to myself. People likely would have laughed at me had I compared myself to a religious prophet of Judaism, Islam, and Christianity as well as a legendary king of Medieval England known worldwide. From these universal tales I found hope, when everyone around me questioned my journey. With these stories as my northern star, I never once questioned my quest.

Having a guiding star, however, is not enough to challenge powerful adversaries. A warrior entering into this battle must have strong armor, to withstand an enemy's blows and also the silent daggers from those who one considers allies and friends. Patience and resolve are equally important weapons in one's arsenal. No search ever happens quickly. For some, searches take decades. Knowledge of one's adversaries is also equally important before entering into this arena. One should never underestimate one's foe, particularly those who spend their lives defending ideas that are, at their core, morally wrong. I speak strategically, as one might going into war. In my case, my opponents' tenacity surprised me the most. They were the hardest obstacles to overcome. But I used the tools of a trickster. I found a way around my foes and into the fortress, through a backdoor even they could not control. In the end, I outfoxed them.

From the start of my records search to the present day, I am amazed how fiercely the many supporters of adoption defend keeping adoptees' birth records sealed shut. They seem blind to their actions that impose the unwanted and unnecessary lifelong sentence on literally millions of people. They seem to forget a basic fact that all adoptees were once the most vulnerable of persons—infants without any capacity to advocate for themselves. They seem to ignore that adoption places adoptees at the will of parties and the state for the most critical decisions to affect one's future—where one is raised and who raises a young child.

This disconnect has seldom registered with the powers that manage adoption law and practices. They at times seem as indifferent as Moses's nemesis and adoptive brother, the Pharaoh Ramses, whose heart hardened in the face of onslaughts from God and who would not free the Israelites until a series of tragic plagues gripped his land.

Those in power have always had the ability and authority to help adoptees more than they ever have. These parties include state adoption bureaucracies, probate courts that manage adoption records, state legislatures that pass laws on adoption, state governors, adoption placement agencies, and even the media. True, this could be said about any government matter.

For the government stakeholders who influence adoption law and policy affecting adoptees, they would have to have cared or had been pressured into acting. They would have to have considered themselves as leaders, not bureaucrats. They would have to have seen themselves as accountable to those who are impacted by laws, policies, and deeds. This is why public recognition of past wrongs matter, and the United States has not reached a turning point compared to other countries like England and Australia concerning adoption practices and lawmaking. Both of those countries have changed, and for the better.

As someone searching for my past, I always believed I had a role as a change agent, not just for myself but for others who could undertake a journey like mine. Historically, those who have been excluded by laws and policies have played critical roles in changing how society perceived problems and solutions affecting its members. This can be found in every major reform this country has seen since the abolition of slavery, to the protection of children workers, to civil rights reform, and now the expansion of legal civil rights to the LGBTQ community.

Since the 1960s, some progress has been made since the adoption paradigm tilted unhelpfully from once being mostly open to being mostly closed for adoptee records seekers. Only nine states allow adoptees access to their original birth records, when before World War II most adoptees could access their records with the consent of the adoption bureaucracy, social welfare employees, and states. In the case of those entrusted with power in state and federal government, the people managing records could always have given far more to adoptees and helped them, so they could live more productive lives.

In my case, parties working in the adoption system never budged an inch or once acknowledged a single wrong. In fact, they believe more than ever they are morally right. But that did not dissuade me from pushing them as hard and as far I could go, or from highlighting the multiple failings of their individual and collective actions. That is one reason why I wrote this book and why I demanded my records from the time I was nineteen until I turned fifty-one years old.

The abolitionist and freedom fighter Frederick Douglass famously described why forceful advocacy always matters to bring about change. Writing before the start of the Civil War about the country's violent opposition to ending slavery, which would ultimately lead to armed conflict, Douglass said:

> This struggle may be a moral one, or it may be a physical one, and it may be both moral and physical, but it must be a struggle. Power concedes nothing without a demand. It never did and it never will. Find out just what any people will quietly submit to and you have found out the exact measure of injustice and wrong which will be imposed upon them, and these will continue till they are resisted with either words or blows, or with both. The limits of tyrants are prescribed by the endurance of those whom they oppress.[1]

In short, I learned that power was never conceded, ever. In the end I have found that adoptees have proven far too willing to tolerate the inequity they have received, for decades now. By writing this book and by taking on each of the individual bureaucrats, agencies, and state officials that opposed me, I am showing as many people as I can that change, as Sam Cook sang, is still a long, long time in coming. I am still hoping it is going to come.

My mythical journey began my second year of college. During my sophomore year, in January 1984, I sent my first official written request for all of the records my Michigan adoption agency had to release to me by law. I cited the statute requiring the agency to comply. The Lutheran Child and Family Services of Bay City, Michigan—the successor agency of my original my adoption placement service based in Detroit—offered no assistance. Its reply also fit a pattern I would see the rest of my adult life. The agency did not give me what it legally had to provide—copies of my non-identifying information in my file that would give me a brief background on my birth parents and their families, and the circumstances of my birth. Instead, the agency lied to me or evaded its legal duties by saying the records were in its Detroit office. That office would reply, wrote the social worker named Pat Lesser. But no other reply or records ever came from either office. Because my academi workload and my economic struggles occupied all of my hours, I let the matter go.

My research resumed in 1987. I had just turned twenty-two. It was a perfect year to start. After I graduated from college, I decided to prioritize my highest goals first. I did not pursue money. I was not interested in a middle-class family life, which I had seen fail spectacularly with my own family. I generally lacked career direction. I knew that I wanted to live in the Pacific Northwest. I also knew that I wanted to live a life with meaning. The more I thought about these goals, the more I realized how important finding my ancestry and biological families were to fulfilling my life's purpose—what Holocaust survivor and writer Viktor Frankl so perfectly called "meaning" from life.

This realization was a gift in disguise. I had a type of freedom that can only come when one is younger. Because I received a generous financial-aid package during my undergraduate education, I did not have student debt. For a while I could avoid chasing money for money's sake and pursue what I always considered to be a higher calling. I would find out who I was and why I came into this world as an underweight, adopted baby in the unwed mother's wing of a Detroit hospital.

My adoptive mother had long cut ties with me financially—and in many ways emotionally—when I was fifteen and sixteen years old. I had taken care of all of my living expenses since then. I bought my own clothes and paid for my insurance. And after I was eighteen, I paid for every ticket between St. Louis and Portland during four years of college. I covered all of my college expenses, including tuition. I paid for my food, rent, and utilities. Being on my own meant I had no interference from my family to pursue what would soon become a full-time quest. I did not know then how all-consuming this journey would be.

Perhaps my dissatisfaction with my college experience and with my former life in the St. Louis area drove me harder. Maybe my disconnect with my mom and sister spurred me to find more meaningful connections, which had long eluded me. I also think my curiosity defined how I interacted with the world.

I landed in Seattle in August 1987, with no job and few ties. After three very difficult months of job hunting, I finally received a part-time job as a paralegal. I also found myself with a lot of free time. That meant I could chase adoption-records dead-ends, false leads, and clues that led down rabbit holes to nowhere. Today I realize just how precious that free time was to my quest and how lucky I was to be focused on success.

In 1987, adoptees had no guidebook for searching. If you were adopted, you were mostly on your own. All you had to draw on was your own end-game plan, innate desire, financial resources that might be available, and mostly tenacity. The latter proved and still proves to be the most important trait for an adoptee to undertake a journey of discovery. It cannot be taught, and it has to be learned by each person their own way.

Some support groups offered help. They used now seemingly old-fashioned communications like printed newsletters, postal mail, and phones. Through these, I found some people in Michigan who were active in the hidden world of adoption searches. I called them long-distance, asking for help. Through their mailings I first learned of the word "triad," to describe the three legs of the adoption stool: the adoptive parents, the adoptee, the birth parents—who is almost always a single birth mother. Adoptee advocates still use the term triad today, though I find it annoying that this term does not convey the underlying law and politics of adoption.

I also realized how the world of adoption searching provided self-therapy for people who clearly had missing pieces that kept them from feeling whole. Their emotional intensity bothered me. I did not want to be like them. For me, searching for my identity would not become an Alcoholics Anonymous or help-group experience. I did not want psychological or spiritual counsel. It was going to be a research project that I would finish, with a disciplined, tactical, and dogged approach that focused always on results. What happened at the end would be addressed when I got there. I had no idea what my family narrative would be.

I did not read any books by adoptees who had found their lineage. By 1987, several well-known memoirs were in circulation—by Jean Paton, Betty Jean Lifton, and Florence Fisher. I was unaware of them until only recently in my life. Stories about adoption reunions were not yet common in the media. With the exception of the smash 1977 TV miniseries *Roots*, which told a moving tale of knowing one's family history and relations, adoptees like me had no cultural zeitgeist or publicized national movement to draw inspiration from.

I always believed that I experienced a natural and insatiable desire to know where I came from and my relationship to my kin. I know of no adoption-search story ever told in which the adoptee does not describe this innate desire and feeling that mirrored what I was experiencing. I was lucky I had a stubborn streak and never accepted what others told me to be true on face value. My adoptive father's lifelong hypocrisy as an abusive, alcoholic minister taught me this as a child. This time, my stubbornness became my best ally.

I recall seeing no other adoptee during this time to discuss my status. I had undertaken an entirely solitary journey. I found it difficult to explain to others. How do you tell people that you are putting your professional development and even lifelong personal development on hold to find information that was being intentionally withheld from you by a state, by the courts, and by social services?

The unjust nature of this power imbalance over one's identity still upsets me, as it did in 1987. How do you convince people who might think you were psychologically damaged if you told them why this search mattered? I also thought most non-adoptees had no ability to understand my innate need to find out my past. I think this as much today as I did nearly three decades ago.

A handful of people in Seattle knew about my search: my two roommates, some of my coworkers at a law office where I worked as a paralegal, and a few college friends. I did not form close attachments during the next two years, which I later learned was a pattern that would typify my life's journey. I have no idea where that came from. I do not believe that is related to me being adopted, even though many stories about adoptees provide a similar point of view.

My obsessive personality proved beneficial. It allowed me to engross myself in a project, regardless of the time I invested. I always had been that way with academic, historic, and current affairs, but this was much more intense. It concerned my origins as a human being, connecting me to my ancestors.

In late 1987, I resumed the search that had fizzled in 1984 because of my adoption agency's intransigence. In my evening hours I visited libraries and made long-distance calls. Home computers barely existed in the consumer market, and the internet was still buried deep in the Defense Department's networks. I used my lunch hours at work. There, I composed letters asking the bureaucracies in Detroit and Michigan to provide me my adoption records. I also received some basic guidance from an adult adoptee in Michigan, who offered insights on Michigan law at the time.

Once again, I pressed my demands for non-identifying information. State law denied me access to what adoption bureaucrats creatively call "identifying information." These top-secret, hidden facts included my original name, the names of my birth parents, the names of my grandparents, and my family's history as it was recorded in the adoption agency's files. These facts that nearly everyone takes for granted were considered "sealed information." The law prevented me from having it. Three decades later, the law still banned me from getting part of this information and a copy of my original birth certificate, except in the rarest of cases with a court order that had to prove "just cause."

Getting the non-identifying summary information took repeated efforts. I quickly learned that my first failed efforts were not a fluke. I found that all of the bureaucracies involved in my adoption worked intentionally to both delay and deny information to adult adoptees, even the information all adoptees born in Michigan were entitled to by law. I also realized that I was on my own and would need to be creative and resilient to overcome entrenched bias and resistance.

In March 1988, I called the Lutheran Child and Family Services office of Detroit. That office claimed it did not have any records of my existence. I found out later this was either a bald-faced lie or bureaucratic incompetence, or maybe both. The social worker who replied told me to contact the Wayne County Juvenile Court, Probate Division, also in Detroit. As I found later, a treasure trove of documents was actually in their care. They had my complete file in their office, which I saw in person later in 1989.

In April 1988, I also requested the same information from the Michigan Department of Public Health, Office of Vital and Health Statistics (now housed within the current Michigan Department of Health and Human Services). That office by law manages all birth records, including the creation of amended birth certificates. The Adoption Unit office wrote me back the same month saying, "there is not much I can do for you." The office told me to pay them a fee to fill out a form, so I could get a copy of my amended birth certificate. The office's letter did not use the word "amended" for my record of birth and did not acknowledge I had two birth certificates on record that the responding official could review in my file when they wrote me back. It is important to remember that the official had the identifying information in his or her possession at all times, and willingly withheld it, because of state law and also because of the harmful agency culture that promoted hiding birth records forever from adoptees.

For its part, the Wayne County Probate Court in April 1988 initially refused to give me my non-identifying information that I was entitled to by law—yet another delaying tactic by another group of adoption bureaucrats. I had filed my request a month earlier. This marked the third refusal to find or share information with me in less than two months by a bureaucracy that held my original birth records. That office demanded a copy of the denial letter from the adoption placement agency to prove that office did not have my information I was entitled to by state law.

Their repeated efforts to withhold records, which the law required them to release, showed a consistent pattern of deny and delay. Their deeds and false words made it impossible for me to trust anything they said to me again, ever. I was a problem and someone they wanted to go away. As of 2016 and 2017, not one thing had changed based on my experience with the new generation of adoption bureaucrats who still hold records in my file they will not copy for me.

After I sent the probate court a copy of the letter from the adoption agency that denied having my records, the court sent a copy of the two-page non-identifying summary. This is what most adult adoptees to this day use to decipher their entire genealogical past and birth family lineage. The office kept what it called an "adoption social history file" on me. The probate court employee, Margaret Hamer, went out of her way to suggest the information might not be valid: "This information is old information, as of 1965. This information may not be accurate. Opinions expressed must be viewed in the context of the time. There is no other non-identifying information available." I later learned after I found my birth mother that my file had other adoption records of me, none of which were released because they were classified by the officials as "identifying information."

Hamer's communication said I could pay a small fee and enter my name into the state's adoption registry. That is the passive system that lets birth parents and adoptees provide their details to a database. If a match is found, the state tells you. The action is entirely at the discretion of the state, with little or no oversight from any third party to ensure birth parents and adoptees are being treated equitably and in accordance to law. I have little faith auditors even check this system today. Registries, like Michigan's, have proven to be broken systems that, in nearly all cases, fail to create matches and in the end do not help the interested stakeholders. I paid the ten-dollar fee and filled out the paperwork in May 1988, but also demanded my identifying information—the records in my file.

In July 1988, Hamer wrote me back saying that the Central Adoption Registry, which today still manages this system, did not have any record of consent from my birth mother. She rejected my request for identifying information. "Release of identifying information occurs only with consent/permission filed by the birth parent(s). No consent is on file: therefore no release of identifying birth information."

Unfazed, I continued to press my claim, writing directly to the probate court again for all of my original records in January 1989. Hamer wrote me back again the same month, saying, "Providing you with a full and complete copy of the adoption file is prohibited by law." For the moment, the trail stopped cold with the bureaucracies. I now had other crumbs to sift through starting in May 1988.

Every trail on my journey of discovery began with my non-identifying information that was so hard to come by. These provide a summary of file records that show the age, physical characteristics, ethnicity, race, religion, some medical information, education levels, and short life histories of my birth parents. My two-page summary also has the date, time, and place of my birth. My document is similar to copies shared with tens of thousands of other adoptees, though records will vary depending on the social service that placed adopted children with new parents. I was confronting the enigma faced by thousands of adoptees—digesting the information to make sense of who I was and using it like a cryptic pirate's map to find my birth family.

The first paragraph in the two-page document begins with the heading "history of child." The very first words, my original birth name of Scott Douglas Owens, are whited out. This short history notes my birth date in the spring of 1965. I was delivered by low forceps. I weighed a meager five pounds, twelve ounces. By weight, I was nearly premature, and thus have a higher risk of lifelong health complications. I was circumcised at the hospital. The records do not say if I was in my birth mother's care or breastfed during my first three days of life. That information would tell me if I had received one of the most crucial maternal health benefits a baby can receive to achieve optimal health as a child and adult. My reading of the document today is greatly informed by understanding of health and public health, and it raises a lot of warning flags.

Three days after my birth, I was transferred to what is now called the Detroit Medical Center Children's Hospital of Michigan because of vomiting. I was x-rayed. The test showed I had no problems. That measure seems extreme for a newborn baby. Even a few X-rays on young children doubles their risks of leukemia, according to a 2010 study from the University of California at Berkeley.[2] The records say I was a "normal baby." The social worker for Lutheran Children's Friend Society, Jeanne N. Arnett, who I later learned wrote my summary, noted I was "a long, thin baby with small features, brown hair, blue eyes and fair complexion."

Later I learned from medical records I was given after I found my birth mother that I had dropped to a dangerous five pounds seven and a half ounces a week after my birth. I was able to climb back up to a meager five pounds, eleven ounces upon my discharge—less than I weighed going into the hospital for what appeared to be specialized care. The adoption records in the social service agency called me "normal," though by weight I was practically a prematurely born baby, at risk of greater medical problems. I was seen by a personal doctor of the foster family I was assigned to twelve days after I was born. The examining physician who signed the discharge to the adoption placement service notes "the above-named child was recently examined by me and was found to be in good physical health. From a medical standpoint the child is recommended for adoptive placement."

The non-identifying information summary states my birth mother "voluntarily released the baby to the Lutheran Children's Friend Society for the purpose of adoption," three weeks after my birth. To this day, I do not know the circumstances of how she made this decision. From this point on I was never supposed to have seen my birth mother again, nor any member of my biological kin.

The summary information for my birth mother, her mother and father, and her twin brother span one paragraph each. My birth mother was born in 1940. Her ethnicity was described as "Welsh, Scotch, Irish." The summary neglected my mother's Finnish background from my birth grandmother, perhaps because of systemic bias against maternal ancestry. The summary describes her physical characteristics—she had medium-brown hair, hazel eyes—and that she generally had good health. She apparently was a mediocre student, with just a C average in college-prep classes. The name of the junior college she attended was whited out. She lasted only a year. She took a seven-month course to be a medical assistant and some extension courses at a university, whose name was also whited out. She worked for two years as a medical assistant at a university—again name blanked out—and in a university lab somewhere in Europe. She was a dental assistant at the time of her pregnancy.

My maternal grandfather, according to the records that are not whited out, was born in 1916. He completed a high school education and worked as a journeyman sheet metal worker. He also had been a teletypist and clerk. I learned later he was born in Big Rapids, Michigan, where his paternal family had a homestead. My maternal grandmother's birth year was listed, 1909, but the city where she was born was whited out. She was short, at five feet tall, and suffered from epilepsy because of a childhood fall. She too only had a high school diploma. Her jobs ranged from department store to administrative work. The records did not mention her Finnish ancestry or that she was born in Hancock, Michigan, on the Upper Peninsula. Many ethnic Finns like my impoverished, immigrant great-grandparents settled in this area at the turn of the twentieth century.

The background for my mother's twin brother lists his physical build, hair and eye color, and possible health issues. He was a B-average student who ran track and played tennis. The name of the university where he earned a BS in natural sciences was whited out. He reportedly was married, but had no children at the time I was born. I learned later he had attended the University of Michigan, School of Natural Resources and that he had a son, two years younger than me, my first birth cousin. I am the eldest child of the two boys born among the twins.

The paragraph for my birth father simply labeled him "paternal." It lists his paternity status was "alleged." He reportedly was twenty-six at the time of my birth, a year older than my birth mother. The summary said he was of Scotch, English origin. He was called "a good looking fellow, five feet, eight inches tall." He had dark hair. The name of the university he attended was whited out, but he attended his undergraduate and dental programs at the same school. The records show he was doing a dental internship at a Detroit hospital and specializing in general dentistry. One of his relatives later told me he did difficult reconstructive work in a psychiatric ward with patients who had tried to commit suicide by shooting themselves in the face.

The records also list the state of his birth and that he had two older sisters—a mistake. He had three sisters. His parents were described only as "short, heavy set people," based on a photograph my birth mother saw. This also was inaccurate. His parents were short, but not heavyset. His father, my paternal grandfather, in real life was lean, and I resemble him more than nearly all other members of his family. I learned later from genealogists the family origin is Dutch and German.

On all of her letters, the probate employee Hamer copied Wayne Avery, Adoption Supervisor of the Juvenile Division. In March 2016, I located Avery and interviewed him by phone. I told him I was doing research for a book about my adoption experiences. I asked him to describe what he thought about adult adoptees like myself who wanted birth information about their biological families.

He said he worked in that office in the late 1980s. He called himself and his colleagues professionals who promoted the best interest of all parties involved in adoptions, including placing children for adoption. He said all of the court's staff treated their work seriously. "On the workers' side, it's scary," said Avery. "We weren't allowed to give out information. Before we would do a decision on anything, we would go to a supervisor, who was the head of adoption. I would never give out information. I wouldn't have given out information unless I got it confirmed." Avery did not recall how many requests for information from adoptees came to his office. He did not remember my requests and Hamer's responses to me that always copied him in 1988 and 1989.

Avery said when he worked for the court, all adoption records were stored in a secure area, with only limited access to approved staff. Birth records were treated as highly sensitive documents. Avery claimed his court always sought to protect the child and parents when it denied birth-records requests like mine. Avery did not reveal he had any knowledge of recent historic studies of US adoption that showed adoption records were once open and accessible to adoptees and birth parents, and that the overwhelming majority of adoptees and birth parents, and even adoptive parents, wanted an open system and to let birth kin find each other.

Avery's most startling comment to me mirrored statements I had heard already from two sets of relatives on my birth father's side of the family in the past decade. They all referenced an unproven urban myth that adoptees want to harm or even kill birth parents. Such fear-based myths are repeated by proponents of closed adoptions during legislative debates or appear as derogatory, troll comments in articles discussing equality for adoptees. Avery cited unspecified national examples that happened during his tenure at the court, like of a birth parent not wanting contact with their relinquished adult children and even birth parents being tracked and killed. He stated this as if it were fact—though it never happened—and highly relevant to his work to keep birth records sealed tightly shut to all adoptees. Even in 2016, his comments showed he had no remorse for his stereotyping, or that he was even aware he was demonstrating historic prejudice.

There is no evidence in any published history of US adoption law that shows the overwhelming majority of adoptees seek anything more than to be reunited with their kin.[3] However, defenders of closed records have made repeated and unsubstantiated claims from the 1960s onward that adoptees or birth mothers might wish to exact revenge or extortion. Adult adoptees seeking their records have been denounced by opposing attorneys and adoptive parents, who claimed the information could be used by the adoptee to "find and murder" biological parents or that granting a records request was the equivalent of giving away a "hunting license."[4]

During the 1980s a supposed mental condition among adolescent adoptees called the "Adopted Child Syndrome" made its way into popular discourse, and the condition is still discussed today in articles, blogs, and even textbooks. Its alleged pathologies included "genealogical bewilderment," compulsive pregnancies, and other behavioral problems.[5] Some unethical lawyers used this theory in their defense work in several murder trials that decade. These stories were circulating in the news cycle when Avery and his staff reviewed and then rejected my requests for help, with the sole exception of their delayed release of non-identifying history.

Some enterprising defense lawyers tried to show that adoptees accused of killing their parents suffered from a mental health issue called Multiple Personality Disorder. According to the argument fabricated by psychologist David Kirschner, the Adopted Child Syndrome could prove adoptees encounter more psychological problems in their childhood and adolescence unique to being adopted. The manifestations were promiscuity, lying, stealing, substance abuse, and more, all showing a "toxic potential of adoption."[6] The theory argues adoptees acted out of "extreme disassociation." Though this entirely fictional and discredited theory attracted national attention from the tabloids, he later revealed he prepared the concept for a trial at which he testified in 1986. He admitted he had not done proper research and the sensational theory was in fact a product of his imagination.[7] Yet, the damage had been done and fed the old stereotypes many clung to.

The stereotyping of adoptees dusted off the much older stereotype of the bastard. It also highlighted that the adoption system, despite its initial good intentions in the early 1900s to prevent harm to infants born outside of marriages, did not erase the underlying reality faced by adoptees.

Adoptees face an unfortunate double burden of two stereotypes from the public—as bastard and adoptees. This happens with little acknowledgment from those who stereotype adopted persons. Generally, those who are labeled as different in some way are characterized as being both deviant and pathological, particularly for adoption. Adoptee and sociologist Katarina Wegar wryly notes adoptees "can appeal to the public for sympathy in their quest for records, yet in some sense they tend to remain freaks, to be pitied and even feared."[8] For many adoptees in America, the stigma associated with the "bad seed" stereotype erodes their political and social stature among those who have power. As one scholar on the stigmatization of adoptees and their branding as "bad seeds" notes, "Americans may know little about adoption, but they do know this."[9]

If you were to ask Americans if they harbored fear or prejudice against bastards, they likely would say, no, of course not. But if you look at how our society actually treats bastards and illegitimate persons through laws restricting rights on adoptees—the group known to everyone as bastards—you will find clear examples of bias that likely is still rooted in these older, archetypal sentiments.

Growing up, as someone always conscious of my status as adopted, I knew I was different. I had parents to whom I was not biologically related. I also had a mother, almost certainly a single woman, who gave me up in Detroit, in 1965. I was the bastard of Detroit. Even though I carried this narrative in my head for as long as I could remember, I never elaborated with friends what made me different. I was self-conscious mostly of how different I looked to both of my adoptive parents.

Seeing my life through the lens of the word "bastard" felt inevitable. Technically, I was born a bastard and will be one until the day I die. That is my birthright, and I own it completely. However, my perspectives on civil rights surrounding the legal treatment of adoptees were drawn from my understanding of US and international law and political struggles by civil rights groups in the United States and abroad. Like the founding members of Bastard Nation, my own deep, personal experience helped to inform views to promote equality for millions of bastard-born Americans. In our case, we arrived at the same point of view through a shared experience and larger grasp of power and politics.

As a bastard, I have always been keenly aware of the word's literal and derogatory meanings. It is a word many find offensive and insulting, which is why it remains an insult of choice. My half-sister, on my birth father's side of the family, who I last saw in 2014, physically cringed when I called myself by that term. The word's etymology is packed with historic meaning and universal human prejudices. If you are to ask an American man what a likely curse he might use to a man he wants to demean, "fucking bastard" surely will be in the top-ten arsenal of verbal slings. Data miners have actually shown in a survey of curses posted on Facebook that "bastard" was among the fifteen most commonly used curse words used by both sexes in the United States.[10]

As a high school student in the St. Louis area, where racial tensions were fairly high for minority whites such as myself, I was bombarded with racial epitaphs on an almost daily basis. The standard put-down like "fucking hunky" or "dumb-ass hunky" was somewhat mild—you normally could blow those off with a shrug. You knew the stakes were higher when the phrase went more like, "Yo, you goddamn fucking bastard!" The word "bastard" then was usually the exclamation point, and the cue that the temperature was hot. That is when I really knew to exit the situation as quickly as I could.

The word has medieval origins in Europe, starting in the eleventh century, with written sources attributing it to northern France. The term *bastardum*, in some dictionaries, is linked to the (medieval) Latin word *bastum*, or packsaddle. This supposedly suggests a bastard was a child born in the saddle, or in French, *fils de bast*. Thus it likely evolved to indicate birth outside of a marriage bed, in transit.

In Europe, prior to the early thirteenth century, nobles and powerful men were able to inherit noble or royal title even if they were illegitimate. However, during the thirteenth century, the words "bastard" and *spurius* came to mean a child born to anything other than a legitimate marriage, as it was defined by the canon law of the Catholic Church. This also included children born to parents both of the highest rank and married to each other, if the pope denounced the marriage as illegal.[11]

In addition to French and German variations of the word, "bastard" (in Latin, *filius nulius*, meaning no one's son) has been common in the English language since before William Shakespeare's day. In English society, which used primogeniture that limited inheritance to just the eldest son under English law, the bastard was viewed as a product of sin, without title and property. He or she was cut off from family. Many writers in Shakespeare's era referred to bastard using imagery of filth, disease, corruption, and plague, which continue well into the twenty-first century.[12] In Western literature, the archetypal bastard has been portrayed consistently as a usurper or murderer, often associated with patricide. Other common bastard references draw from use many of the same stereotypes from the Elizabethan era. A bastard is someone who is contaminated with a disease or who bears a deformity.[13]

Today the term is used widely in everyday English language around the world, usually derogatorily. One of the most popular television shows on the planet as of 2017, *Game of Thrones*, has given the slur new life, with a cast of bastard characters who are as vile as any ever created for the small and big screen. The show's sadist Ramsay Bolton and lunatic teen-boy King Joffrey Baratheon come straight from bastard-central casting. On the HBO Network show, adapted from George R. R. Martin's popular *A Song of Fire and Ice* fantasy series, the word is used repeatedly as the meanest insult a man could hurl at another in the fictional realm of Westeros. The discourse from the show, since it first aired in 2011, has seeped into our daily social media lives on countless websites and YouTube. And this is just one of many ways we keep the stereotype alive and well.

The still-prevalent framing of bastards as damaged goods, who also are capable of heinous and violent crimes, distorts and ignores the grim historical data that illegitimate infants and persons faced. Throughout history, illegitimate children and their mothers were the victims, not perpetrators, of crimes and the ones who paid the price for societal attitudes, including with their lives. These outcomes are found in population health records, which provide data on health and mortality of infants and children.

British writer Ruth Paley, author of *Was Your Ancestor a Bastard?*, notes that in England, before the twentieth century, illegitimacy left a lethal legacy, including single mothers abandoning their bastard infants, who were commonly known as foundlings. "Lots of foundling children were illegitimate," she said. "And look at the assize records for the 19th century and you'll find that half the murder victims were little babies. We don't think twice about illegitimacy now; it's really hard to get your mind around the idea that the shame was once so awful that women were prepared to kill their babies."[14]

As a modern social institution, adoption laws only date to the nineteenth century in the United States. Labeling illegitimate children as societal threats and bogeymen, however, far precedes the US adoption system and the laws that govern it. Ideas of birth-driven—now considered genetic—identity are historic and rooted deeply in most cultures over time. Bastard children call into question property ownership, lines of familial and political succession, moral standing of parents and entire religions, and more. Each society over time has addressed these fears, often brutally and lethally for the unlucky illegitimate. Normally, society ostracized the "bastards," or just outright killed them not very long ago.

The United States inherited European and English legal traditions, which prescribed clear rules how infants would be classified as legitimate and illegitimate in the eyes of society. Roman law, canon law of the Catholic Church, and English law all adhered to the rule that only children born inside of approved marriages were deemed legitimate. Those who were conceived outside of wedlock were not. While there have been changes to parts of family law that cover how children are legitimized, the basic principle behind legitimation is still mostly unchanged.[15]

Anthropologist Bronislaw Malinowski's Principal of Legitimacy asserts that "no child can be brought into the world without a man, and one man assuming the role of sociological father." The man serving that role does not necessarily have to be the biological father. He also can be the guardian and protector—the male link between a child and the rest of the community.[16] Using this sociological perspective, the appearance of children has to be prevented for whom no adult male, permanently allied to the mother, can be held responsible as the father. This is required in order to safeguard the future of any given society.[17] This societal need is both ubiquitous and historic.

Malinowski first published this idea in 1930. Others who have studied the issue since note that illegitimacy is a category that will be found at many points in the past of every society, as well as in all present societies. Many have since challenged this idea, pointing to high levels of out-of-marriage births in parts of the Caribbean and, since the late 1970s, in the United States. But the idea of legitimacy prevails, even though it is not adopted in practice.[18] Sociologically, illegitimacy is and always has been regarded as a negative—the breach of an established rule, never considered an outcome of an approved sexual or reproductive behavior.[19]

Bastards and illegitimate children have always faced societal scorn, and they paid severe and deadly consequences for it. Today, a likely contributing factor to poor health outcomes for adoptees is societal stigma, and its multivariate impacts on unmarried mothers and their illegitimate kids. Despite the political correctness of the term adoptee, the underlying truth known to everyone—from the adoptive parents to the adopted children to society at large—is that adoptees are, sociologically speaking, bastards. Adoptees, more than the public, are the most aware of their different social status. It is a fact I always knew, and so did nearly everyone around me, including peers my age. Today, such children still bear the stigma as being born illegitimately, despite the high prevalence of children born outside of marriage that has made their status ubiquitous.

Historically, illegitimate infants in recent history have been among the most vulnerable population groups, documented in birth and mortality records. In fact, the historical study of illegitimacy—or bastardy as many demographic historians call it—is among the best documented of any topics in history because the research has relied on mostly reliable demographic data, such as baptism and death records, in Europe from the 1500s on, as well as in pre-twentieth-century America.

Cambridge historian Peter Laslett, who contributed to an exhaustive study of the topic in 1980, notes that many cultures have for centuries viewed illegitimacy as "pathological." Many of these cultures perceived mothers who gave birth to bastards as "victimized, disordered, even mentally abnormal."[20] The numbers from these old data sets from across Europe and early America from the 1500s onward often paint horrific outcomes for birth mothers. Outcomes could be worse for the infants who died at rates that suggest infanticide in many instances.

In the eighteenth and nineteenth centuries in the United Kingdom, infants who were born out of wedlock were about twice as likely to have died before reaching their first year of life compared to their peers born in sanctioned marriage. Poor and unmarried pregnant women frequently took refuge in the country's notorious workhouse, which housed and fed the poor and forced them to do often-brutal labor—captured in the writings of Charles Dickens's *Oliver Twist*. Many of the children confined to them faced early deaths. In 1760, four in five infants born in workhouses or left there by their birth mothers died before reaching their first birthday. By 1834, there were nearly forty thousand children living in workhouses in England and Wales—most subjected to a bleak existence, if they were lucky enough to live beyond childhood.[21]

Records collected in the English market town of Banbury in Oxfordshire, between 1561 and 1838, provide a lethal picture of existence for bastard-babies born there. The number of bastard children with baptism and burial records made up 18 percent of all recorded persons—a high number. However, the rates of infant deaths were at best catastrophic for those unlucky to be born a bastard. Records show that 70 percent of all of these bastards born during these 277 years died before reaching the age of one. Only 21 percent lived to the age of one, and just 5 percent reached the age of five. A mere 1 percent of bastards made it to the age of thirty.[22]

Other findings of higher infant mortality can be traced in the records of births and deaths of infants over the last hundred or more years in Europe. Jenny Teichman, author of *Illegitimacy: An Examination of Bastardy*, reports "there is a persistent and significant difference between infant mortality rates of legitimate and illegitimate children." Her study found that mortality ranges for the two groups ranged from 50 to 150 percent higher for both English and Norwegian illegitimate infants, looking at national records between 1914 and 1973 at four different points in time. Teichman notes even at English public hospitals through the 1960s, doctors and nursing staff "refused anesthetics to unmarried women in childbirth 'to teach them a lesson.'"[23]

A bastard's prospects in the English colonies in North America were not much greater than those born in Europe. Infanticide likely became a common practice in the United States in the 1700s. Virtually every colony in North America passed legislation that declared, unless witnesses would swear to seeing a childbirth, the mother of a dead infant would be presumed guilty of murder.[24] Things did not improve, even through the end of the 1800s. Nearly a century later in the early 1970s, infant mortality in the United States was 73 percent higher for children of unmarried mothers than their peers from families with married parents.[25]

The findings also are not unique to the Western world. One seminal study on the sociology of illegitimacy published in 1975 found that as of the mid-1960s, in every nation globally that tracked child health data, fetal and infant mortality were higher for illegitimate than legitimate children.[26]

While the penalty for illegitimacy as measured in infant mortality rates did fall in the last century, data from the first years of the twenty-first century shows illegitimate infants in England and Wales are still 30 percent more likely to die before their first birthday than legitimate infants.[27] Remarkably, evidence shows children reported as illegitimate but registered to both parents living at the same address are still 17 percent more likely to die in infancy.[28]

Today excess infant mortality tied to illegitimacy remains a legitimate health concern. Multiple risk factors contribute to the outcome. Single parents have less disposable income. They likely have worse housing. A single parent likely works full-time. Children likely are weaned off healthy breast milk earlier. The stigma of illegitimacy and societal scorn directed unfairly to unmarried mothers might reduce their ability to keep their children healthy. Unmarried women may also have come from poor social positions, and thus be more vulnerable to having a child out of wedlock.

But what about adoptees, who were relinquished by these single mothers? My subpar health as a child made me a likely candidate for the early mortality statistics seen in England and Wales. My mother's diminished social status, isolation in pregnancy, and the stress of having a child as a single woman likely affected my health, but I cannot say that conclusively.

My original birth records show that I was at higher risk of being unhealthy, being born almost prematurely. Had I been born four decades earlier and given up to adoption in one of the deadly adoption orphanages for illegitimately born children, I am sure I would have died.

In the early 1900s, before reformers from groups like the Child Welfare League of America and other benevolent groups intervened, illegitimate babies were boarded and trafficked at so-called baby farms in the United States. One highly publicized 1914 report called the *Traffic in Babies,* by Dr. George Walker, reported on what amounted to charnel houses for unwanted, abandoned, and illegitimate children. These reportedly operated to "save" the single women from the disgrace of being unmarried mothers. The description by Walker is noteworthy because of his focus on maternal and child-health practices that are unquestioned today. His report focused on health risks posed by separating infants from their mothers. He also described how poor public health practices for abandoned babies served as the functional equivalent of homicide. Walker wrote:

> Day after day, month after month, they received healthy, plump infants into their wards and watch them hour after hour go down to death. They know that practically all of those that immediately after birth are separated from their mothers will die; yet year after year they keep up their nefarious, murderous traffic. We do not attempt in this study to settle the many complex problems relating to the illegitimate; but we believe that the facts show that society's method in many instances is one of repression and

virtual murder. This is a hard word, we grant, and we would fain substitute a gentler term; but, after all is said and done, that which we have recorded is virtual murder, and slow and cowardly murder at that. It would be far more humane to kill these babies by striking them on the head with a hammer than to place them in institutions where four-fifths of them succumb within a few weeks to the effects of malnutrition or infectious diseases.[29]

Even with the mortality rate of relinquished, out-of-wedlock children as high as 80 percent, this fact did not curb the practice of punishing the children born out of wedlock by professionals and religious leaders. Some doctors, nurses, midwives, clergymen, and hospital administrators actively referred the disgraced mothers, who had sex out of marriage and became pregnant, to these lethal, for-profit baby shops.[30] Some hospitals even took a cut from the baby trade that ferried bastard babies to their likely deaths. Walker's summary notes hospitals had different methods of disposing of unwanted babies permanently: "There is an old woman, called 'Mother—', who carries the babies from the hospital to this institution; she gets $5 for this service. At another hospital, the nurses have charge of separating the infant from its mother; they make all the business arrangements; receive the money; and send the baby to Institution No. 1 by an old black woman, who carries it in a basket."[31]

These acts all occurred a mere five decades before my birth. They demonstrate how powerful stigmas against bastard-born children were in recent memory—strong enough to create a system that ensured the likely deaths of bastard infants in institutional care. Adoption, as a cause championed by Progressive Movement reformers from 1910 through 1930, was a solution that offered a way to eliminate the stigma, mortality risks, and lifelong barriers posed by illegitimacy. It was supposed to prevent this type of outcome, though the immediate health impacts of being born out of wedlock were already expressed in my body before I was two weeks old.

When I interviewed the obstetrician who delivered me and told him how I was born underweight and early, he said he was not surprised by my health outcomes during my first two weeks of life outside the womb. "Many of the girls' babies were premature," he said of the out-of-wedlock children born in Crittenton General Hospital, where infants destined for adoption were born in Detroit in the years surrounding my birth. "Many girls out of shame tried to hide their pregnancies."

The doctor told me the young pregnant girls who stayed at Detroit's Crittenton House near Crittenton General Hospital likely had not taken proper care of themselves and their fetuses in the early stages of their pregnancies. They were trying to hide their status, he said, and this meant some did not get the proper prenatal care that would have helped them and their future children. However, they still received competent care from a recognized maternity hospital well-known for training in obstetrics and gynecology. He described most patients from the Florence Crittenton Home as first-time mothers. He assured me that all had outside medical care and "were taken care of by us while they came in for childbirth and postpartum care."

According to the US Department of Health and Human Services, a healthy pregnancy is one of the best ways to promote a healthy birth. This includes early and regular prenatal care, which improves the chances of a healthy pregnancy and reduces later risks to infants for chronic diseases. Maternal-health experts strongly recommend that any woman who believes they might be pregnant should schedule a visit with a health provider to start proper prenatal care. Proper prenatal care with good nutrition for a fetus is essential during all three trimesters.[32]

It would be naive to think that contemporary American society has escaped patterns long-established in most cultures throughout time. In my view, the stigma against illegitimate children today can be seen in their treatment over time as a new class of pariah persons—adoptees. As a large population they theoretically have become "legitimized" by law as normal with a new label, but that does not change how individuals, families, and societies treat them at the individual and macro level.

Adoptees will forever be bastards and illegitimate children. Everyone knows that when someone says they are adopted. It is still a reason why it is taboo to talk about one's adoptive status publicly and why the intake staff at medical offices become visibly uncomfortable, and avoid talking to you, when you tell them their forms asking for family history are insulting because you are adopted.

An adoptee's taboo status reinforces biases they face from state record keepers, who do not serve adoptees' interests in states that discriminate against those seeking their birth records. There is no reason why officials managing my adoption records, like Avery and Hamer, would treat me without fear deeply rooted in societal discrimination against adoptees.

Researchers in the fields of neuroscience, psychology, criminal justice, law, sociology, and anthropology have long investigated prejudice and how humans practice it, often unknowingly. Investigators have even begun looking at how prejudice works at the neurological level. New York University psychology professor David Amodio, an expert on the neurological roots of prejudice, notes that prejudices and stereotypes often operate in combination to influence social behavior. According to Amodio, "both forms of bias can operate implicitly, such that they may be activated and influence judgments and behaviours [*sic*] without conscious awareness."[33]

For Avery, his claim that adoptees posed a safety risk let him transfer an old prejudice onto the adoptee as a perceived threat. It likely unmasked how he internalized society's deeper fears about what being a bastard means in the eyes of those who scorned them. He likely believed that adoptees truly were potentially harmful. In fact, in nearly all societies over time, those born illegitimately have been the historic victims of prejudice and well-documented harm.

My experience with the adoption bureaucracies jaded me when I was deeply engrossed in the search. At the time, I thought the treatment was grossly unfair and also inherently discriminatory. Those sentiments have grown even stronger since then because I see so little change. I always believed that a system that denied persons the most basic information about who they were was unjust. No rationale for protecting the so-called privacy of birth mothers—and society-enforced shame heaped upon them—can defend a practice that is so basically unfair to an adopted person.

In the 1980s, I did not fully understand the culture and cult of secrecy that had evolved since the 1950s in the United States. Had I been born in the United Kingdom or two decades earlier, I would have immediately known the answers to my questions when I was eighteen.

I have shared this story with good friends who I trust and who I know understand the complexities of being adopted. One recently told me, everything you did, every letter you wrote, ever lead you chased, was an essential chapter in your journey. On some days, I agree. I believe I am better for having learned the hard way how entrenched bureaucratic systems work and how adoptees are treated as second-class citizens by those who have power over them. On other days, I wonder what kind of life I might have lived had I not spent two years searching and wasting countless hours charging the adoption fortress that has still never opened its doors.

Chapter 10

Flying to Detroit

I'm going to have to get used to the idea I got a grown-up son now.

—Rudy Owens's Birth Mother, 1989

My adoption forced me to become a private detective. I acquired that profession's skillset out of necessity. I developed informal personal networks, talking to people who had conducted adoption searches in Washington state and Michigan. I learned how to navigate records systems, with people, public agencies, organizations, and libraries. I learned how to make up a story on the phone when I called someone, if I knew telling the truth about who I was and why I was asking for information would trigger fear. I had learned already from strangers and those I knew that people viewed me with both suspicion and fear, because I was both an adoptee and, yes, a bastard.

I used detective tricks I had picked up watching the *Rockford Files*. They really worked. I learned to never make people who helped you feel nervous or afraid. This was my underlying rule of information acquisition. I also learned early on who likely would be a friend, but not always. Luckily, enough adoptees, some sympathetic women, and a few personal connections paid off.

I possessed two pages of non-identifying information that were drafted on a typewriter and shared by my adoption agency. From them, I had basic information that provided the foundation for my search. Because the information was literally whited out and then photocopied,

I could count the typed spaces of each blanked-out section using the lines above and below the redacted spots. This simple counting method proved to be the most critical step in my detective case. They gave me likely answers to key missing facts. I knew the following details that could open doors for more information:

- My birth mother and her twin brother graduated from a high school in Detroit, and because of the way the name was typed out, I could count the exact number of characters of the school name.

- The year of my birth mother's graduation was likely 1958, because she was born in 1940. That would limit my search to one or two high school yearbooks—if I could find them.

- My birth father was a dentist and had attended a major Midwestern university. This meant he likely could be found using dental registries and university yearbooks.

- My birth father had three sisters, so I might be able to find them using a high school yearbook, but the chances would be slim without my birth father's name.

- My birth grandfather was a sheet-metal worker, which offered little possibility because there was no professional organization for this group.

- My birth mother's brother studied natural resources, likely at the University of Michigan. There could be professional registries, events, and contacts in the field in Michigan—if he was still there.

When I started, my most promising lead was the name of the university where my alleged birth father earned his undergraduate and dental degrees. But without his name, how was I supposed to identify the man among the thousands of students who attended the university? I decided to trust my eyes. I would look at the pictures of every single student in each university yearbook.

Thanks to my connections at the college I attended in Portland, the school did an interlibrary loan for that yearbook. I had presumed he was a 1961 graduate for his bachelor's degree, given his date of birth and the narrative in my meager description of his life history. In the fall of 1988, I drove from Seattle to Portland to take a look. I sat for about two hours flipping through every page and looking at every photo of every man. I photocopied every page with photos, each smaller than a square inch. They showed an almost entirely white student body, of mature looking Midwesterners. I still have the copy I made of the yearbook.

Almost every man had short hair and wore a coat and tie. One by one I looked at the tiny mugshots. One stood out, of a thin-faced man. I thought for sure he was the one, judging by his cheekbones and eyebrows. I asked friends to see if they agreed with me. They did not. I could not be sure. I found out later that I was wrong. I had glossed over the man who was actually my birth father, once I learned his name in 1989. I went back to the yearbook and gazed at his face on page 99. "Really, him?" I thought. Later, in 2007, when I found and met his sister, my biological aunt, I went to the university library and photocopied the 1964 yearbook showing his group photos for the Delta Psi Dental fraternity. But even those photos barely showed enough to confirm what he looked like. I marked the yearbook search method a failure.

I pursued other leads, however improbable. One of the contacts I had made who worked on adoption records searches said sometimes the US State Department would scoop up original birth certificates in their records on citizens, including during passport processing. I could do a federal Freedom of Information Act request on myself and maybe get lucky. I sent my request to the State Department in December 1988. In March 1989, the department replied to my request for records. The reply said only one record was found, my passport application from May 1985. My records show the State Department only had my amended birth certificate, issued by Michigan on May 13, 1965, not my original certificate. I scratched that effort as a failure too.

My notebook from this era is filled with lists of names and telephone numbers. Each represents possible clues and people to contact. Some were names of dentists and orthodontists around the country. My notes have an action item to contact a research team at the University of California at Los Angeles (UCLA) doing twins research, thinking somehow my birth mom and brother may have been involved. I have the names of five twins researchers. I have names of staff of the Society of American Foresters in Michigan. I searched through a directory of certified physician's assistants at a university library. My notes show names of the Nursing Board, the Michigan Board of Dentistry in Lansing, the Physician's Assistant's Task Board, the Michigan Education Association, the University of Michigan Health Center, the Health Occupation Council, and names of multiple medical centers in the Detroit area.

I was preparing to ask Wayne County General Hospital for records of their dental interns. I reached out to the University of Michigan natural resources alumni, hoping they might be able to help me find my birth uncle.

My contacts also suggested contacting the hospital where I was born to ask them for a copy of my birth records, as well as the Church of Jesus Christ of Latter-day Saints (the Mormon Church), for possible records. I considered writing to my birth facility, Crittenton General Hospital, and pretending I was my birth mother's brother, and then ask about records. I didn't know at the time the hospital had been torn down more than a decade earlier. Today I am amazed by all of the rabbit holes I considered going down. Almost all of these ideas and leads failed. After nearly two years, the chase was wearing me down.

Imagine the frustration I encountered multiplied by the tens of thousands of adoptees looking for their past. These searches can last ten, twenty, even thirty or more years. Totaling all of these wasted years shows how the systems in place for legal and birth records are completely indifferent to adoptees' rights. It is why adoptees feel so profoundly insulted by those who dismiss their basic legal and human rights and the records requests that non-adoptees have fulfilled without question.

I had another promising lead. I used the typed spaces that fit in the whited-out spot on my non-identifying information sheet that listed my birth mother and her twin brother's high school. If I found a list of high schools, I could determine which ones were exactly the same number of typed characters to spell the school name. I called the reference desk at the Detroit Public Library and asked if they had a list of high schools in Detroit. I learned that only one institution in the city had a name exactly the same number of characters that matched the blank space on my non-identifying information sheet.

In the end, that clue mattered the most: a high school name, and little more. I figured because my mother had a twin brother, they would be easy to find looking at a high school yearbook. Luck smiled upon me. The Detroit Public Library also had an extra copy of the 1958 high school yearbook in its special collections archive. If I could review it in person, I could see if there were twins. That would almost certainly provide the names.

That still left major unknown issues. What if my birth mother had married someone and took her husband's name? What if she and her brother no longer lived in Detroit or Michigan? The only occupation I could track from my birth uncle was forestry, and he could be a professional member. My birth mother, according to the non-identifying information, did not have a clear profession. She likely could not be tracked using professional registries.

By this point, I had grown frustrated. I had no more leads from the state, from the Wayne County Probate Court, or from Lutheran Child and Family Services. The Wayne County Probate Court's letter from January 1989 had slammed the door forever on me, saying my original birth records were sealed by law. The two adoption registries I had joined, the voluntary one in Washington State and the official registry run by the State of Michigan, yielded no matches. Without a name of a birth parent, I could never begin a proper search for any of my relatives, and thus, my ancestry.

So, in March 1989, I made a leap of faith. I bought a round-trip ticket to the city of my birth, timing it for the eve of my twenty-fourth birthday in April. I once again contacted Lutheran Child and Family Services. I asked to meet them in person. I wanted this agency, which continued to deny me records and had lied to me before, to know I was a real person being denied information they kept in their file drawers. This must have triggered a remote feeling of sympathy in the social worker I would eventually meet.

She gave me, per my request, a final order of adoption that did not list my birth name or birth mother. She also had reached out to my former foster parents, who had cared for me for nearly a month before I was placed for adoption. She wrote me back and included their names, telephone number, and address. This information was not protected by law. Once again, persistence in the face of repeated denials made a few inches of progress. To my surprise this couple said they would be happy to meet me after I called them. Unfortunately, they had no information about my birth mother. As foster parents, they were not allowed to know the parents of children they cared for, because, even to foster parents who cared for relinquished infants, this adoption system promoted secrecy.

I lined up temporary lodging at the relatives of Seattle friends. I brought copies of all the documents that described what little I knew. And I took my first real leap of faith that had no promise of success. I determined that I had to make this trip, or forever be haunted by regret of what I should have done and did not do. My meager income and savings made this trip feel like Don Quixote's battles against windmills. At the very least I could meet the foster family who raised and cared for me for nearly five weeks.

I flew out of Seattle the second week of April 1989. On the plane, I saw a movie that seemed more than coincidental. The flight screened the 1988 comedy *Twins*, starring Danny DeVito and Arnold Schwarzenegger. The brothers were the result of a genetic experiment and were separated at birth. DeVito's street hustler character learns about his mother and brother and vows to find them in Los Angeles. In the end, the two siblings learn of their relationship and meet their biological parents. The film seemed to me like a positive omen that I was on the right track. Maybe this madcap trip would prove as fruitful as the journey of these improbable two brothers looking for their identity and past.

I arrived at the Detroit airport in the late morning. I wasted not a minute. I rented a car and immediately drove to downtown Detroit's main public library. I remember seeing the signs of Detroit's former glory in the Wayne County Courthouse Building and the signs of the city's emerging and catastrophic decay in the Brush Park neighborhood near the city center, where old and elegant brick homes were gutted and burned out. I went to the reference desk and requested the 1958 high school yearbook that I was 95 percent certain would have my birth mother and uncle's photos. The librarian returned with the twenty-one-year-old document. That book cracked my two-year-old detective case.

At this point, everything sped up into light speed, it seemed. I nervously thumbed through the pages, once again looking for a face that resembled mine and images of a set of fraternal twins, a brother and sister. There were ten pairs of siblings shown for the senior year. But two photos stood out. There they were, right in front of me. I had found pictures of my kin. I could not believe I spotted my birth mother and uncle's faces in a span of minutes. The case was now wide open.

There was no mistaking my birth mother. She had my mouth and my hair. She looked Scandinavian—a reflection of her Finnish heritage. Her hair was cropped short, just above her ears. Her gaze is away from the camera, with a wide-open smile. She had thick lips, a lot like my own. It was a black-and-white photo, and students wore the fashion of their era. "So, that is what a real relative looks like," I thought. "Goddamn, there is someone in the universe who looks like me!"

I also found several other photos of both of them from their high school activities. My birth uncle ran track, and I bore a very striking resemblance to him when he was younger—we both had long necks and skinny bodies. I photocopied the pages that showed them and also the names of the class officers. I would need to contact those officers to learn if they still knew of my birth mother and her brother. The officers might also know if my birth mother's surname had changed through marriage. Some might be living in the Detroit area.

So now I had two names. I next had to find where they lived. They could be anywhere. They could be dead. My biological mother likely could be married and have a different name. My biological uncle likely would have the same name. But would the class officers know? I copied down their names. I also copied down the name of seven high school counselors and the names of the two editors of the high school yearbook.

By then it was not quite one o'clock in the afternoon. I had made more progress in one hour than I had in nearly two years. I next stopped at the Detroit office of Lutheran Child and Family Services, in Southfield, literally across the street and border with Detroit on the now infamous Eight Mile Road. I had an appointment to see the social worker who

I had contacted in March. This was the same office that a year earlier falsely told me they had no file about my adoption from its predecessor agency. I wanted to meet their staff in person, so they could see me as a human being and learn that my journey of discovery mattered.

The office was located in a bland, two-story office park building on an ugly stretch of a commercial and business district. When I arrived, the social worker in her forties invited me to her office. She was polite, but still unwilling to share anything more than she had shared already. The information amounted to two pages of non-identifying information and a final order of adoption without my original name or birth mother's name.

I sat in a chair opposite her. On her desk, I could see a case file in a manila folder, with dozens of pieces of paper inside it. The folder was facing her, but I could read the folder's file name upside down. It had the same name of the woman whose picture I had instantly recognized in the yearbook hours earlier. I now confirmed that the agency had lied to me a year earlier when it said it had no files on me. I also had 100 percent confirmation that I had been successful in finding my birth mother's identity. I did not let the social worker know I had found a match at the Detroit Public Library. I did not mention how her office had been untruthful when I first asked them for help. I only told her I would be looking for clues in Michigan, starting with my foster family.

The next stop on my road trip of discovery took me to Mount Clemens, Michigan, a township about six miles north of Detroit in the working-class suburbs surrounding the metro area. The wife in the foster couple was retired, and the husband was home because of a work-related injury at a soda-bottling plant. We made an appointment to meet that afternoon.

When I was born, in the mid-1960s, foster families took care of infants relinquished for adoption, like myself. This was considered a best practice. The American Academy of Pediatrics in 1960 recommended that children being considered for adoption were given temporary placement in foster homes.[1]

The friendly couple were in their early sixties. They looked healthy and happy. They invited me into their modest, single-story home—welcoming a stranger they had last seen nearly a quarter of a century earlier. The pair told me they had several children of their own, all grown. They had always cared for children for social service agencies as foster parents, they said, including the one that placed me in their care on April 28, 1965. I stayed in this home through May 26, 1965. On that day, my adoption placement with my adoptive family was approved by the adoption agency. The wife said, "I instantly knew who you were from when you were a baby."

I sat stunned. I felt an immediate connection with them. These were the people who still knew who I was by my physical appearance as a newborn. They were the caregivers who ensured my well-being for some of the most critical weeks of my life. It made me think just how important physical appearances are to the parent-child bonding experience. It also made me realize I lacked that crucial connection, never having looked like anyone I had known my entire life.

In records I later received, I was given a "running record" of the time I spent with my foster family from the adoption agency that handled my placement. My foster parents used their personal doctor to examine me after my hospital discharge. Once in their care, I had stopped vomiting while drinking bottled milk. The records show the wife noted "the holes in the nipples were so large that it is no wonder that he vomited because the milk came out too fast." The records also show I finally began to gain weight after being well under healthy birth weight. The records note, "The boarding mother said he was a very beautiful baby with blue eyes, rose colored skin, and reddish-brown hair. . . . There were no sleeping or eating problems displayed by the baby. He seemed to be a very good, alert child." These were really good people, and I knew I was lucky they had me under their wing.

The couple told me that for nearly thirty years, they had taken care of more than two dozen foster children for adoption agencies. They opened their home because they cared about children. I felt humbled by their generosity. In the last fifteen years, many of the adoptees they helped were African American or mixed-race infants born prematurely or with drug addictions because of substance abuse by young mothers. Those children had the greatest needs, and helping them required enormous compassion and resources, they said.

Hearing how adoption had changed since my birth made me realize that I was luckier than many of my fellow adoptees. At least I was not exposed prenatally to harmful, addictive drugs like crack. Today I still do not know how my birth mother managed her health during her nearly forty weeks of pregnancy. She may have been very healthy. Or she might have used substances like tobacco or alcohol, like many mothers did before the 1970s, without the important health education mothers now receive about healthy prenatal care.

Neither the husband nor wife ever met my birth mother or my adoptive family. They told me that the adoption agencies always hid that information. They had no records that would help me. They were thankful we had finally met. They told me how much they loved seeing how a young baby they cared for had grown into an adult they could host in their home again.

At five o'clock that evening, I started calling the class officers of my birth mother's high school. This was still the era when you could use directory assistance, and when phone directories contained extensive listings. I knew I would have to make up a story when I called. If I told them the truth—that I was an adoptee looking for his birth family—they would grow immediately suspicious. They would be more trusting if I made up a story that seemed probable, but not make them realize they were sharing valuable intelligence.

I pretended to be the young-adult son of a University of Michigan forestry graduate. I made up names for myself and my imaginary father. I fabricated that I was hosting a reunion event, and needed to find a missing student, my biological uncle. Except I did not know where he lived. I would ask if the former officers could help me find out where he was. It was a type of tactic I had used many times before. People did not want to hear words that would scare them, and adoptees—then and now—frighten others when they are looking for their past.

Before six o'clock in the evening, my first day in Detroit, I hit pay dirt, again. I found that a person with the same name as one of the high school officers still lived in the Detroit metro area. She believed me when I called her, and said she could not help me find my birth uncle. However, she told me his twin sister had just returned to the state in Ann Arbor after living away for nearly half a decade out of state. Oh, and her name had changed. She now had a married name, which she shared with me. Maybe I could find her, she said.

I could hardly contain my excitement internally. On the phone, I expressed frustration still not being able to track down my birth uncle. But, perhaps I could call his twin sister. To this day, I still do not think this woman knew she had changed the course of my life in such a positive way. I wished I could have thanked her, again and again.

The Ann Arbor phone directories made it easy to narrow down the names to just two women with the same last name. At the local public library that night, I combed through directories from the past decade and the most current edition. I found the gap when one of the women with the name left Ann Arbor and then returned in 1987. So now I was getting real, real close.

That night, I wrote a two-page letter to a stranger who was also the woman who brought me into this world. In that note, I explained to a mother I had never met that I was her son. I described who I was. I wrote how I had grown up in the St. Louis area. I explained I had gone to college in Oregon and now lived in Seattle. I provided a short history of how long I had been looking for my biological family. With as much clarity as I could muster, I succinctly explained why finding my family mattered. It was important for me to know who I was and where I came from. I wanted to know my ancestry and the people in my family tree whose genetic material lived in my cells and DNA. I included recent pictures, one showing me smiling and involved in outdoor activities that I loved pursuing in the mountains of the Pacific Northwest. I told her I would be in Michigan for another four days. Could she meet?

I planned to leave a package at her home. However, I did not know which of the two names I found in the phone directory, listing numbers and addresses, was the right one. I first had to confirm with my eyes that I was leaving my story letter with the right woman. Receiving a letter like the one I had written is a once-in-a-lifetime event, so I owed it to my birth mother and a stranger to do this right.

There was and never will be any how-to guide to handle reunions among kin separated for decades. That has not prevented the growth of a cottage industry since the 1970s of so-called "adoption intermediaries"—social workers, therapists, and counselors who claim to offer expertise on how to connect family members separated by state-imposed adoption secrecy rules and laws. I have never given these go-betweens much credibility, because they belittle birth families' dignity with a presumption those families cannot manage their lives and their emotions without interference from parties who have no meaningful stake in the reunions. To me and many other adoptees, these stakeholders are the classic definition of "parasites." I believe I handled my situation responsibly and thoughtfully, as have thousands of other adoptees and birth parents who met without anyone helping them out.

The next morning I drove to downtown Ann Arbor from the house where I was couch-surfing outside of Detroit. I wanted to see for myself if one of the two possible women with the same name in Detroit could be my birth mother. This woman ran an art shop. It was located in downtown Ann Arbor. I figured even if she were my biological mother, she would never assume the person walking into her space could be a long-relinquished son. Part of me wanted to believe my birth mother could be an artist. When I went inside the business, I saw a woman who could be my birth mother's age, forty-nine. But her facial features were not mine. I knew she was not my kin.

I asked her if she knew the other woman in town who had the same name. Not personally, she told me, but others had come in making the same mistake. She asked, why did I want to know. For some reason, I trusted her. I told her flat out I was adopted and believed her namesake double in town was my birth mother. Instead of acting uncomfortably, she told me she had friends who also had been adopted and understood why I was looking. She told me the other woman with her name worked at another store, very close, off State Street, near the famous University of Michigan Law School.

I immediately went to that store. I walked around, but decided I should not stay long. It was a woman's clothing business. I had no fake story I could use to find out if the woman who I presumed was my birth mother was working that day. I did not see anyone who might look like me. This was not the right time or place to meet. At that moment, the chances were extremely high we might recognize each other.

Using the address I had found in the phone directory, I drove the short distance to her apartment. I didn't knock or ring the bell. I put the envelope with my letter and photographs under her door. It was now a matter of hours before I would learn how she would handle a major life event. I knew it would be jolting. It also seemed like the most honest way to do this.

By this time, barely forty-eight hours had passed after I had landed in Detroit. I had found out the name of my birth family and the identity of my biological mother. I also had met my foster family that had cared for me for weeks as a very small infant. It was dizzying how rapidly my fortunes had changed, all because I had taken the bold leap in coming to Michigan. It also was several days shy of my twenty-fourth birthday. If anything in my life had been preordained to happen, this was it.

I decided not to call her until the evening. I learned later from a relative that the letter and its contents arrived as a life-changing shock. My sudden appearance out of nowhere, with no warning, created fear and anxiety, and perhaps other emotions she never shared. She spoke to her brother's son, my cousin. They had a close relationship. She began sharing some of her story about my birth with him—things he had never known. I heard about this piece of the reunion story years later. With my birth mother, information about her past and her giving me up for adoption were secrets she has shared with just a few people.

I called her in the early evening. I said, "Hello, this is Rudy. Did you get my note?" Indeed she had. She did not reveal the intensity of the emotion she may have been feeling. She sounded calm. After a few awkward minutes, she proposed that we meet in Ann Arbor for a beer. I said that sounded fine. About an hour later I was at a local pub, where I finally laid eyes on my closest biological kin.

My birth mother looked healthy, though not athletic. Her dark blonde hair was still short, like her high school yearbook pictures. I had her hair. She was sitting with her nephew, my cousin two years younger than me. We both had what I call "blockheads," an older insult against Upper

Peninsula residents with Finnish ancestry. He was about three inches shorter than me, and two years younger. He was stockier and heavier. He looked like I would if I did not exercise regularly.

We mostly shared stories. They involved strangers who were also my closest kin. My only tools to navigate this reunion were an open mind and empathy. I talked about growing up in the St. Louis area and moving to Oregon, and then Seattle. My cousin was trying to finish his undergraduate program at East Michigan University. My birth mother talked about her marriage to her one-and-only husband, who had passed away many years earlier. She had taken his family name and never had children with him. He ran a supply company, and he provided well for her. In the years after he passed away from a heart attack, she left the state with a new partner. He was younger, working in research. They eventually split up about three years earlier. She returned to her home state of Michigan and long-time home of Ann Arbor. Again I had been lucky she had moved back to her home state when I had visited.

I mostly remember my birth mother and cousin offered me a condensed story of their family history. I had been waiting for a moment like this for years. My birth grandmother had Finnish and Swedish-Finnish ancestry. She was born near Hancock, Michigan, on the Upper Peninsula—one of five children. Many Finns settled here at the turn of the twentieth century. The men worked in the copper mines. Her parents hailed from Finland and arrived as poor immigrants. My grandma's father appeared to have been a laborer, and also ne'er-do-well taken to drink. He died in 1934, at the age of fifty-seven, during the Great Depression. Her mother lived to be seventy-three, dying in 1969, probably never knowing I was born. I learned the family had a family tree of Finnish relatives that dates back to the late 1700s, when Finland was under the iron hand of the Russian Empire. One of my distant relatives even served as a sharpshooter for the Russians in the Russian-Turkish War of 1877–78.

My birth grandpa came from Welsh and English immigrants, one of three children. Up until the early 1900s, everyone in his family had been farmers. The family line kept moving slowly east as the country expanded in the 1800s. My great-grandparents included an Owens and a Baker. My great-grandmother ended up living until she was ninety-three, passing away in a nursing home in Detroit in 1977. She probably never knew I was born either. I have her very, very large nose, as I later learned from family pictures. I hope I have many of her genes, because she was tough as nails. The Owens-family homestead is located near Big Rapids, Michigan, which I would soon visit a few days later.

We ended the evening early. The next day I visited my birth mother at her apartment. She shared some photos of her and her former husband, her twin brother, friends, and other family members. She gave me the address where she grew up in Detroit, which I wrote down. She showed me the detailed family tree that shows all of the family members on her Finnish side of the family back to the late 1700s. I still have a copy of that today. That is when my fascination of Finland began, and I later embraced the term *sisu*. I put a sticker on my truck. The Finnish expression roughly translates to stoic determination and guts. It seemed fitting as a word to describe the journey that connected us.

I asked her if she would sign a state consent form that would allow the State of Michigan Office of Vital Statistics, the Wayne County Probate Court, and my adoption agency to release my adoption and birth records. She agreed. She told me ever so briefly about my birth father, a dentist resident at Wayne County General Hospital. Theirs was a brief romance—or whatever the sexual and intimate relations were—and he later denied paternity. Her father later confronted him in anger while she was pregnant, but my birth father never changed his story, his entire life. But now, finally, I had his name.

I told her I needed some time to decompress from the events, and I think she did too. Before we parted ways, she signed a consent form that would allow the state to release my identifying information and birth records. I immediately mailed the consent form to the Lutheran Child and Family Services. They in turn shared with the state's adoption registry and the Wayne County Probate Court. From each of them I received a written letter later that month acknowledging all of them now had proof my birth mother had consented by law to release all my adoption records. By law, these entities would now have to share what they never wanted me to see—my original records with my birth name, birth mother's name, and details most persons take for granted who are not adopted. After two years, they had finally relented. It all seemed like a huge waste for everyone.

Now on my own, I toured Detroit. I also drove to the street in northwest Detroit where my birth mother, her brother, and her parents lived in the 1950s. It was a clapboard style, two-story tract house, built in 1949. That was during Detroit's heyday, when working in a factory could provide a family a ticket to the middle class. Every house on the street, near River Rouge Park, looked identical. They were modest, built on small lots. Every street had sidewalks. This house was located across from an elementary school and nice park.

Ironically, they lived very close to where my adoptive parents lived in the city. I have since wondered if my biological grandparents and adoptive family met by accident in River Rouge Park on a Sunday walk, or at a local grocery store. Would they have known the little toe-headed boy in my adoptive parents' stroller was their grandson they had never seen? I think this could have happened. I have wondered how often this may happen with other adoptees and their kin, all over the country.

I learned later that my grandparents sold their house in 1968, a year after the deadly Detroit riots of 1967 that saw forty-three persons killed and two thousand buildings destroyed. They moved to a neighboring suburb city, like tens of thousands of other white Detroiters. By then I had moved with my family to St. Louis. My biological grandparents were part of the white flight that continued the next two decades.

After finally meeting my birth mother in Detroit, I took a two-day road trip to northern Michigan to see some new landscapes and to think how my life had dramatically changed. I now had a past. I was in a state where my birth mother's parents were born, grew up, raised a family, and retired. This was home to me. I stopped in the city near where the Owens-family homestead resides. It felt very rural even today. It was mid-April and still cold. So I had relatives who lived here. I wondered what it would have been like to grow up here before the Depression.

I went back to the adoption agency when I returned to the Detroit area. I wanted the social worker I had met to see the person who had been denied information days earlier, and to know he found his kin. I wanted that to sink in, so she one day might learn from how she denied an adoptee his basic right to his identity.

By then she had received the legal paperwork I had mailed. She seemed to marvel at my success of having found my birth family so quickly. She never offered any apology for not sharing information with me that literally was underneath her fingertips when I was in her office. It had not mattered I had flown halfway across the country, with perhaps no chance of success. Though she did not show any visible contrition, I think she tried to make up a week later for her duties as a social worker—bound by law to hide adoptees' and birth parents' identifying information from each other.

A week after I returned to Seattle, she sent me proof that my birth mother had consented to release information by the state's adoption registry—a critical document that was essential in my future legal battle with Michigan. She gave me detailed records of my medical and hospital history. She gave me copies of court records, which she wrote "are normally not shared." She also gave me a copy of my original adoption decree, with my original birth name. She wrote that she "enjoyed" meeting me and wished me well now that I knew my birth family. She also added that the State Registrar still refused to release a copy of my birth certificate by law—something I would ask for again in 2016.

I met my birth mother one more time when my road trip ended. This time her twin brother and his wife joined her. They were excited to see me. I was a new family member, a long-lost nephew. They drove in from out of town. We had lunch at a local restaurant in Ypsilanti and posed for pictures. One is of me in between my birth uncle and my birth mother smiling, arms around each other. Our resemblance is unmistakable. My birth uncle was already going bald, but my birth mother's and my dirty-blonde hair glowed in the cool afternoon light of Michigan.

When I returned my car to the rental agency, the same two young African American women were behind the counter whom I had met my first day. "So how was your trip," one said. "It was incredible. I had the most amazing trip to Detroit," I responded. They were both taken aback. I liked Detroit? They saw I was genuine and then laughed. Hey, all right with us if the out-of-towner likes the tough town of Detroit, they probably thought. They had no idea what had just happened to me.

I came back on a return flight on a Sunday. I had just turned twenty-four. I would be entering the next quarter century of my life with knowledge of my ancestry, going back centuries.

Right after I came home I received a letter from my birth mother. It was the most confessional note she has written to me during our twenty-eight years of knowing each other. She wrote it when she was likely the most raw and exposed by my bursting into her life unannounced. She naturally talked about the emotions that were churned, from happiness to worry.

My birth mother also described how the reunion occurred on my timetable, not hers. It was something I had long planned to do. For her it was a sudden, unplanned life change. She wrote, "I'm going to have to get used to the idea I got a grown-up son now. I hope you will give me time. Thanks for the great week. P.S. I'm glad we could share the week together. Hope you had a great birthday."

Later, by mail, she wrote a very simple explanation of events for me, and a slightly more detailed summary of how she met my birth father. I still have that note, written on her former husband's business stationery. It was only four sentences long, and that made up the entire history of their relationship she ever shared with me to this day.

She wrote that she met him in July 1964 at the home of a lab tech during a party for staff at Wayne County General Hospital. He worked as a resident with the hospital. She said in October that year, she met him at another party and told him she was pregnant. "He didn't believe me," she wrote. On one occasion two decades later when I flew out briefly to Detroit to meet her, she shared a completely different version of events with me. That version of events was very ambiguous and open to multiple interpretations. It left me more than confused and still wondering about the circumstances how my biological parents came together, leading to my conception.

I wrote a poem about that later. It is a story of my origins that I read from time to time. The poem is called, "I am Taboo." I have never shared the full poem with anyone, and yet it is my best poem. I would love to share it in a crowded room one day—but I never will.

My final stanza captures how I still think about my origins, as an unwanted, illegitimate child in an era when they were very common. In those sometimes-darker moments on contemplation, I know that I alone had to own how I would respond to the path that life put in front of me. Only I could make meaning from this experience. I wrote:

Can sit and stew, cuss and chew.
I am taboo, it's so damn true.
Guess I knew, with hindsight too.
But you can't undo just who made you.
That path ahead, it's yours to choose.
So start anew, there's much to do,
And there's nothing, just nothing
That stands in your way.

Chapter 11

Out of the Darkness: The Son Emerges from the Shadows

You're not my son . . . Get off my property.

—Rudy Owens's Birth Father

The two months after I found my birth mother opened new doors and relationships that would evolve in the years to come. They also revealed bitter truths about my status as an illegitimately born child that I naively ignored until I confronted them head on. In less than eight weeks I met both sides of my biological families who had been unknown to me my entire life. Those encounters left crisp and painful memories, as if they happened yesterday.

Events unfolded quickly. During these months, I would receive family visitors and embark on another flight, to another city, where my kin called home. When I arrived at the doorstep of one of two people who brought me into this world, my birth father, I did not hesitate to knock. To an observer even familiar with my story, my actions might have appeared naïve or foolhardy. To me, they represented the only logical outcome and right thing to do. To this day, I have no regrets about my decisions made in the spring of 1989.

A few days after I returned from Detroit, I received a call from an older man with a gravelly voice. He told me his name—a French literary one that I had never heard of. He was my birth grandfather. He and his wife, natives of Michigan and the Upper Peninsula, were thrilled that I had come out of the shadows and back into the light. They wanted to meet me. They were going to buy tickets and fly out to Seattle in late May 1989. First, however, my birth mother would fly out to see me earlier that month. It was the only time she ever traveled to where I lived. It also marked the most honest and open time we communicated with each other.

Her trip lasted three days. We visited Seattle's tourist destinations, making the most of our time. We went up the Space Needle. We rode a ferry to Bainbridge Island, across the Puget Sound. We continued to get to know each other. She gave me some older family photos that showed her and her extended family—our family—over time.

Both of us were still getting used to something entirely new, for which there was no script. The person you are sharing dinner with, at a nice waterfront restaurant overlooking Elliott Bay, is also someone who looks uncannily like you. Yet you still know nothing about them. You have little in common because you have not shared a life together. You just have fragments and a desire to make things work out.

My birth mother may have been more like me than I had originally guessed. She was guarded about her secrets. She never shared any new information about my birth origins. The only tale that I recall from her trip concerned her seeking legal counsel. She told me she found one of the few women attorneys in the Detroit area to represent her in a paternity case against my birth father. She told me she eventually let that go. I do not know if that was true.

I do know my birth father was already courting another woman at the time. She became his bride. The two were married in Detroit in December 1964. He had moved very fast from bedding a woman in the summer of 1964; to breaking off whatever relationship they had; to denying paternity when confronted by my birth mother and her father; to finding a new romance. And all of this happened while he was doing a busy dental residency.

The smiling picture I have of the two newlyweds—shared with me by his sister years later—makes me wonder how my birth father navigated his world. What circumstances led to my birth as an all but certain accident that should never have happened? This was before the era of widely available birth control and eight years before the United States Supreme Court legalized abortion. Whatever happened, my birth mother did not share much more. Decades later, in April 2016, I finally asked why she gave me up. It was the only time I ever asked her to explain this life-changing decision for both of us five decades earlier. She told me she has never spoken to anyone, not even her closest friends, about why she relinquished her only child. She made no exception with me, her son.

During her 1989 trip, I asked if she would pose with me for frontal and side shots. I wanted to have a visual record to share with everyone that there was a person out there, a parent, who I looked like. One shot has us looking at each other. The photograph captures our side profiles. Our lips are very similar and pronounced. I have a larger nose. Our chins have the same curve, more like her father and my birth grandfather. Our hair color and hairstyle looked similar, though she had curlier hair, like her mother.

For me the photo provides a remarkable image of biological similarity. I still gaze at that photograph in amazement that I am a person with a clear past and ancestors with whom I share a binding and biological connection. I also used that photograph decades later to show the Michigan adoption bureaucracy and circuit court that my claims to having a birth mother were real, and therefore my request for final birth records should no longer be denied.

About a week after my birth mother left, I met her parents, my maternal birth grandparents. He was seventy-three and she was seventy-nine, almost eighty. Both were retired blue-collar Michiganders. They looked like my birth mother. My birth grandmother was barely five feet tall, and my birth grandfather was just a hair above five feet seven inches. She had red and gray hair, kept in a beehive bonnet, which long had gone out of style. He was already bald and wore a cheap sun hat.

They dressed in outdated Sears clothing that celebrated polyester and golfing fashion from the 1970s. My birth grandmother's health was already sliding. She suffered from diabetes and was hard of hearing. She likely was suffering from some early form of dementia. My birth grandfather had a slow style of speaking, pausing long on words, almost unconsciously. When he yelled at his wife because of her hearing disability, it made me uneasy. Yet she always smiled and never seemed angry when he did. So these are my people, I thought. There were no hidden princes or Nobel Prize winners in this family tree. They were mine and nothing could change that.

They both told me during our first night out to dinner that they were thrilled I had come back into their lives. My birth grandmother told me that for nearly a quarter of a century people asked her how many grandchildren she had. She said she always bit her lip, and said "one." Her other grandson, who was younger than me, was my birth cousin, son of my birth mother's twin brother. She told me that story several times this trip. For her, this reunion clearly had special meaning that let her make a connection with her heart. She would no longer have to tell a shameful lie that had bothered her all these years. From this time on, my birth grandfather went out of his way to let me know I was every bit his grandson as his daughter's son. He repeated this fact to me as long as he lived, right up to the day he died in 2002.

As I look back upon this first meeting nearly three decades later, I think this trip helped them make amends for their actions years earlier, which they may have regretted. In 1965, they did not intervene by adopting me or raising me. Informal adoptions, which include family members like grandparents, occur among non-white groups such as Alaskan Natives, Native Americans, and African Americans in higher percentages.[1] Historically, those groups have experienced the deep trauma of forced family separation. My birth cousin told me my birth grandfather had found the adoption agency for my birth mother. Given the social stigma of the times, my birth grandparents likely were deeply ashamed their daughter had become pregnant out of marriage. That made them look like failed parents. The attitudes of the mid-1960s allowed children like myself to be legally turned over to adoption agencies, who took full legal responsibility for me once my birth mother ceded all legal connections to me.

This happened hundreds of thousands of times from the late 1950s through the early 1970s. Sadly, overly restrictive laws in most states still actively prevent reunions like the ones I was lucky to have with my birth mother and grandparents. These out-of-date laws never allow for elderly grandparents to come to terms with their peripheral roles supporting the secretive world of closed adoptions or their later redemption, like my birth grandparents had. Unlike many grandparents of children given away, mine finally saw a grandchild they thought would be lost forever.

With the exception of my birth grandmother's confession, they did not share how they felt about their experience of losing me to the adoption system. For now, it was all about talking and connecting. In their eyes, I was better than they had wished for. I had not become a professional success by age twenty-four. My prospects for a brilliant career or even marriage looked minimal. Still, I looked fine to them. That thought comforted me. I remained closest to my birth grandfather for years after, simply because he always accepted me the most vocally and publicly after 1989 as his own flesh and blood. I think he saw me as a form of redemption. If he felt shame for his actions in the past contributing to my adoption, he never shared them with me.

They described living their whole lives in Michigan, raising a family with twins. My birth grandfather, who only had a high school education, pulled off a feat that few would try. He took a year-long contract with a company that helped build the Thule Air Base in northwest Greenland in 1959. That fascinated me. Maybe my desire to see the world had its roots in his wanderlust. His desire for adventure was only to be realized during a frigid trip to the top of the world, building a secret military base that housed nuclear-armed planes at the height of the Cold War.

He later sent me his slides of his time in Thule. I still have a picture of him, which is hanging by my computer, looking street-tough in real Michigan workman's clothes, next to a sign that says Piktufik Blvd., with Thule's landmark island and rocky butte in the background. When I visited Greenland three successive summers in a row, from 1998 through 2000, Greenlanders would ask, why did you come here? I always replied, "My grandfather helped to build the Thule Air Base." The practical Greenlanders would always nod their head in agreement, as if this made perfect sense because my visits to Greenland marked a family custom.

By the time Memorial Day arrived in 1989, I also had completed the search for my biological father. That proved to be the easiest discovery of all. This contrasted sharply with my failed efforts the past year and a half. American Dental Association records were published in an annual list kept at the University of Washington Library. With the name my birth mother gave me, I found him in less than thirty seconds after opening the book. There he was, a practicing dentist living in the San Diego area. Within an hour, I had found his home address, business address, and phone numbers through the white and yellow pages for the city. Some additional checking on his name and background turned up likely relatives in his home state in the Midwest.

I called about a half dozen people who had his Dutch-German name. A woman answered and told me she once called him, to see if they were related. They also met in person. He treated her very rudely. She called him an "asshole." I had that word in quotations in my notes from that time, since she said it so emphatically. Even before I met him, a pattern emerged. His rough edges were coming into focus. He was a birth father who denied paternity without regrets. He was smart and daring, starting a new life as a highly skilled medical practitioner in sunny southern California. According to stories I heard about him, he was unpleasant to anyone who crossed him or whom he wanted to leave behind.

I went back to the college yearbook copy I had studied for hours and found his smiling senior year photograph on page 98. I saw little resemblance except in the eyebrows, and maybe hairline. He was dark haired, unlike me. I copied that picture, pictures I took of myself with my birth mother, photos of me outdoors, and bundled them with a letter. I explained that I was his biological son. I wanted to know my medical history. I wanted to know my family history and genealogy. I was not seeking to have a relationship with him, but I did want to meet him and get as much information as he could share.

I sent the letter to his office, not wanting anyone else to see it. At the time, I did not know if he had a family, but I did not want to risk a possible spouse seeing the note. To this day, I have no idea how he reacted. But it appeared to arrive like a thunderclap. The ripples could be seen in his family's actions over many years. Decades later, I pieced together the broken fragments of the chaos I created from brief tales by one of his oldest sisters and from one of his two daughters.

He likely never told his wife, family, or daughters that he might have had another child. He may have believed that he was not my father. In 1989, he embodied the American success story: a family man living the good life in San Diego. His public identity came wrapped in the American myth—the loving father, business owner, medical professional, former ROTC officer, and upstanding citizen. A bastard coming out of the past posed an existential threat to that narrative.

I can imagine him opening a manila folder. Inside are pictures. One is of a man who is twenty-four, who looks like him and more like his father, but has dirty-blond hair. That man is his son. *That young man's purposes must be for financial gain*, he thought. *He is up to no good. His letter is a ruse.* I can only guess these thoughts crossed his mind.

This view ignores that my birth father turned his back on his responsibilities decades ago. He shunned a woman and their child, at a time when abortions were illegal. He entered into a marriage having lied about his paternity and his actions that could undermine his marriage. He likely chose a suitable marriage partner to keep out of the draft pool, just as the Vietnam War was beginning to heat up.

Most of all he had refused to own what he had done. He left the shame and lifelong burden of having had an illegitimate child on my birth mother's shoulders for the rest of her life. If he suffered a sudden midlife crisis because of this unannounced US mail, he had brought it upon himself. While I may have triggered a crisis that threatened the glittering life he had built, I did not feel guilty asking this man to look in the mirror and confront his past and the twenty-four-year-old son he helped bring into this world.

I sent that letter in early May. Having heard nothing for a month, I bought a last-minute flight to San Diego. I chose a three-day holiday weekend and to wait no longer. I vowed to meet him in person, and do it that weekend. As I flew down the West Coast on that sunny late spring day, I was amazed I had literally crisscrossed the country twice in less than two months on my voyage of self-discovery. I could not have guessed my life would be taking these turns less than three months before.

I did this without assistance from any agency and in the face of resistance from authorities who tried to keep people like me from knowing anything about my biological roots. I was busting down those barriers while finally putting together pieces of my life that had been intentionally hidden from me.

If I had not been so determined, the policymakers who passed adoption legislation and the adoption-system bureaucrats, who constantly thwarted adoptees searching for their past, would have won. They had wanted to deprive me of these stories and these moments forever, simply because I was adopted. I doubt if state officials overseeing adoptions and adoption-agency staff ever considered me to be a fully realized person. In their view, I did not deserve equal legal and human rights. I was unworthy of the most important information and life experiences most of us take for granted. This reality is why many adoptees like me openly embrace the term bastard.

I arrived on a Friday morning, May 26, 1989. I quickly found my birth father's house and his office in a city just south of San Diego. I still have a picture of his former practice. The small, single-story commercial office had his name on it, with his DDS credentials. I decided not to meet him there. I then drove to his home near the San Diego US Navy Base.

He first came here as a naval-reserve officer in 1965, after his residency was completed in Detroit in 1964 and 1965. According to one of his relatives, he was assigned to the psychiatric ward at Detroit General Hospital. It was a harsh rotation. He did complex reconstructions of people's jaws after they had tried to commit suicide by shooting themselves in the face. San Diego was an easier rotation in his career, apparently. He completed his naval service in 1967 with an honorable discharge as a lieutenant commander in June 1967. The closest he ever got to the Vietnam War was taking care of naval officers on ships off the harbor. He must have liked the sun and beach, like so many of us do.

He returned to San Diego with his family after practicing a couple of years in his home state. The eldest of his two daughters was born there. They moved to San Diego when she was still young, before his second daughter was born five years later. I am two and seven years older than each of them respectively.

Their house was bigger than I was expecting. He had done very well for himself. When I looked up the house on Google in 2015, I found it was on the market, selling for $1.4 million. In 1989, it was not cheap to call this neighborhood home. I took some pictures of it. I wondered if this was what private detectives spent most of their time doing. I was too nervous to approach the house my first day. So, I went to the nearby high school on a hunch that my biological father might have other children. At that time, I had no idea that I even had two half sisters.

The high school library was still open before shutting down for the weekend. Again, I made up a story. I said I had graduated six years ago and worked on the publication. Could I take a look at some recent yearbooks to see how the books looked? The helpful school librarian handed me copies of the past six years. I quickly found one that had the senior high school picture of my oldest half-sister and the photograph of her younger sister in a later yearbook. I knew they were my kin instantly. They looked more like me than he did.

Wow, I thought. So I have two half-sisters I never knew even existed. And they were California girls with brown hair, living a life I for years only thought existed in TV shows like *The Brady Bunch*. Except this was not a fairytale story. It was a messy tale. It was a drama complicated by lies my birth father had been living for nearly a quarter century, and a system that hid records from adoptees like me.

During this trip, I felt deeply aware that this unfolding story would have a cathartic moment like a Greek tragedy. In the end, this tale did not involve me gashing my eyes out like Oedipus, when he learned he had killed his father and wed his mother. Luckily, life is more boring.

It was sunny the next day when I drove to his place mid-morning. I felt nervous. I was approaching someone who likely was still rattled by the letter and photographs I had mailed him. I knew that confronting a man at his doorstep, with his family likely present, would not end well. But I had to do this and look him in the face and tell him I was his son.

I parked the car a block away. I entered the gate to the two-story, Spanish-Mexican styled home and rang the bell. A young woman opened the door. She had brown hair and brown eyes and looked a couple of years younger than me. She wore shorts and a T-shirt. It was my oldest half-sister. I do not think she knew who I was or what was about to happen. I still wish I knew what happened the day after we met. It was the first time we had ever met face-to-face, and it was the only time I would see her in person until I knocked on her door in San Diego more than twenty five years later. She asked what I wanted. I asked if I could speak with her father.

In a few seconds a good-looking, dark-haired man stood at that doorway. He looked like he was sweating from doing yard work. He was wearing shorts, and his arms and legs were tan. He was about an inch and a half shorter than me. I noticed he had dark, hairy legs, like me. That is what I remember most, and it made me realize where that physical trait came from. He too had brown eyes, like his daughter I just met. There was a touch of gray in his hair. He was about fifty years old at the time, and fit. Using his first name, I said hello. It's Rudy Brueggemann. I'd like to talk.

He closed the door behind him and stood glaring at me with his arms crossed. "Get off my property," he said. "You're not my son." He informed me that he had already been in contact with his attorney about my letter and that a reply was coming to me from the law office. My note he received three weeks earlier had asked him for information about my family history and family medical history. I do not think he ever called his attorney. No letter from him or an attorney ever came. I also think he never believed I would have the audacity to show up at his home on a holiday weekend, with his family around. I tried to start the conversation again, but he cut me off. "Get off my property," he said again, coldly. His muscular arms were crossed, his body rigid as he glared at me.

Salvaging this train wreck looked impossible at that moment. It had gone worse than I was hoping. There was no further point in talking. I turned away and headed back to my car, head drooping, lost in thought. I felt numb and empty. Outside, around me in beautiful San Diego, it was hot and bright.

I drove straight to La Jolla Shores. I waded out into the cool Pacific Ocean and caught wave after wave after wave. I stayed in until my lips were shaking. I remember little else about what happened that day. A group of amazingly beautiful black women in bikinis were dancing in the parking lot, and they smiled at me when I came out. I must have looked like a ghost. I could not even smile at their easy come-ons and joyful, sexual teasing—and I remember them being some of the most beautiful women I had seen in years. It would be twenty-five years before I returned to this very spot, with a completely different mindset.

My housemate met me at the airport. It was one of the few times I really needed a hug in my life. I probably looked like crap. I do not think he knew what I was feeling. I was not even sure myself. I had little to say except that my birth father had rejected me and his relationship to me.

I wanted to believe that kinship and blood ties mattered more than anything else, even the reality of my story. I had not been ready to accept that my life was just another version of an ancient but recurring story on how certain people are treated, just because of their station at birth. I thought the power of blood kinship would overcome a lifetime of decisions made by the man who had unprotected sex and disregarded the outcome. I had to accept my entire life was not the fairytale world that society had told me it was.

Instead, this was a different tale—an illegitimate man's life journey. Mine was a bastard's story: my mother's pregnancy and decision to relinquish me; me being placed with a foster family and becoming for a few weeks the ward of a charity; and finally, being adopted into a new family, which was not my biological kin

My birth father's actions had already been played out tens of thousands of times before, with no consequences for a man who impregnates a woman he did not marry or intend to marry. The remaining bastards like myself were simply collateral byproducts, with no legal rights to the father. We were scorned by society and also denied rights by state governments who refused to give us our identity documents. And if we bastards dared raise our voice, society had ways to diminish our stature, deny our rights, and call us mentally unfit. He could wave me away and never suffer for a second.

It turns out very little had changed for bastards from the time that the Black Plague ravaged Europe. Centuries-old Catholic Church doctrine through the modern era and even English common law about bastardy well into the twentieth century had determined children born of unmarried parents or an "invalid marriage" were illegitimate. They were *filius nullius*, subject to social and legal discrimination. I would keep fighting my bastard status for years, until I later accepted and embraced my true self. But that never changed the reality of what happened in San Diego. It taught me exactly who I was by a man I spoke to for less than thirty seconds.

That short trip to San Diego confirmed I was a dispensable person. I was no one. I really was *filius nulius*. I literally was an abandoned baby, with no rights and no power, and even no name. And when I finally came to confront a man whose genes I inherited as his biological son, I still did not matter. I was still no one in the eyes of a prosperous business owner, successful dentist, ROTC veteran, and upstanding San Diego family man. I never spoke to my birth father again.

Chapter 12

After the Discovery: Figuring out a New Identity

Did you really believe those stories you were told?

—Rudy Owens's Question to his Paternal Aunt and Cousin, 2007

In her 1968 book on the adoption experience, adoptee-rights pioneer Jean Paton provided one of the best descriptions that adult adoptees confront once they have completed their search. They are transformed, in ways that others are not:

> The Reunion of adopted people with their kindred is not equivalent to other human reunions because of the experience within it, the loss of stigma, which other reunions do not include. Other actual reunions are not linked to concepts of personal change and personal reformation, except for reunion with God when that is experienced or believed possible. Therefore the special curative element in the adoption reunion seems to most people to be an unlikely thing. Examples are, of course, known to many privately, whether or not the full potentials of the situations have been achieved.[1]

Once an adoptee finds they have a whole new family, it takes time to sort out the patterns of family events, holiday rituals, and vacations. Did I send birthday cards? Yes, to my birth mother and birth grandparents, while both were still alive. How about Mother's Day cards? Yes, both mothers each got one, every year. Where did I go for holidays? In my case, I always spent time, when I could afford to travel from the Pacific Northwest and Alaska, to the St. Louis area. That is where my adoptive family called home. My adoptive mother was still mom. My adoptive sister was still my sister. My stepdad was still only my stepdad, and never anything more.

Between 1989 and 2015, I visited Michigan ten times to see members of my birth mother's family. The last time I saw my birth grandmother was in 1992. At that time, I was finishing my first year of graduate school in North Carolina, and flew to Ann Arbor for a weekend visit when the spring semester ended. My birth grandmother's overall health and mental health had taken a slide since I had last seen her in Seattle in 1989. Her hearing was failing. My grandfather sounded abusive to her, yelling when she could not understand anyone. Nothing felt easy. The trip caused more stress than I needed. I wondered to myself, this is my birth family, do I want to keep in contact with them?

I met with my birth uncle and his wife, who would soon pass away. My birth cousin still lived in the area. We had meals and mostly sat around. It still felt strange to be around each other. By now, three years had passed, but we all acted awkwardly. We had no history to build upon. I had stayed in touch on a semi-regular basis with my birth grandfather and my birth mother by phone. The calls were always short. My birth grandfather always spoke warmly to me, despite his gruff, Depression-era exterior. On many of those calls, he repeatedly let me know, *you are my grandson.*

My birth grandfather was the only person who offered me some emergency and desperately needed cash when I had less than fifty dollars at one of the lowest points in my early adult life. I owed more than $14,000 in student loans. I was twenty-eight years old and finishing my MA at the University of North Carolina at Chapel Hill in July 1993. I did not know who I would ask to borrow money, to just buy food or gas for my truck. My adoptive family—meaning my adoptive mother—never helped me out this way, ever. She never contributed anything to my college and graduate school education, or on any expenses for them. I footed the bill for every expense: travel, food, rent, tuition, insurance, everything.

My birth grandfather must have heard something in my voice during one of our calls. He sent me just enough money to get me out of the state and to my first job as a newspaper reporter after grad school in California. His unsolicited kindness taught me something about family I never knew. Sometimes, your family backs you up when you have no one else to turn to. It made me wonder again if blood was thicker than water when you hit rock bottom. Up until that point, my adoptive family showed me it would not offer a helping hand if I hit such a low point. I accepted that. Luckily, I was able to land on my feet with my birth grandfather's modest gift.

I regret that I missed my birth grandmother's funeral in 1994 after she had a failed surgery. I lived on the opposite end of the country, and I had very little money for anything but necessities. My cousin later told me that our grandfather had put her in an assisted-living nursing home before she had passed away. The action divided the family. His father, my birth uncle, never forgave him, and their rift continued until my birth grandfather passed away. Even to this day, my cousin told me that wound still has not healed.

My birth grandfather wrote me a note saying she had passed away, with his typical stoicism. He included her obituary. That obituary listed the names of her grandsons. In that account, my name was included. I had officially become part of the family now. We continued to write and talk on the phone. He advised me to invest in the stock market and also to keep traveling. My less than straight career trajectory that allowed for overseas travel never worried him. "You have the right idea, do your traveling while you are young," he wrote. "You can talk about it when you are old."

During the late 1990s, I made a couple of trips to Ann Arbor. I never stayed with my birth mother. Each trip lasted a few short days, and they mostly proved unmemorable.

I never told my adoptive family about these and other Michigan trips. It felt like a taboo topic. This unwritten code minimized what I communicated when navigating between the two families. Occasionally my stepfather, in his moments of anger at me, would tell me how I treated my adoptive mother so poorly by doing anything with my birth family. He viewed any of my visits to Michigan as an intentional wound to his wife. The hidden code still guides how we interact today.

I also began using the Internet to search for family information. The search engines were still in their infancy, and I joined tens of thousands of adoptees searching online for family clues. I occasionally did searches on my birth father and my half-sisters. My birth father had stayed almost entirely off the grid of searchable online information. He probably stayed offline because he was a dentist and did not want his patients to know anything about his life. I found he spent a lot of time in Palm Springs based on the few facts that popped up—a fact I later confirmed from his family. It also appeared he had divorced from his wife in the late 1990s.

I also found a telephone number for my oldest half-sister. After many excuses, I finally found the guts to call her in September 1998. When she answered, I said, I am your half-brother. I would like to talk. At the time she was working as an attorney in San Diego. She said, "You do not want to know this guy," referring to our father. "He has a lot of problems," she said. She also told me she was not interested in talking to me or getting to know me. We ended the conversation in less than five minutes. It marked another rejection from my paternal family, from someone who was as close a blood relative as possible—a half-sibling. I found it hard to accept she did not share my curiosity about our relationship.

It was the only time I would speak with her until we met at her San Diego home in 2014. Over the intervening years, I had assembled a cache of information I wanted to share. I wanted to tell her my story and allay any fears she had about me. My never-sent packet had pictures of me on my travels to South America and Asia, statements I made before finding my birth family, copies of my original birth records, my adoption decree, photos of me and both of my mothers and my maternal grandparents, and yearbook images of her father.

This rejection stung. Why would kin so close be so unwilling to know or meet one of their closest blood relatives? I learned some of the answers later, but not all. I still believe my existence as my birth father's oldest child, denied as his own before I was born, created a family conflict that never healed. My existence personified the problem. It also served as a bitter reminder of complexities and threats that a bastard poses to any family. The bastard challenges the meaning those family members invest in critical relationships as father and child, husband and wife. I also had no idea at the time of my pariah status in the family or the crazy stories that her family were saying about me. The story lines made me out to be either a blackmailer or a man bent on violence. These tales further illustrated for me that the bastard-bogeyman was not a myth, but a deeply rooted archetypal fear.

About once a year I sent my birth father a note, telling him what was happening with life and asking him for information about my family history. If I was abroad, which was often, I sent a postcard. Most of these notes I sent to his business. I sent and signed a few postcards to his home, just wishing him well and signing my name, Rudy Brueggemann. I still hoped he might change through persistence alone. I doubt he read my communications. One of them, which I mailed in August 1999, included copies of a Seattle Times newspaper series about an adoptee finding his birth family.

I wrote:

[The articles] concerned the importance of knowing one's family history for medical reasons. As a highly-trained health professional yourself, you obviously know that these are legitimate concerns . . . I hope they will provide you somewhat neutral rationales why it's important that you share our family's medical history with me. I don't know you, and you give me every indication that I shouldn't want to know you. But you're still my biological father. I can live with that too. I have no idea why you're so afraid of me . . . I'm basically a decent person, and that may be hard for you to accept.

As with every other communication I made, he never answered me. It had been ten years since I had last seen him, with his arms crossed on his stoop and an angry expression on his face.

Though my birth father refused my requests for family information, I still had other ways to learn the family's history. I reached out to others with his surname. I wrote to some of them and left messages about him on genealogy websites. On one of them in 1999, I posted my birth father's name, and his background. I said I was an adult adoptee seeking information on the family's history. That connection later led to me finding a reply six years later by a man with the same family name. He was a de facto genealogist for the family, from his home in Arlington, Texas.

After I wrote to him, he sent me the family history of my biological father, with records going back to 1858, when my great-grandfather was born. He even showed me how he had entered my name into his semi-official online family tree. I finally had knowledge of my paternal past. Like my birth mother's side, the lineage featured mostly poor farmers and trades people, who eventually settled in the Midwest. My birth father's mother even came from my former home state, Missouri.

This online entry about my place in the family tree sparked a harsh reply by one of my birth cousins, the niece of my biological father. I later met her in person in 2007. In 2005, however, she wrote to the man who shared our family history, "He is not the son of my uncle and showed up on his doorstep one day and was a very strange fellow who wanted money from my Uncle (that is a whole long story in itself), but it appears to me that you might be compiling a book, and I would not like this gentleman's name listed as his son, and that is not correct." I knew she had either made up the story about me as an extortionist or heard it from someone else, perhaps my birth father's wife. Over time, even her views changed when we met in person.

In the decade after I found my birth families, I felt closest to my biological grandfather. Nothing I did bothered him. He did not worry that I was not chasing a middle-class life, with a family and a comfortable middle-class job. He always showed that he respected me, even for being different.

Our pattern continued this way for years, until I received a note from him on January 24, 2002. He drafted it like all of his letters—on a typewriter—and signed, "Grandpa." Something was wrong. He normally wrote out his first name. He wrote, "This is the money I promised you in my will. I spent a long time making this money grow. You can spend it or make it last . . . It can be the foundation of your future. It has responsibilities. You will figure it out. Make the most of it." It included a check that, in the end, I socked away and used entirely to help pay for my graduate studies in public health nine years later.

I flew out immediately to see him in early February 2002, landing in Detroit. The winter weather was snowy and cold. Michigan felt bleak and lonely. I drove about five hours to his house in a little town named by its former Finnish immigrants. He had no hair left on his head. He stooped over with his age. He spoke at an even slower cadence. His house looked clean, but he had been all alone since 1994, when his wife, my birth grandmother, died. It must have been horribly lonely in that small town, with winters that lasted until April.

When I woke up the next morning, I peered into my birth grandfather's room. It looked as if he was not breathing, and I thought he had died that night. He already knew he was close to death. I left him later that day, knowing he was likely going to die soon, and this would be the last time we saw each other. I still have a picture I took of both of us on my mantle. We are sitting on his sofa, me smiling and him stone-faced, slumped over. It was our last picture together, frozen in time.

Three weeks later, my birth cousin called me to say our grandfather died peacefully in his sleep. My birth grandfather had seen his death coming, and made sure in his own way before he died that I knew I was his grandson. The church bulletin for his funeral provided a simple history of his love of fishing, his passion for euchre and hunting, and his long membership in the Lions Club. The bulletin listed me as a surviving grandson, with my biological cousin. Once again, I officially had become part of the family. I regret never having changed my surname to Owens while he was alive. That would come later.

In 2007, I planned another work trip taking me to Canada. I traveled there once a year for training. At the time, I was living and working in Anchorage for the Government of Canada since 2004, for its Department of Foreign Affairs and International Trade at the Consulate of Canada, Anchorage. I usually included side visits to see my family in St. Louis when I took these cross-continental work trips from my new home in the north. On this outing, I mapped out a detour first to a Midwestern city near where my birth father was born. I flew out of Ottawa to Detroit, and then I caught a short commuter flight to my destination.

Just before the trip, I had contacted my distant relative in Texas, who had added me to our family tree. When I called him, he told me my birth father had passed away in 2004 in Montana from cancer, at the relatively young age of sixty-five. It was the same year I moved from Seattle to Anchorage. The obituary reported he was survived by two daughters. I was not part of his official history that was published in a Midwest paper nor in the newspaper in Montana.

The obituary praised my birth father's public virtues: eagle scout, ROTC program, skilled dental professional, retired with honors from the US Navy, loving father of two girls, and admired colleague by his peers. It said he was "an enthusiastic fly-fisherman, an opera buff" and had "many close friends from childhood and college." The obituary painted a kind of life narrative one expects, minus the fact he had fathered a son and denied that to his grave. The news finally erased my slim hope he might one day acknowledge me. It turns out he made that decision forty-two years earlier in Detroit, when I was conceived. I had been naïve assuming he might change.

For several weeks before my trip, I communicated with two local genealogists who lived in the city where my birth father had grown up. For reasons I never understood, these two women threw themselves into family research on my behalf that went far beyond basic kindness. One of them knew my birth father and had attended primary school with him.

She last saw him when she was eleven. From her I learned that my birth father doted on his dog and spoke to it in Italian. She also told me my birth father had serious health issues requiring liver-transplant surgery—which I learned later was the result of contracting hepatitis from an infected dental patient. I also heard about small-town gossip concerning my paternal biological grandparents. Everyone who knew my birth grandfather, a small-town local veterinarian, called him "doc." He and his wife fought often. Tales of her behavior suggested the possibility of mental health issues in the family and the chance I could have inherited, or might one day display, some of these problems.

One of two local historians also agreed to act as an intermediary to reach out to my biological aunt, who still lived in a nearby city, not far from where her family grew up. At the time she was eighty and being helped by her daughter, who was my older birth cousin. This was the same birth cousin who had called me the "very strange fellow who wanted money from my [birth father]" on a genealogy website two years earlier. Apparently, blood kinship curiosity may have finally overcome the archetypal fear of the dangerous bastard.

I called my birth aunt in early April. We had a surprisingly candid conversation. I learned that both of her parents came from extremely large families. She mostly provided medical history, which was a relief. She told me about her brother's hepatitis and resulting liver surgeries and transplants. She had to take care of him for a number of years. She said their father died of prostate cancer at the age of eighty-two. That too was a good sign for me. It was four years longer than the average male life expectancy in the United States that year. Her mother, my birth grandmother, died at seventy-seven from shingles and was less healthy. Apparently, her mother's parents were healthy, though she herself had lymphoma.

This trip became one of the most fun chapters in my long adoption journey. I arrived late in the afternoon in early May 2007 in the medium-sized Midwest city, not far from my birth father's family home. I immediately went to the local library and found my birth father's obituary in the paper of record. I toured the city and then went for one of the most memorable, exhilarating runs of my life along a river trail—probably buoyed by the excitement of knowing I would finally meet two birth relatives on my birth father's family side the next day.

I drove out early the next day to the small town where my birth father's family of three sisters and himself called home until they all became adults. My two genealogist allies greeted me at the local historical society on the main street of this small city, with a population of nearly 1,200 souls. Both women were in their early sixties. They never explained why they wanted to help me, but I think it was their basic small-town, Midwestern goodness and the curiosity of meeting an adult man who came back to find his local roots. Perhaps I was a novelty, with a twist. Perhaps I was mythical, and myths are meant to draw people into a story that is essentially a universal desire to know one's self. Maybe they had family stories similar to my own, and this way they could share in them with a kindred spirit.

They gave me pages of an old US Census printout showing my paternal family history going back to the early 1800s. They included old newspaper clippings showing life events of my birth father's family. So without any help ever from my birth father's family, I had finally obtained information about half of my bloodline. My paternal family narrative looked remarkably similar to my birth mother's family—farmers slowly moving west across the upper Midwest until they found communities to call home. I later contacted a distant relative in Chicago who was related to me through my great-great-grandfather. It felt deeply satisfying to know I had roots, and where they were historically. From these clippings I finally learned my birth grandmother died in 1981 and my birth grandfather in 1982.

The town's main street had old brick buildings and closed storefronts. My birth grandfather's house stood off that street, now converted into a historical home open for events like weddings. They had the keys and offered me a tour. It was a block away. The three-story former ancestral family home was considered a "wedding cake" style house dating from the late 1870s and painted gray. It stood empty. My two hosts let me in, and I walked through every room taking pictures. One must have been my birth father's bedroom. Everyone left this house after the 1950s, once the four children had grown up and moved away.

We next walked to the local high school. Photos of all the students who graduated each year hung on the school hallway walls. There I saw pictures of one of my birth aunts, from a 1940s-era class picture, and one of my birth father, from the late 1950s. He wore a tie and had his hair greased back, in a classic 1950s James Dean style. I took pictures of them to have some visual record of my kin. I knew this would be the last time I visited this town.

I profusely thanked these Midwestern researchers. They provided texture, where there were shadows. They gave me roots that had not existed for more than four decades. From these two strangers, I obtained more information about my kin and my family history in one morning than I had my entire life from any family member from my birth father's kin.

My next stop was a town about thirty miles away, where the youngest of my birth aunts lived. We had arranged to meet at her home, with her daughter who was my birth cousin. Though she was eighty, my biological aunt still lived independently.

I arrived midday at my birth aunt's house. She and her daughter were there to greet me. I looked at their faces, and I know they looked at mine. We shared a remarkable resemblance, particularly me and my birth aunt. We drank tea, ate some snacks, and sat in their dining room in no particular hurry to go anywhere. The pictures I have tell the story still. My birth aunt and I posed next to each other. I was runner-skinny then, training for a marathon, and she looked full of life for a woman her age. We both displayed beaming smiles, knowing that two family members who had never connected finally met. I have her chin and my face has a similar oval shape. Our noses looked practically identical. My birth cousin, who was about a decade older than me and an artist, was heavier than her mom. She too had the same family nose. We both wore the same goofy grin in our posed shots.

The doubts or fears they had about me for nearly two decades soon began to melt away as we talked about each other's past. I told them I was living and working in Alaska. I think my geographic distance from them and their families relaxed them. They also appeared pleased when I told them I worked for the Consulate of Canada, in Anchorage. Maybe they felt comfortable around me because of how I looked. I was clean-cut, and I looked like someone who took care of himself with exercise and good food.

They had brought family photo albums to share with me. Through these photographs, I could catch a glimpse of a family I never knew. I saw pictures of my two other birth aunts, my birth father's older sisters. I saw family reunion pictures of my birth grandmother's clan in Missouri from 1957. My birth father stood out in that, with his greaser style and rakish grin. The men all had crop tops and every woman wore a dress. They showed me pictures of my birth father's December 1964 wedding in Detroit, which surprised me. It was the first time I saw a photograph of the woman he married. It was taken four months before I was born. They also had childhood photos of my half-sisters, when they were young, living in San Diego. I took pictures of all these family photos, which I later added to my own family albums.

Both of my relatives alluded to the family schisms, similar to what my half-sister had told me on the phone. They never fully explained these divisions. I could tell they disliked my birth father's wife. I learned that my birth father and his daughters were estranged for years, as my half-sister had once told me. Clearly my half-sisters, as the California girls, were not favorites with the family that remained rooted in the Midwest. The two sides of the family never communicated with each other, they said.

All told, we spent about four hours together. Toward the end of the visit, my birth cousin finally told me that for years the family had known about my existence. This revelation surprised me. She did not reveal how long. Was it immediately after I met my birth father? Was it for the last ten years? I was the dark secret that was whispered about. From her words, I pieced together that I was a dangerous character. The tales contained exaggerated threats I never made, harm I never posed—something I know were lies because I never committed those terrible deeds. Their family legend, fed by their suspicions, made me out to be a lowlife bent on revenge. My birth cousin did not share all of those tales. But she gave me a clearer idea of how I lived in the imagination of my kin who never had met me.

Standing in my biological aunt's living room, I realized our conversation had turned into confession and repentance. At this moment, we confronted together the hard truth about an illegitimate baby who grows up. That bastard looked like them, found the family, and came back like some character out of an Alexander Dumas novel. In fiction, that could be as vengeful as the wronged Count of Monte Cristo.

Except I was not that character or any of those bogeymen. I was someone who wanted to meet others who shared the same ancestors and DNA. I looked both of them in the eye, and I asked, "Did you really believe those stories you were told?" Each of them smiled. They paused and said they never did. I could see the relief in their faces. Their words served as an apology and act of atonement at the same time. We shook hands goodbye.

The next day, I drove to my adopted family's home in St. Louis. I never told them why I had taken a detour before coming there. I think my adoptive mother and stepfather suspected I was up to something. As with all things related to my birth families, we just avoided the topic.

A week later, I received a richly detailed email from my birth cousin. She told me my birth father eventually died of carcinoma, which put me on high alert to sun exposure ever since. His liver transplants had destroyed his immune system, and he spent his remaining months in Montana in 2004, dying after what appeared to be a painful last few years. My birth cousin avoided talking about family history. Half of her email focused on my birth father's love of dogs and his life history with the different dogs he owned. Sometimes, it is easier to talk about things we all love, like dogs, than the family from whom we have grown estranged.

Her email included as many historic family photos as she could find, with the genealogy information for each of our kin. It was her way of telling me, "You are one of us. We are family. You are my kin and birth cousin." The graduation photo of our grandfather resonated the most. It shows him when he finished veterinary school, just before the start of the Great Depression. I have that photo printed out now. It has been on my refrigerator doors wherever I have lived ever since. Everyone who looks at it comments on our physical similarities. My half-cousin wrote, "I think that you have a resemblance to grandpa in this photo, most significantly in the lips." This was the last time I heard from my birth cousin. I have not spoken to her or my birth aunt since that memorable trip. I have sent her a couple of Christmas cards, but she never wrote me back.

When I returned to Alaska, I shared the story with my good friend. He worked as a doctor in the Indian Health Service, and had grown up next door to me in University City, Missouri. He was one of the few people I told about this trip. He congratulated me for making this family connection. Just before Thanksgiving a year later, on November 24, 2008, my same friend was brutally killed. A snowmobile operator had run over him while he was dog sledding near Kotzebue, Alaska. His death devastated the Alaska Native community and his hundreds of friends. The utter meaninglessness and randomness of his tragic killing profoundly shook me to the core.

I realized that my time on this planet, at forty-three years of age, was finite. I too could be killed at any moment by a drunk on the road, in Alaska or anywhere else. I looked at my life's goals. I asked myself, what really mattered? What would provide meaning for the remaining days, months, and years I had left? I circled back to the idea I had been plotting for a year. I would change my name. The day my friend died, I ran out of excuses to delay this decision.

I never liked my adopted name, Martin Rudolf Brueggemann. I was not Lutheran or a practicing Christian. I had stopped using my Lutheran-based first name, Martin, in 1983. My adoptive father chose that name. He also caused real harm to my adoptive mom, my adoptive sister, and me growing up. I did not want to die taking his legacy to the grave. Most of all I wanted to rid myself of the family name, Brueggemann.

The Brueggemanns were not and never would be my family. No one from that clan stood by my adoptive family in our neediest times. None intervened when they saw my adoptive father spin out of control while we were with him. When it mattered the most, they never showed that me or my adopted sister were true family members. What's more, my adopted mom had changed her surname to my stepfather's family name when they were married in 1983. The time had long passed to change my name officially.

I chose to honor both sides of my adoptive identity with my new name. I kept Rudolf, the name I had been using since I was eighteen, using the abbreviated "Rudy." I had long become Rudy. I liked it because I had claimed it as my own. I decided to take my full legal birth name of Scott Douglas Owens and make Scott-Douglas my middle name. Owens would be my new family name. I still regret starting this process after my birth grandfather passed away.

On May 26, 2009, I filed my paperwork with the Anchorage Superior Court to legally change my name. The court set a final hearing date of August 24, 2009. I would have to appear in front of a judge and say why I wanted to create a new identity. The court required applicants to advertise the proposed change in a business paper. This likely was required to expose scofflaws who were seeking to avoid debt or maybe a criminal past. I paid $150 and advertising costs to get on the docket.

The application also required petitioners to justify their request. I wrote for the court, "I am an adult adoptee who is not biologically related to the Brueggemann family. My birth mother, who I have known for twenty years, gave me the name Scott Douglas Owens at birth. I wish to reclaim my original and biologically true family name as well as my current middle name. Owens is a fine name; I am an Owens."

I took two hours off of work on the trial date. The drab, gray-colored court building was two blocks from my office. I joined others in the room before the judge, a woman, and listened to other petitioners. The judge asked me a few questions. I repeated for her nearly verbatim what I put on my application for wanting a new name. She agreed, pounded the gavel, and the deal was done.

On that summer day in Alaska, forty-four-and-a-half years after I was born in Detroit, I legally revived the person who was christened as a baby when he came into the world. I had retrieved my identity that a national system had worked decades to erase—forever. The adoptee born Scott Douglas Owens had now become Rudolf Scott-Douglas Owens. This would be the name I carried till my last living day on earth.

I felt ecstatic. I celebrated by having a salmon party for a dozen friends. I drew a picture of a tombstone that said, "RIP Martin Rudolf Brueggemann." It was a festive night. One usually does not change identifies in life. In my case, I had done it twice. The first time occurred without my consent, as an infant, at the whims of state government and social service intermediaries. This time, I controlled the outcome and became who I always was, while honoring my long, complex life as an adoptee.

I was not the only person who wanted one's name to connect to one's family past. That night I emailed one of my good friends about my name change. I told her about the hearing and others in the hearing room with me earlier that day. I wrote: "Funny thing was, in the court today, there was a woman ten to fifteen years older, clearly in her late fifties. She told the judge she wanted to change her name to that of her biological father (family name). I was kind of stunned. I was thinking I was the only person out there, and I wasn't, not even in Anchorage. Go figure. The world is funny, and you can never figure everything out. I guess I came away thinking, I bet the judges see this stuff all the time."

Chapter 13

Battling Michigan for Records

To each of you who were adopted or removed, who were led to believe your mother had rejected you and who were denied the opportunity to grow up with your family and community of origin and to connect with your culture, we say sorry.

—Australian Prime Minister Julia Gillard,
Apology from the Government of Australia to
Australian Birth Mothers and Their Children, 2013

Adoption has been many things. It was a grandiose scheme to reform "fallen" and mostly white women, who could be redeemed by relinquishing their infants and hiding the outcomes of unprotected sex. It has been a means of creating a family, among kin but also among strangers. It was, in the United States and to a lesser extent Australia, England, and Canada, a massive experiment never before tried in the mid- and late-twentieth century, to place infants from single mothers with parents with whom they had no natural connection. It was a large-scale vital records and public health undertaking that created new identifies for adoptees, while hiding original birth records after the 1950s. It was a means of wiping away individuals' pasts and their sense of place in history with their tribal, blood kin. It was a way of addressing horrific public health issues seen in the first decades of the twentieth century, due to mostly Christian-based religious prejudice and social stigma, which allowed infants to be placed in baby farms that were often recipes for early mortality.

In the United States it was an odd public, medical, private, religious, and charitable partnership. Leaders in each of these fields created the large national system that moved children from one parent to other parents or guardians through a large network of maternity homes for mothers, foster homes for infants, and hospitals. It was also a maternal and child welfare system that involved the full participation of public health, health care, and social work professionals.

Above all, adoption has always been a bureaucratic process. The complexity of placing and tracking millions of adopted children from the 1940s onward required multiple agencies to manage the records of everyone involved and to ensure adopted children had safe, healthy outcomes. This is demonstrated by the multiple health exams I received, in different states, by multiple doctors. It is seen in the rigor of the state and court record keeping that followed me through my placement with a new family. It is evident in the tracking that occurred between the time I was born, cared for by a foster family, and then fully relinquished from state oversight.

Through the 1970s, these actions took place in hospitals, doctor's offices, and records offices. Almost no one in those facilities raised serious questions about the system's underlying goals and purposes. Instead, they each did their job to make adoptions work. By the time I was born in April 1965, the process of having babies change names and move custody from one parent to possible foster parents, and then to another family, had become normal, when only three decades earlier this happened on a much smaller scale, mostly in Western countries. Few spoke publicly about or on the record about these practices. Those running the adoption system did not carefully examine the larger issue of how the institution of American adoption separated hundreds of thousands of young people from their birth families. In the end, these groups supported a process that prevented the most affected people in adoption—birth parents and adoptees—from getting information about their biological kin.

Birth parents and adoptees were the first groups to challenge the adoption model. They started to push back against what they saw as a system of privacy and shame, for mothers and adoptees. By the 1970s, a critical mass of young adoptees had moved into adulthood. But unlike their peers a generation earlier, they had to confront sealed records. Their efforts to find their birth documents and meet their biological kin sparked what became known as the Adoption Rights Movement (ARM). Its leaders included Jean Paton, writer Betty Jean Lifton, and housewife turned activist Florence Fisher.

Fisher wrote about her experience in her 1973 autobiography, *The*

Search for Anna Fisher, describing her twenty-year search for her birth mother. Fisher, with her group the Adoptees' Liberty Movement Association, also unsuccessfully sued the state of New York to open birth records with a federal lawsuit in 1977. Though the effort failed, it attracted national attention. Fisher used the language from the 1960s of "rights." Fisher's demand for open records was unrepentant. She openly called herself "militant" and declared, "We demand free access to our original birth certificates and the records of our adoption."[1]

Researchers during this time began to document for the general public that adoption was a lifelong process for the adoptive parents, birth parents, and adoptees. Researchers also began to debunk the myth that searching for one's past was pathological. Instead, they showed it was innate and natural to have a curiosity about one's genealogical past.

The fights of the 1970s highlighted the still-ongoing policy debates about adoptions. They showed how adoptees perceive the issue differently than the organizations that depend on adoption being unquestioned and structured around closed records and secrecy. For adoptees, the issue is deeply personal. It entails searching and asking for records about one's kin and asking the most basic question of all concerning an individual's identity. Sadly, the issues have changed little since the 1970s, when the ARM began.

Fisher, who helped to spark a national movement, told *People* magazine in 1975, "I had to know who I was. It's that simple, because life begins with birth, not adoption. I knew that until I looked at my mother I would never feel whole. I couldn't go on living with lies, with closed doors, being told I didn't have a right to know my own identity."[2] These are lines you will find repeated on blogs and stories published almost daily today. Four decades after Fisher made her statement, adult adoptee Jon Casebere told a Fort Wayne, Indiana, newspaper in February 2015 that he spent eighteen years navigating the closed-records system, not meeting his birth mother until he was thirty-six. "I chose not to have kids because I didn't have any family medical information to go off. That was obviously a personal choice," he said. "Having my original birth certificate opened many doors for me. I have medical info, a better sense of self, where I come from. Honestly, it made me feel whole."[3]

Adoptees who are not blood related to their adoptive families may always have close ties with those relations. They call each other family. But adoptees are also hardwired wanting to know their genetic and ancestral family and kin. Those relations for an adoptee are also family, and the family members of an adoptee may find this reality impossible to grasp, intellectually and emotionally. The research published on this topic over the past several decades has found this desire to be normal, not a mental health problem, despite mental health professionals' claims through the 1970s and beyond.

The social services systems in the United States have not accepted the underlying evolutionary issue that drives this desire to connect, despite the evidence that is accepted widely in fields of evolutionary biology, genetics, and evolutionary psychology. A good part of the wider population also remains misinformed by taboos surrounding bastards and illegitimacy. Messaging from pro-adoption groups with political agendas greatly shapes public opinion. The messages focus on their care "for the children," "unwanted kids," and "loving families," which also mask these groups' advocacy activities to keep birth records sealed.

This reality is part of my story. It is something many people would prefer not to discuss openly. Politicians invested in adoption as a political issue—related to the abortion debate and the groups who participate in the transglobal business of adoption—are the most reluctant of all. I experienced this problem during the search for my biological family in my twenties, and then repeatedly years later with my adoptive and stepfamily members. My family members, during the many years after I found my biological family, continued to question me and sometimes criticized me for successfully finding and getting to know my blood relatives and genetic-family ancestry. To this day, I no longer explain my motives to them and keep that part of my life private.

There is also a well-organized movement that strongly opposes adoptees, from the Left and the Right. The most organized groups are Christian and conservative. Their voices drown out advocates for open records in sheer volume, firepower, and funding. Foes on the left-liberalism spectrum include the ACLU. The ACLU is motivated by misguided privacy advocacy, which ignores that the original intent of the adoption system was never to hide birth records from adoptees or birth parents. Another left-leaning opponent is Planned Parenthood, which believes access to abortion might be impacted by changing laws allowing access to birth records by birth parents and adoptees.

The Christian Right features more powerful voices and is better funded than advocates trying to unseal adoptees' original birth records. They work in legislative settings and in the court of public opinion. They include uber-right think tanks such as the Heritage Foundation and Family Research Council, which advocate the Republican Party line that sees adoption as a cure-all to social ills like sex out of wedlock. Other right-leaning constituencies are The Church of Jesus Christ of Latter-day Saints and its subsidiary organizations, who work in social services and pregnancy prevention. The power of the Mormon Church is so pronounced in Utah, that Mormon women face a reenactment of the coercion and conditions faced by millions of single mothers in the three decades after World War II, the boom years of American adoption.[4] Other proponents of secrecy are the American Center for Law and Justice, the Christian Broadcasting Network, the American Life League, the National Right to Life Committee, the Christian Coalition, and the Eagle Forum.[5]

In a purely theological sense, adoption fits within the personal value system and theological worldview of activist and evangelical Christians. In the minds of those conservative-leaning Christians, adoption is a perfect fusion of their beliefs in God's adoption of Christians into his family and their manifestation of the gospel by supporting adoption or adoption of unwanted children—particularly "overseas orphans." In the past ten years, many such adoptions have been exposed as outright baby stealing.

As the Christian researcher David Smolin notes in his analysis of the US-based Christian fundamentalist adoption movement, "To be 'adopted' by God is to have God truly as one's Father and to share in the intimate love of God the Father for God the Son. Adoption is at the center of God's salvation, a great act of redemption in which sinners are forgiven, justified, sanctified, and made into a 'new creation.'"[6] What's particularly alarming, notes Smolin, is how Christians misinterpret scripture and exploit vulnerable mothers and children in poor nations in their pursuit of their calling. Anyone who dares to criticize the institution of adoption anywhere, from the global adoption movement to current U.S. adoption practices, is a person who rejects the foundational Christian gospel message. In short, adoption critics are apostates and non-believers who are their adversaries.[7]

Writer Kathryn Joyce's 2013 study of the frequently exploitative, unregulated, and highly lucrative overseas adoption industry run mostly by Christian groups, called *The Child Catchers: Rescue, Trafficking, and the New Gospel of Adoption,* concludes that evangelical Christians play an oversized role on adoption policy at home as well. Their advocacy is shaping both national and state adoption policy. For these advocates, adoption is considered the moral, Christian, and only just answer in the longstanding abortion debate.

For adoptees who have been denied equality for decades by discriminatory adoption laws, this is a particularly troubling development. Instead of seeing change, adult adoptees today encounter a modern bureaucracy in the adoption agency networks and at state agencies, some staffed by hard-core evangelical Christians. These actors have internalized the missionary-driven values of Christian adoption advocates. Evangelicals' perspectives have now infused the entire culture of modern adoption in the United States. Joyce writes, "The language of rescue and salvation—language that has its genesis and its most literal interpretation in evangelical adoption efforts—now also colors how adoption is discussed in secular society as well."[8]

From my interview with the former Wayne County Probate Court supervisor, who did not release my records, I learned the adoptions records staff he managed back in the late 1980s included devout Christians. Fundamentalist Christian adoption agencies in the Detroit metro area like Christian Families of Southfield focus on adoption counseling for pregnant women, overseas adoptions, and consultation with state officials. That is in addition to handling adoptions for Christian families only, costing about $15,000.[9] Christian-based agencies make up the majority of adoption placement services in the state, with two of the largest being Bethany Christian Services and Michigan Catholic Charities.[10] The MDHHS has also created the Community and Faith-Based Initiative on Foster Care and Adoption, to promote even closer relations with faith-based adoptive services statewide.[11]

The role of Christians and Christian groups in adoption policy-making statewide remains as powerful as ever. Legislation, passed by the GOP-led Michigan State Legislature and signed by Republican Governor Rick Snyder in June 2015, allows state-funded faith-based adoption agencies to deny gay parents service if they want to adopt children or foster children. Though many liberals and critics of conservative policy largely criticized this as an anti-gay bill, most commentators failed to note the reach of Christian adoption activists in shaping state adoption policy, through a discriminatory measure. They achieved a major and heated legislative win that easily weathered a burst of national and public criticism.[12]

When I called Governor Snyder's communication office and asked if the administration could speak publicly on his views on adoption policy issues, his senior communication advisor refused. She said she would only take written questions. The advisor did not answer any of those questions that asked if adult adoptees had legal rights to vital records without restrictions. She did not reply if Snyder believed all persons in Michigan had the right to receive equal treatment under the US Constitution and state law regarding access to original vital records. Snyder's office only said for the record, "The Governor does not have a position regarding adoption records in Michigan so I am unable to answer your questions."[13] She further suggested I lobby the legislature, ignoring the fact that her boss was responsible for the day-to-day administration of all state agencies, including senior managers who oversaw vital records for every adoptee ever born in Michigan.

Adoptees have never had a strong bench of support against pro-adoption organizations in Michigan and elsewhere. The adoptee rights groups that are engaged on the political stage or as solitary advocates working at the state level lack funds to mount national public relations campaigns outside of social media from the individual groups themselves.

For thousands of adoptees, the only people they have been able to turn to were other adoptees or sympathetic friends, maybe a few family members, or perhaps themselves. I have leaned on friends, but not my adoptive family. In my efforts, the most helpful people have been other adoptees and, not surprisingly, women sympathetic to the issues facing birth mothers and children relinquished for adoption.

Laws that helped to create this culture remain one of the key underlying problems. As 2017 ended, Michigan still had among some of the most confusing and regressive state laws nationally of the states that allow some record sharing to adoptees. Most adoptee and birth parent advocates consider the state's type of closed-records system for adoptees born during the boom years of adoption (1945–1980) as regressive, discriminatory, harmful, and incredibly insulting to adults. Michigan uses a tiered system that allows some adoptees to access some birth records, but denies that right to other adoptees based on their year of birth. All of the statutes governing adoptee birth records treat adult adoptees like children, empowering state bureaucrats to routinely communicate with adoptees that they do not have the equal rights of other citizens born in Michigan.

Michigan, by statute, penalizes and bans any state official from sharing original birth record information, except through narrow exceptions such as a "court order." Those are ominous words to most people outside of the legal system. What's more, state law as of 2017 still promotes a dual vital-records system that creates amended birth certificates to resemble original birth certificates. Michigan also conscripts public health officials—the essential deputies in the adoption identity shell game—to enforce the adoption birth records illusion: "The director of public health shall furnish to the adopting parent or parents a certified copy of the new birth certificate that shall not disclose the adoption of the person. A birth certificate issued to an adopted person shall not refer to adoption and shall conform as nearly as possible to the appearance of birth certificates issued in other cases."[14]

Michigan statutes also prescribe a so-called "confidential intermediary system" for some adoptees and birth parents. This model purports to have a dubiously qualified person be a broker between blood relatives and conduct a search for biological kin, supposedly to protect the interests of birth mothers and adoptive families. Legal scholars, adoptees, and open-records advocates have considered this system broken for more than two decades.

The very notion of intermediaries has long insulted adoptee advocates. More than forty years ago, adoptee rights leader Fisher said it was "absurd and unacceptable to any adult adoptee who considers himself a human being and not an object. The intrusion of a social worker, or, indeed, any person, into a reunion between parent and child is an obscene violation of the privacy of all parties."[15] Adoption law scholar Elizabeth Samuels's review of both adoption registry and intermediary programs found both were failures, in terms of outcomes and for the parties they allegedly were supposed to help. As of 2001, fewer than 2 percent to 5 percent of birth mothers and adoptees used them, and they have been poorly run and understaffed. Samuels notes the parties most impacted—the birth moms and their kids—call them unworkable.[16]

Jean Paton, the early and preeminent US pioneer for adoptee rights, was unflinching in her criticism of intermediaries more than twenty-five years ago. During testimony on state adoption laws in Colorado in 1991, Paton said:

> When the records were put under seal, it was an experiment in Utopia . . . It was a destructive error, and should be remedied by a sweeping cure, not this intermediary dabbling. I fear that this new quite colonial type of search, a state structure and bureaucracy will be formed which will be immovable. Thus, freedom to the adopted person will never come. The process of being made to consent to having a stranger approach one's parent instead of going oneself is most demeaning. It encourages adopted people to continue to think of themselves as inferior people. That is what is wrong with it, and it is very wrong.[17]

My own experience with registries to find my kin failed on two occasions. I used the state of Michigan's passive registry system, run out of its Central Adoption Registry, starting in June 1988. I entered my name into that passive registry system that tried to connect birth parents and siblings. An adoptee would be told only if a birth parent filed a statement with the state. The Wayne County Probate Court told me no birth parent statements of consent were filed. My birth mother for whatever reason never signed up for it. She may have desired to put this behind her, but the system was not a well-publicized system, particularly in the pre-internet days.

When I lived in Seattle during those years, I also used a privately run, little-publicized system run by the Washington Adoption Rights Movement (WARM). I had at best a slim hope my birth mother might have signed up for it, too, if she was in Washington State. I had no idea what state she called home at the time. Still, I paid $250—a large sum with my meager income in 1988 dollars—to support it. The group returned the funds after I found my birth mother on my own, with a nice note, "We are so happy to hear your search and reunion is complete and with excellent results."

Theoretically, a passive system like Michigan's Central Adoption Registry or an active system like Michigan's confidential intermediaries, where a paid person searches for a birth family member, should connect birth parents with their children and vice versa. But the passive registries need both sides to enroll in a system that all parties know about. This rarely happens. Active registries can never begin to address the demand for search services given the number of adoptees and the fact that twenty-six states, including the District of Columbia, have completely closed-records systems. No system could ever accommodate the need, given the limited resources. One of the most well-known national systems is run by ALMA, which asks for a fifty-dollar fee to connect parents and their children placed for adoption.

Research since the 1990s has found these systems to fail. The data show mutual consent registries have very low rates of matches. State and local passive registries have success rates, at best, of 4 percent and a median of 2 percent, and are mostly underfunded and understaffed.[18] So, there was little if no statistical chance the registries I used would work. I continue to call state-registry systems a fig leaf to help cover political agendas of Christian interest groups supporting alternatives to abortion. I believe they should be scrapped, only when birth records are opened to adoptees and birth parents.

Michigan's web communications regarding adoptions state, "For those adoptions that occurred between May 28, 1945, and September 12, 1980, the release of the original birth certificate is contingent upon a court order." The state's adoption statute also criminalizes the release of sealed information by any state employees to anyone, including adoptees born over this thirty-five-year period, as a misdemeanor offense. For this class of adoptees, myself among them, a birth certificate and other birth records are treated as secretively as CIA and NSA classified documents. Adoption records may even be more secretive.

For an adoptee in this group to get original identity documents in Michigan, except a birth certificate, they must have had a birth parent sign and file a form called a "statement of consent" with the MDHHS. All adoptees will be denied their requests without that form. If a birth parent is dead, the adoptee must first prove their death with state bureaucrats. This condition represents a form of legal absurdity for most adoptees, who likely have no probability of even knowing their birth parents' identities, let alone if they are alive or dead. The state also poorly communicates that it offers the adoption intermediary program.[19]

Michigan adoptees born before May 28, 1945, or, on or after September 12, 1980, are treated slightly more like adults, but are still wrapped in a shameful shroud of secrecy. If the state's Central Adoption Registry does not have a signed statement from a birth mother or birth sibling requesting anonymity—what adoptee-rights advocates commonly call a "disclosure veto"—the state MDHHS can provide identifying information. The registry first must provide a "clearance form" that the adoptee can use to request his or her original birth certificate.[20]

Adoption law expert, Professor Elizabeth Samuels, through her research, has shown multiple examples on how the promoters of adoption from the 1940s and 1950s always meant to have birth records available on demand to adult adoptees. That was the recommendation of the first Uniform Adoption Act, enacted in 1953. The position of the United States Children's Bureau also supported this view—and the acknowledgement of the importance of kinship—that an adopted adult has a "right to know who he is and who his people were."[21]

Michigan maintains an adversarial relationship with Michigan-born adoptees, based on their records-keeping practices and their staff's actions that I have witnessed over the years. In July 2016, I attempted to interview State Registrar Glenn Copeland, who oversees the department's vital records and health data services section. The MDHHS refused to allow him or anyone else to speak to me about the department's management of adoptees' birth records and requests by adoptees to get their original documents. MDHHS issued a press statement to me that defended their strict enforcement that limited the release of adoptees original birth certificates: "It is our responsibility to carefully adhere to any and all laws of the state of Michigan. Michigan law includes specific provisions on the sealing of birth certificates in certain circumstances, such as following an adoption . . . The vital records office is required to adhere to the law regarding the release of original records."[22]

In response to twenty-seven questions I sent to the MDHHS about their practices, the tracking of birth records requests by adoptees, and more, the department only answered five of those questions. The department did not reply if it discriminated against adult adoptees in the management of vital records. It refused to answer questions how it managed or it tracked adoptee "troublemakers" who challenged the department's authority—emails I requested by a public records request show I was marked for tracking. It could not even answer simple questions about the state's adoptions record unit that handles adoptee records requests—the Central Adoption Registry. It refused to answer who managed the agency or if it ever had been audited. Finally, the department did not answer if it was aware of national adoption laws in countries like England that allow all adult adoptees to get copies of all of their original birth records when they turn eighteen.

In its reply, the MDHSS revealed it even failed to track how many requests for birth records by adult adoptees are denied by the MDHHS. "The total number of these official requests would not be known but is believed to be very close to the number released."[23]

From a management perspective, the department's refusal to count requests for original birth records amounts to professional incompetence, given the ubiquity of adoptees in the United States, who number five million, or maybe more.[24] Poor records keeping by professional records managers seems more bizarre, given the decades-long efforts by adoptees to access their records and the highly visible nature of the political battle over records. The department's acknowledgment shows that in Michigan at least, adoptees still do not matter and thus will not be counted by those entrusted to oversee the state's public health system. As practitioners in public health and health frequently say, "what gets measured gets done." Or, what is ignored remains a problem.

The state also refused to provide a written estimate of how many Michigan adoptees may be living who were born between 1945 and 1980. These are persons for whom state law requires court orders to get birth certificates. According to the MDHHS, the department only began counting the number of released birth certificates in 2009—decades after adoption became one of the most widespread practices in family formation in the United States. Since 2009, only 549 original birth certificates have been given to adoptees as of late July 2016, according to the MDHHS.[25] Assuming Michigan had similar adoption rates as neighboring Illinois did the year I was born, that means in 1965 alone, about one in every twenty-six persons born in Michigan was adopted.[26] If these numbers are added for the thirty-five-year period, then the small proportion of this number of released birth certificates for Michigan adoptees comes into sharper focus.

The message from these vital-records keeping practices by Michigan's public health professionals is very clear. Adult adoptees, you still do not count. The state can continue to ignore your rights and treat you like a nonexistent person or problem, not a person deserving respect and equality.

It is unsurprising many adoptee advocates like Paton over the years have expressed consistent frustration by the system they encountered, given the obstruction and legal barriers they have faced. Nor is it surprising adoptees have embraced the still-common slur "bastard."

The boldest adoptee-rights activist group, Bastard Nation, formed in 1996. The nonprofit organization has reclaimed the word "bastard" as a brand of empowerment and rejected the stigma of illegitimacy. Its URL is bastards.org. Its logo on its social media and bumper stickers show the words within a circle, like an egg, with sperm surrounding the orb like a sun.

Bastard Nation's main planks call for equal access by adoptees to original government-held birth and adoption records, fighting negative stereotypes of adoptees, and giving voice to the adult-adoptee experience.[27] I do not belong to this group, and I do not even know anyone who is. I have never even met anyone affiliated with the organization. I also do not support it with donations, nor buy its products. However, I support its core position statements because they are rooted in basic moral and equal rights and in valid research that shows open records provide the best possible outcomes.

Ideologically, I fall into the camp of persons who own the full meaning of the word bastard. Lauren Sabina Kneisly, a writer who was also adopted in the 1960s like me, best summarizes what it means to be an adoptee-bastard in the United States. Her website, *Baby Love Child*, offers a list of five criteria what being a bastard means in a political, activist, and self-awareness sense among adult adoptees.[28]

1. A bastard understands to the core that no one gets left behind. They have learned the lessons from history and incorporated that thinking into their actions.
2. An adoptee advocates changes in the way adoption is currently practiced as well as the political climate in which adoption sits.
3. Bastards have been "bastardized by the state," and socially, in overt and covert ways. They have received and still get unequal treatment by the state, or by governments. They are aware of that inequity, and work to change it. They are "in it for the long haul," and they refuse to let anyone ever treat them as "illegitimate" again.
4. Bastards own the words long used to shame them, much like queers, and use them with pride, "defanging any of the terms' corrosive power."
5. Bastards exist in a dark cultural space, being products of a form of "illegitimate" reproduction, a child born of "unwed motherhood," a child of a "shameful secret" pregnancy, the progeny of "love 'em and leave 'em daddy" or "absent" or null father.

To me it is remarkable how someone I have never met, but who comes from a similar experience of American adoption, shares some of my core and lifelong beliefs that motivate how I engage the world around me and define myself politically and publicly. It is another reminder of how the institution of adoption affects adoptees in unforeseen ways throughout their lifespan. This fact is still not widely acknowledged the way we recognize how being born poor or living in households that have an adult smoker can affect a person's opportunities for success or health during their lifespan. The legal, health, and public health fields have overlooked the political treatment of adoptees through laws, despite the prevalence of adoption in American society. It is not an accident that adoptees' status as likely bastards would allow society and state governments to ignore them politically.

Because I successfully found my identity and biological family when many others have not, I have not participated in advocacy with groups like Bastard Nation. I do not feel trapped in a morass of not knowing my family history and being denied that information for decades like so many other adult adoptees. I escaped from that rusty, cruel cage.

Some of those who have persevered in their searches were likely stronger and more resilient than their peers. Or, they were just luckier. I consider myself all of the above. I also possessed a deep reservoir of physical stamina, which is absolutely necessary to keep pace with a normal work life, and a second life as adoptee records hunter. An adoption-records chase often is a multiyear if not multidecade marathon. One cannot expect change quickly. An adoptee who does find his or her past must be in it for the long haul.

Successfully finding one's past frequently depends on the quality and accessibility of the original birth records, what non-identifying information is made available by the adoption gatekeepers, and the time and resources a busy person can devote to a daunting undertaking. If you are poor, you likely will not succeed in this quest, unless you live in one of the nine states that allow adoptees unfettered access to their records. To learn about who they are and where they came from, most adoptees must pay a heavy price, in time, emotional energy, and money. The task is daunting in most states, where their social service bureaucracies and the medical community who were involved have taken extraordinary and discriminatory measures to keep adoptees' origins secret.

I also credit my success to my stubbornness, street smarts, and plain good fortune. Along the way, I got used to hearing I was ungrateful and that I "had issues." On my journey, I became immune to the word "no" and to the more polite refusals to help me by Wayne County Probate

Court records keepers in Detroit. I always rejected their legal grounds for saying no. Knowing your opponent has no moral standing or authority and rejecting their legal claims can empower a person to keep fighting for what is right.

Most of all I got used to people, agencies, strangers, family members, coworkers, and classmates telling me to be grateful and happy for the family that adopted me and just get on with my life. Most of those people knew nothing about my adoptive family. If they did, they might have used other words. Some of them may simply have been voicing a hidden bias against me they may not have recognized. As an adoptee, I am proud that I never accepted what others consider to be the status quo or what they perceived to be legal and normal for me. In the end, an adoptee searching for the past and their identity must be comfortable being alone in the wilderness, for years if not for most of their life.

Even one of my best friends who has two adopted sisters to this day still criticizes me for thinking too much about adoption, because her sisters do not think or act like me. In her eyes, I am the problem, not the system that created the problem.

In the end, I also proved craftier than the gatekeepers and my bureaucratic opponents. Through the process I gained a measure of wisdom that can come from no other source than personal experience. Asking who my biological ancestors and parents were and looking for answers was what a normal person can and should do. Nothing could be more natural. But if you try to explain that to any person but an adoptee, you can quickly sense the body language of confusion, and in some cases distrust. The very act of looking for answers assigns one labels. I learned early on not to talk about these things because of how uncomfortable most non-adopted people are with an issue they would prefer to remain in the shadows as a taboo subject.

Even my adopted sister has criticized me. She never had the drive and resources to search for her biological family because of other challenges she had to navigate in her personal life. Even she suggested I work on "my issues." This comment makes me laugh and sigh. It embodies the defeatist self-critique adoptees have internalized from society. Many adoptees like my adopted sister, and adoption champions of all political stripes, are not even aware how they have internalized this point of view.

I feel blessed and fortunate for the positive outcome from my family history and birth records search. However, I remain frustrated that none in authority who promoted legal secrecy and the medical labels and stigmas have ever stepped forward publicly to say they made serious mistakes to generations of children seeking just to "know thyself." If they have, I missed it. If someone can show me a book by or interview with obstetricians and maternity nurses who delivered the millions of adopted children, highlighting their professional involvement in a system that separated family members forever, I would like to read it. No one has identified—to my knowledge—any personal confessionals by retired or active social workers who convinced hundreds of thousands of single pregnant mothers to relinquish their children from the 1950s through the 1970s.

The politics surrounding adoption have played out far differently in countries that promoted the system actively after World War II. In Australia, tens of thousands of birth mothers who surrendered their children for adoption in coercive situations received a federal apology in 2013 from Prime Minister Julia Gillard. The government and Gillard offered the apology to single, young mothers from 1951 to 1975. Thousands were coerced to relinquish their children. She said in a widely covered speech that is on the government's website and YouTube, "We deplore the shameful practices that denied you, the mothers, your fundamental rights and responsibilities to love and care for your children. You were not legally or socially acknowledged as their mothers. And you were yourselves deprived of care and support. To you, the mothers who were betrayed by a system that gave you no choice and subjected you to manipulation, mistreatment and malpractice, we apologize."[29]

Gillard's formal statement also included remarks to the children who moved from one family to another and then lived a life asking, who am I, and from where do I come. To those adoptees, the Australian head of state also said, "To each of you who were adopted or removed, who were led to believe your mother had rejected you and who were denied the opportunity to grow up with your family and community of origin and to connect with your culture, we say sorry."

Australia's national reconciliation effort was modeled on the country's 2008 formal apology that acknowledged the forced adoption of nearly one hundred thousand children from indigenous and aboriginal communities from 1869 to the 1970s, known as the "Stolen Generations." As a result of Australia's efforts, a national consensus has been reached that adoption can provide benefits, but can also be coercive and abusive to natural families, and that every attempt should be made for family preservation before an adoption is allowed.[30]

More recently, in November 2016, the head of England's and Wales's Catholic Church, Cardinal Vincent Nichols, offered up a nearly identical apology to more than five hundred thousand birth mothers who relinquished their babies to adoption with the support of Catholic social service agencies. The cardinal stated, "The Catholic Church understands and acknowledges the grief and pain caused by the giving up of a child through adoption."[31] The apology atoned for what many birth mothers in England, like their peers in Australia, have called forced adoption in the United Kingdom after World War II through the 1970s. Nichols's public statement attracted national attention on the eve of a documentary on Britain's ITV station called *Britain's Adoption Scandal: Breaking The Silence*, which aired on November 9, 2016. The program profiled some of the experiences of the half a million birth mothers who had adoptions arranged through the Catholic, Anglican, and Salvation Army churches, along with other organizations.

Australia's reconciliation and public efforts followed by those in England present a radically different approach to the national dialogue and policy directions of the United States. All three modern, English-speaking democracies practiced similar national programs to promote adoption as a national social-engineering experiment after the Second World War. In the United States, thanks to the outsized influence of the evangelical-right in state governments and Congress and the role of Christian faith in national culture, adoption is still viewed as the proverbial "win-win" option. It is not widely seen by the public or those in elected office as an experience that likely harmed a generation of mothers and their children.

In her analysis of the global adoption industry and its champions among evangelical Christian groups in the United States, Joyce says these national differences reveal the adoption industry's success in shaping the national consensus and dialogue in the United States. She notes the system obscures unsettling facts that hide the underlying role of money for the groups who perform adoption services. Domestic adoptions can cost $15,000 to $40,000, and large agencies can haul in as much as $10 million a year.[32]

These developments are particularly worrying to some birth mothers from my birth mother's era, who have been fighting with little fanfare for years to receive recognition similar to what all Australian birth mothers of the post–World War II generation received from their national leader in 2013. According to former birth mother activist Karen Wilson-Buterbaugh, "We're getting older, and we're terrified we're going to die . . . without getting some acknowledgement that a crime was committed against us . . . The [adoption] industry's biggest fear is that someone's going to listen to us. We don't want this to happen to another generation."[33]

There has been no repentance demonstrated at the state or national level in the United States by anyone—in the political, social service, or medical sphere. The unequal treatment of birth mothers and adoptees is not even considered a serious issue in a national dialogue dominated by income inequality, immigration laws, institutional racism, police practices, overseas wars, gun violence, drug use and abuse, LGBTQ priorities, prison overcrowding, trade policy, health-systems failures, and more.

Having followed adoption as a religious, cultural, social, political, medical, and legal issue most of my life, I see no triggering event or groundswell of support for former birth mothers. I can detect no broadly shared national compassion for adoptees that could coalesce around a formal apology statement by any of the principal promoters of adoption in the decades after World War II. In the minds of many, adoptees are still bastards, and single mothers were the fallen women who had given up their flesh and blood. They are still not worthy victims, even in our therapeutic culture of celebrating uplifting life stories on television and through the self-confessional novel.

Apologizing has always been difficult for any leader. It is harder to do that when the topic involves the way adoption and abortion intersect with Christian teachings and morality in the United States. Christianity's basic tenets are central to today's unresolved problems for adoptees and birth parents. Adoption was promoted nationally because of shame derived from the country's largely Christian values. It was also aggressively promoted through the teachings and the care systems used by many faith-based charities to transfer children from single mothers to agencies, foster families, and ultimately new families.

Throughout history, some practices enacted by state governments and the US federal government have always harmed victims. That happens with all governments. For me it is naive to expect a national leader in the United States to acknowledge publicly that our adoption practices—beloved and cherished by the Christian Right and enshrined as a platform in the Republican Party—have flaws that deserve a national debate. The national mood still tilts toward treating adoptive parents as saints and adoptees as blessed innocents, so long as those adoptees never challenge laws and rules governing adoption nationally and in most states.

Even if a government apology like Australia's to birth mothers and adoptees never comes, it is due. I just wish someone involved in this enormous, decades-long system would have the guts to say: "We made mistakes along the way. We know it. We are sorry."

In my experience, I do not think there were bad people who willingly set out to harm my birth mother, me, or our larger family. I think there were good intentions that were never thought through. Among the millions of other affected families, there also were less noble intentions among hundreds of thousands of others who allowed the social stigma of illegitimacy to override every other option for a single mother.

Adoptees like me were collateral byproducts, which a system would place in the right homes with the right parents. In my birth family's case, I still do not know how this family crisis played out and never will. Nationally, adoption turned into a flawed experiment that was never questioned or changed, even once it began affecting millions of families. It never gave full and lasting moral consideration to adoptees or birth mothers.

Though I am not Australian, I still felt deeply moved the first time I heard a national leader utter words in a public setting that spoke directly to me and my adoption story in the United States. She offered her words in the plainest possible language—in my opinion, she told her nation that inherent rights of former child adoptees should be restored. Prime Minister Gillard said to the applause of a full house, "More importantly, we will remember the lessons of family separation. Our focus will be on protecting the fundamental rights of children and on the importance of a child's right to know and be cared for by his or her parents."

Chapter 14

Birth Certificate, the Final Battle

Sometimes, you need to make a stand and stay in the fight because it is the right thing to do. Anything that really matters in life has never been given freely. What matters the most is earned and gained through perseverance, struggle, determination, collaboration, and effort.

—Rudy Owens, Statement on his Court Order Request
for his Original Birth Certificate, 2016

The first day I began writing this story, I knew I had to complete an unfinished chapter in my adopted life. For me, nothing could be more symbolic of completing this lifelong journey than holding the true and correct record of my birth in my hands. That is when this odyssey would finally end.

When the state seized control of my identity—after I was legally severed from my ancestors and birth family—and surrendered me to an adoption agency and then placed me in a foster home, it wrongly claimed my birth certificate was a sealed record. But the original record of birth is not, and never has been, a top-secret record.

The state never had the legal and moral right to hold my past from me or the right to prevent my birth families from knowing about me. My true birth certificate shows the world that I exist as someone with a past. It shows I have an identity that I alone own. This document is and always has been mine by birthright.

But Michigan, like other states that restrict adoptees' records, also has understood the raw power that controlling this and all birth documents has over people deprived of their personal and family history. That power gives the state mastery over a mostly powerless group. The state demonstrates that power when it withholds scraps of records that have almost talismanic properties.

By societal and legal consensus from the 1960s on, my past was found to be so secretive that few people would ever know the truth, especially not me. I was expected and repeatedly told to accept the national social experiment called adoption. I was repeatedly lectured and informed I would never see papers that said who I was and where I came from.

But that experiment failed through the political evolution of adoption into a cult of secrecy and a political wedge issue for the Right and for evangelical Christians. Adoption as a social and political institution continues to fail adoptees and their birth parents. It denies both groups the right to know their kin and, in the case of adoptees, the fundamental right to know who they are.

Even though I had beaten the system with creativity and sheer dumb luck in the 1980s by learning who I was, I really had not won. In my case, Michigan still could justify its past and future actions by defending views now considered historically antiquated. Yet, those views remain enshrined in state adoption law and defended by a small army of government workers, who never have cared about the rights of adoptees and discriminated against them for decades, under the paternalistic smoke screen of a morally troubling philosophy that "the law is the law."

When I renewed my demands for my original birth certificate in March 2016, the state still claimed this one sheet of paper had to be kept secret in a locked box, withheld from me because of a law. I also knew I would be going into battle for the legal document that proved I existed as a person with biological kin and ancestors. The state also took up its battle stance, with the many resources it could muster.

The state asserted its paternalistic power without showing any evidence, policy rationale, or benefit exactly how the state or my birth mother and birth families are helped by these actions. Michigan discriminated against me as an adoptee, solely to preserve a perk of power and to demonstrate that the state could arbitrarily exercise that power over even law-abiding persons. Withholding documents showing my original identity also reaffirmed the state's broad legal authority to create children with a "clean slate" and no real family history. In my case, the state exercised its power without demonstrating compassion, leadership, or even common sense.

For decades, Michigan had always done everything it could to defeat adoptees like me, claiming "the law" was on its side. So it is no surprise the state defended its practices with me again. The records, including emails from senior state officials released through my state Freedom of Information Act (FOIA) records request in June 2016, showed my legal claims posed a perceived threat to Michigan's legal model. On my website, I later published a forensic analysis of the state's emails revealing how state managers reviewed my birth record request and the extraordinary measures the state took to deny it.

The current system promotes discrimination against Michigan adoptees based solely on their birth status and their year of birth. Officials from Governor Rick Snyder's office and many branches of the MDHHS hurriedly responded when my request for my birth certificate called them to account, with a demand for both justice and my record. By copying the state's media with my request, I set the state's machine into motion.

My struggle against Michigan has always rooted in equal and civil rights. I did it on behalf of all adoptees who seek their records and their past. For that reason, it matters to everyone.

A birth certificate is the most important legal document for any American and every person born anywhere in the world. In the United States, it proves you are entitled to the benefits and privileges—and responsibilities—of being a United States citizen. One cannot obtain the most critical documents to navigate modern life without this sheet of paper: getting a US passport, obtaining the standing legal identity document in the United States—the driver's license, applying for a Social Security card, or enrolling as a child in school. One literally cannot live a modern life, including opening bank accounts, voting now in many US states, accessing benefits, obtaining a job, and accessing all forms of education throughout one's life without the cornerstone proof of legal existence that a birth certificate provides.

Globally a birth certificate is named in the United Nations Convention on the Rights of the Child as a basic human necessity. Without a certificate, anywhere in the world, a child can be denied basic human rights. They cannot get jobs, open bank accounts, obtain credit or inheritances, participate in social benefits, or be involved in political and civil affairs.[1] That is how important birth certificates are.

Vital-records keepers in the United States through the late 1940s never intended to prevent adoptees or their birth parents from getting the information contained on the true birth certificates. The secondary or so-called amended birth certificates given to adoptees and their adoptive parents when they were adopted were intended to hide a child's status as "illegitimate" from society. Today, no other persons in the United States are denied this record and the essential human right associated with it.

As I finished this book, I turned fifty-one years old. I have known who my birth families are for more than half of my life. Because I successfully found my biological family and ancestry, I had obtained all other records of my adoption. This includes my medical record from my first few weeks after my birth, my adoption decree, and my social service agency reports from my adoption files.

Because my birth mother signed a release for the state to allow for the release of my identity documents to me in April 1989, the Michigan Department of Public Health, Office of Vital and Health Statistics sent me a letter legally acknowledging I met the state's rules to access my birth records. It notes that identifying information can be shared with me. The social service agency that handled my adoption has signed documents including a "notice of release of identifying information from adoption records," which proves identifying information can be released to me. Even the Wayne County Probate Court, which denied me my birth records for two years, sent me a note on May 12, 1989. The court acknowledged in writing it had "received notice from Adoption Central Registry regarding consent to release identifying birth information as filed by your birth mother on 4-21-89."

Common sense should dictate that the state must then release my original birth certificate. The state never used that standard in how it treated me. Back in 1989, the social worker who released copies of my identity documents wrote me a note on May 26, 1989. She said the state's public health agency told her "original birth certificates of adoption are sealed and not available." Thus, my original birth record sat, in a file or box, in a state building somewhere in Lansing. Even though the state likely was violating its own rules, I decided to get on with my life having found my families and received most of my records.

For years I let this sleeping dog lie. However, that dog awoke as I began compiling research on the larger story of how states deny equal rights to illegitimately born human beings who are adopted. So, in March 2016, I decided to challenge the state's immoral and illogical position to promote secrecy at the expense of common sense.

I would do that by asking for my original birth record. What's more, I would do that publicly, not privately, by publishing the records of our communications to document how the state treated adoptees who asked for their records. I chose to shine the light on how the state defended an irrational system of controlling records that were never intended to be secret in the first place. The public could decide for itself if they agreed with the state or a person challenging the state's authority.

Michigan's statutes treat adoptees as citizens with lesser and different rights to original identity documents than all other state residents. As of 2017, the state's adoption-records rules are among the most restrictive among the sixteen states that provide birth records to some adoptees, but with access restrictions.

Making matters worse, Michigan's statutes are so poorly worded, few can understand their meaning, including those entrusted by the people of Michigan to manage the state's vital records. Even the state's deputy state registrar, Tamara Weaver, in emails released by a public records request, shows confusion among the state's senior vital-records managers. In less than twenty-four hours, Weaver offered two conflicting interpretations of the muddled statutory language that covered my request for my original birth record. In March 2016, she wrote, "It's not in statute that this individual can get his record via court order . . ." A day later she offered the opposite interpretation that ". . . we do accept court orders to release the record . . ."[2]

If state officials who manage vital records cannot interpret their own legal mandates, how can adoptees and outsiders fare any better? The state's statutes do not share in plain language how an adult adoptee born from 1945 through 1980 can obtain copies of his or her birth documents, including a copy of the original birth certificate. The state has taken wide liberties to interpret the law in a way that promotes discrimination against adoptees. The state claims an original birth certificate can only be released by a court order, regardless of the circumstances in each case.

The unstated but clearly desired goal has been to prevent thousands of adoptees from getting what is theirs—their original birth certificate. To date, the state has succeeded, as Weaver boasted in private emails she shared with her boss, State Registrar Glenn Copeland. In preparing a rejection letter to my request for my records in March 2016, she highlighted the state's success limiting the release of original certificates of adoptees to less than two dozen a year. She informed her boss Copeland by email: "Why doesn't he just go in front of a judge to have him give an order. We probably get 1 or 2 every month from this era . . . and we give it to them."[3] In a prepared statement released by the MDHSS in July 2016, the agency further claimed it did not track how many times it denies requests for birth certificates. Worse, the state only began tracking the number of birth certificates released in 2009, amounting to only 549.[4] That means the state has no public record spanning decades showing how many adoptees have demanded their birth certificates.

The state singles out adoptees born during the postwar adoption boom but before the 1980s as persons who do not deserve their identity information. The sections of the law applying to this class of persons are the most confusing in the state's adoption laws. In Michigan, adoptees born on or after May 28, 1945, but before September 12, 1980, are not entitled to their original birth certificate except by court order. Adopted Michiganders born before May 28, 1945 or after September 12, 1980 are entitled to the original birth certificate, but only if a birth parent has not signed what adoptee legal rights experts call a "veto disclosure," which denies an adoptee the legal right to have copies of their records. Though both groups of adoptees face discrimination based on their birth year, the law is more restrictive for adoptees whose births happened after World War II. I am in that huge pool of adoptees born during these thirty-five years when adoptions of mostly white, illegitimately conceived children numbered nearly three million nationally.

I made repeated calls to the Michigan Central Adoption Registry in October 2015 to explain that the law did not apply to my situation. The staffer Connie Stevens eventually called me back. She would not answer my basic questions or help me understand their system. Her angry reply to my questions for assistance was to "fill out the damn forms." Because my birth mother already had filled out the "damn form" in 1989, I rejected her bureaucratic excuse for professional service. I tried to explain the form was already in their files, and that I had evidence to document that. Instead, she cut me off. It appeared little had changed in Michigan's vital-records system since the 1980s.

I learned later from public records that Stevens likely used a tracking system to flag problematic adoptees who demanded their birth records from state public health officials. Weaver wrote an email to Stevens in March 2016 and suggested that I be added to that system: "If you [Stevens] have a way to tag him, he is not very receptive to anything any of us have to say. His name is Rudolf Owens."[5]

When I was ready to make my request five months later, I went straight to the head of the agency and bypassed all of the bureaucrats below him. On March 20, 2016, I sent my letter and a copy of my adoption records to Nick Lyon, director of the MDHHS. Going to the decision maker is often the quickest way to get a response from any bureaucracy, as my request showed. My case received attention from the state's most senior public health officials.

My letter to Lyon provided the core facts that I knew my birth family. It had all of my identity documents with my original birth name. I wrote, "Laws that your legislatures have passed concerning adoption no longer apply to me, as I have already found my birth families, now for more than 26 years, in 1989. There is no longer any compelling state interest or legal or other rationale that justifies the state of Michigan holding an original record and what is mine by birthright."

I also forwarded copies of my letter to radio, print, and blog news services in Michigan and Governor Rick Snyder's media office. I knew copying the governor's press team would trigger high-level action. No media representative pursued my request as a story, even after I followed up repeatedly with all of them multiple times.

For its part, the governor's office showed concern. FOIA records show my request generated a fast response from the governor's press officer the day it was sent, on March 20, 2016. Communications Advisor Laura Biehl forwarded my email and attachment of birth documents to Angela Minicuci, MDHHS communications director, and Bob Wheaton, MDHHS communications manager. They shared it with other staff triggering a chain of emails and discussions on what to do about me and my request, which ultimately involved nineteen officials in the department and Governor Snyder's office.

On March 21, 2016, it appeared State Registrar Glenn Copeland was open to reviewing "where this case falls in the adoption code and what he would need to do to have his original record released." Within a day, he quickly approved the consensus view of staff to deny me my record. At this time my original documents were still en route to Director Lyon, and would not arrive until March 28, 2016.[6]

Copeland and his team had already decided within a day that my original birth certificate would stay sealed and that I had to go to a court. Catherine Hoover, yet another senior manager at the MDHHS, also wrote an email on March 21, 2016, to the department's number-two official, Children's Services Agency Chief Steve Yager. She said that I needed a court order, so long as there was no record on file from a birth parent that requested she remain anonymous. In my case, their adoption office—the Central Adoption Registry—already had a record on file since 1989 that my birth mother signed the waiver, allowing for my records to be released. It is clear from released emails I obtained that the MDHHS never checked or bothered to look at my file carefully to review the waiver, or simply ignored what they found.

In the end no public health official ever reviewed my documentation sent by certified mail to Lyon. That letter had evidence showing I did not need a court order, which would be a waste of resources for myself, the state, and the court. To this day, Yager, Hoover, and Copeland may never have seen the photo I included of my birth mother and me. I included it to show the *real* people the state was determined to keep from ever meeting one another, while hoping it would trigger a small measure of empathy.

On March 22, 2016, I received a call from Deputy State Registrar Weaver. She did not say she was the number-two official who managed the state's vital records, or that she was already drafting a rejection letter without having seen my evidence. This represented a remarkable lapse in professional conduct by a senior state public health official charged with managing all state birth records.

I was left speechless hearing her talking points; how wonderful she felt that I had found my birth family in 1989. These messages contradicted the state's actions over the decades that sought to prevent any reunion among adoptees and birth mothers. Internal records show she had been instructed to call me and manage the state's denial of my request. She finally asked the question her superiors wanted to know: would I get a court order to request the record.

I ignored her question. I told her I have never needed any order, and had not since my birth mother signed a release in 1989. I made very clear that I rejected the state's legal authority to keep my record sealed, particularly with my identity no longer a secret. I told her the department could already make a decision and release my certification immediately. I also said court orders provided an unjust burden to all adoptees, particularly on out-of-state persons like me who could not afford attorneys or costs for an unnecessary process, which was not even required in the first place.

She then shared the state's simple message that "the law is the law," using that exact phrase. She said my original birth certificate would never be surrendered without such an order.

I replied that her argument amounted to "legal insanity"—my exact words—that defied common sense. I said, "Of course the state could give me a copy of my original document, if it chose to do the right thing and exercise leadership and even interpret the law correctly." I pointed out to her, this was no longer a legal issue because even the state's biased law was on my side. I said at this point, it was a moral and leadership issue. When the call ended, I knew that I had not convinced her. Throughout my years of requesting records, I still have not spoken to any bureaucrat in that system who considered Michigan adoptees worthy of the basic human rights of all non-adopted persons born in Michigan.

Emails I received from my FOIA records request made on June 3, 2016, reveal she quickly contacted her boss, State Registrar Copeland, after the call. She did not provide an accurate record of my legal points, particularly that agencies have wide latitude of authority to interpret and enforce statutes. She failed to mention she never introduced herself by her title—something that could be grounds for a professional reprimand or even dismissal. She seemed pleased to have learned I "couldn't afford the lawyer or take time off to go to the Detroit court for an order."[7]

She suggested that my real goal was "to make a statement." She somehow concluded I may not have wanted my birth certificate—the document I had been asking for and had been denied since 1989. "He has an agenda, nothing I would have said would have been sufficient," she wrote. "I don't think that my offering him his record would have been enough for him, even though that is ultimately what he says he wants. I am fairly certain that if there was a way to give it to him, he wouldn't be happy to have the sealed marker on it, though that is only my opinion."[8]

Two days later, on March 24, 2016, Copeland wrote to Communications Director Minicuci, Lyon's assistant, and other staffers that advice he received from subordinates had determined my birth certificate was still a sealed record, even though its contents were not secret anymore. He claimed, "releasing only one active version of an individual's birth record is a prudent policy." His statement ignored the historic record that all birth documents in this country, including post-adoption and original certificates, were once mostly accessible to adoptees, and that national laws in countries like England release all original birth records to adult adoptees. Copeland's analysis embraced the state's policy to hide all adoptee records behind a "law is the law" shield.

Copeland wrote it ". . . may not seem like common sense, but there are established process in law that govern such releases and it does not make common sense that we should break the law." In an even further twist of logic, he concluded that because I already knew my name and birth family, keeping my record sealed should not matter to me—therefore it should stay hidden. No emails showed any disagreement by his peers with his logic or conclusion.[9] According to his rationale, I did not need my certificate after all—even when I asked for it. What's more, I should accept his department's bizarre view of "common sense," as he defined that term.

Not once in any email released through my FOIA request did any official acknowledge the state had the legal waiver signed by my birth mother allowing the state to release my records. Copies of Copeland's letter to me were sent to Governor Snyder's office. The emails released show his letter represented the official views of both Snyder and MDHHS Director Lyon.

After Copeland mailed his letter, Deputy State Registrar Weaver almost gloated in an email that her department completed its mission to keep my birth certificate sealed. "Glenn signed it and we sent off yesterday, put a big ole stamp on it and walked it across the street," Weaver wrote on March 31, 2016. "[Rudy Owens] is not going to like it, so I would suspect that we may be hearing from him again."[10]

She was right. I would not accept a decision that rejected compassion.

She was correct. I would not agree with views that ignored common sense. She was right. I would not agree that their decision ignored the fact that state agencies have discretion to interpret the law in their rule making. She was correct. I would disagree with a decision that ignored national practices that once allowed US adoptees to have access to their original records. She was right about a final point that should matter to a state agency entrusted with promoting public health and the well-being of the state's residents. I would not accept an answer that ignored evidence-based best practices in this country and around the world for giving adoptees their birth records.

Copeland's letter, dated March 29, 2016, arrived the first week of April 2016.[11] The single-page note framed my birth certificate as a secretive document holding harmful or protected information, even though he shared separately to his coworkers that the information was no longer a secret. The letter resembled a denial the CIA might draft for classified documents.

It used a narrow lens to continue denying me my birth record, maintaining the state's policy direction from the past three decades. The note did not acknowledge that existing state law did not apply to my unique status and situation. It also ignored that I had proven, with legal records, my relation to my birth family and that I knew my original birth name and background. The letter succeeded on one count. It demonstrated Michigan's power over an adoptee who questioned the state's adoption-records system, legally and morally.

Copeland also ignored that my birth mother had allowed the release of my birth records decades earlier—in a legal document the state had in its possession but never reviewed. "Michigan law does have processes in place that would permit us to release sealed records to an individual in very specific circumstances, but those criteria do not apply in your case," he wrote. "Even though you indicated you have already been able to obtain the facts of your birth, in order for us to release a copy of this sealed original, a court would still need to order the release of the record."[12]

Copeland's letter further noted, "As a result, if you provide this office with a court order to release a copy of the record, a copy could be released to you. Please note that the document would be conspicuously marked to indicate that it is a sealed record." Finally, Copeland wrote, ". . . there are circumstances that cannot be accommodated as law simply does not permit certain actions. In this case, complying with your request would violate the law."[13]

Copeland's comments amounted to a rude middle finger, but through polite bureaucratic language. Here is the rough translation to his department's decision: "I couldn't care less about you or your documents, and I do not even have to review them. Go away."

Ever since sociologist Max Weber warned of the powers of bureaucracies in modern societies a century ago, there have been countless stories how public agencies become so obsessed with the rules, regulations, and processes, they overlook the larger good that they are supposed to uphold as public bodies. The lines "I was just following orders," or "the law requires this action" have become veils to mask at-times abusive state actions.

I now had limited choices. No Michigan media had shown interest, and my blog posts, tweets, and video I published online had not attracted public attention. I had no support from the court of public opinion, so I had to approach the state's judiciary. I contacted the Third Judicial Circuit Court of Michigan, Family Juvenile Division. The court is based in Detroit and serves Wayne County. It handles civil, criminal, and family matters. It also processes court order requests for adoption records, as well as infrequent records requests for adoption records. State law forces adoptees like myself, born in Wayne County between May 28, 1945 and before September 12, 1980, to ask this court to compel the state to provide an adoptee his or her original birth certificate.

When I contacted the office that processes these requests for court orders for records, I learned from the office manager that adoptee requests happen "all of the time." The last report published by the court in 2014 said it managed 208 requests for adoption records, or about four requests every workweek.[14] In other words, adoptees and families who ask for information are very normal.

However, even the court official who I called was surprised how intransigent Michigan's adoption bureaucracy was in releasing documents. The woman professed bafflement why adoptee records were so protected. The court manager warned the state's adoption bureaucracy might still ignore a court order coming from her court. She told me the state denied the release of records arbitrarily and that she frequently fought them to defend the rights of adoptees asking for what all others are given—copies of their birth records.

Nearly three months passed before my telephone hearing on June 17, 2016. Getting that hearing required three petition forms and repeated calls and emails trying to firm up a court date. My forms and petitions had to condense the frustration of decades of having my records hidden, to make a convincing short summary for the presiding judge. My statement might be tossed out. What's more, my petition would be heard by a judge whose job was promoting adoptions through the court system.

The majority of US states use records-management practices that most adoptees find demeaning. They force adoptees to prostrate themselves and plea for assistance. Not once did any official working for Michigan or a Michigan court ever show my claims had legal legitimacy.

It is unsurprising adoptees are usually exasperated when trying to explain what it is like to be treated like a pariah. Non-adoptees do not get this, and officials are largely ignorant of discrimination they practice routinely against adoptees. Things have not dramatically changed since the 1970s and later when adoptees seeking records were considered to have mental health illnesses by the mental health profession.

My court experience also reminded me why adoption-records systems fail adoptees and why officials managing vital records do not grasp that fact. The state's media also showed indifference, despite me sharing updates, videos, blogs, and press releases about the state's adoption practices with them. None of Michigan's media I reached out to—the major network news channels of Detroit, the Detroit Press, Michigan Live, a muckraker blogger in Detroit—showed interest in Michigan's failure to surrender my birth certificate. I was an out-of-state adoptee, and the state had much bigger issues on its plate like the Flint water crisis. The two reporters from Detroit who I briefly spoke to were skeptical I even had a basic right to my original birth certificate. I always assumed reporters carried a bias against adoptees, and perhaps even bastards as well. There is no reason they should be different than the general population.

On June 17, 2016, my long-awaited court date arrived with Judge Christopher Dingell of the Third Judicial Circuit Court of Michigan. They arranged a telephone hearing because I lived in Portland. Dingell was joined by a court reporter and a court supervisor. The judge said he could find no record of my birth father's death. I thought that was a strange comment, since birth fathers in most adoption cases denied fathering a child—or "knocking up" a woman without protection, as many boasted.

Fathers abdicating their paternity were a root problem for many adoptions. My own story offered living proof. My birth father denied his paternity when I was inside my mother's womb, just as he denied it when I stood looking at him face to face at his luxury home in San Diego twenty-four years after I was conceived. He denied it through to his last living day. Common sense would seem to dictate that a birth father's interests in an adoptee's request for original records should have had the least consideration when ruling on the interests of the adoptee. I wondered if a female judge would have handled the questioning differently.

Dingell read out loud the facts of the case, stating the hearing would determine if the adult adoptee should be given a copy of his sealed and original birth certificate. Dingell highlighted key facts: The adoptee knew his birth name. The adoptee had changed his legal name to include most of his original birth name. The birth mother had no objection—as shown in documents I submitted as evidence and already on file with the state. The biological father was deceased. He stated there had to be a showing of good cause for the order to be given.

He then asked me, what was I going to do with this information? I had prepared for days for this moment. This was my only chance to tell my story in a court of law. I had drafted ten pages of talking points and facts to make a statement why an adoptee had a legal and moral right to his original records, and to show that denying an adoptee those rights amounted to legal discrimination.

In the end, I made a very brief statement:

I'm going to have it in my record. This information is nothing new. This information is a document that already has publicly available information that I have been sharing publicly for decades now. This is a matter more of me closing a chapter in my life addressing an issue of importance. It is very important for people to pursue issues they believe are both just and right. And I could not in good conscience allow this issue of not having my records finally shared with me where there is no longer any need to keep those records sealed, shrouded in a state of secrecy.

Following my testimony, Dingell said he thought such cases were strange. He said no authority clearly told the court who it should notify of its finding. His confession offered another example of the confusion around the law among the experts who interpret it daily. He also said that he disliked the term "good cause." He stated for the court recorder he would sign the court order. He then hung up the phone. Less than seven minutes had passed. I had, temporarily, won a key victory.

After the trial, the court adoptions supervisor called to tell me the order would be coming, and I was responsible for sending it to the state. The court had no further role. I thanked him and his colleagues on the phone and by email: "Yours is the only Michigan office in the last three decades that has assisted me in my request to get a just, legal, and fair resolution to my common-sense request. Good deeds are never forgotten, even if this is your court's professional responsibility for the state. It still matters, and I will not forget the courtesy provided."

From what I experienced, this court did not want to deal with adult adoptees or these records cases. I still could not tell if the MDHHS would reject Judge Dingell's order. That threat was very real. The court's records manager already told me that the state had disobeyed past orders. Copeland's letter to me intoned they had discretion to disregard the rule of law, in the form of a court order. Lastly, the state's confusing adoption statutes itself made it impossible for anyone to know really what had to happen with a court order, if that was even required, as Deputy State Registrar Weaver wrote to her boss.

The order arrived at my home on July 1, 2016. It said: "It is ordered: that the Michigan Department of Health issue a copy of the original sealed birth record in regards to Scott Douglas[s] [sic] Owens (birth name), birth date, April 16, 1965 and release a certified copy of the sealed birth record to Martin Rudolf Brueggemann, now known as Rudolf Scott-Douglas Owens (legal name change, birth date: April 16, 1965)."

For the final stage of this bureaucratic odyssey, I mailed the order to the vital-records office at the MDHHS on July 2, 2016. I filled out another state form—my fourth since April—and included a forty-six-dollar check. I knew my request would get double-strength scrutiny. MDHHS already had flagged me, calling me "this problem," and had denied my request on behalf of Director Lyon and Governor Snyder.

Despite my uncertainty, I shared the temporary good news with my friends on social media and received sympathetic kudos. I wrote:

> Today, I won a court battle with the State of Michigan that deals with my original birth certificate that was 27 years in the waiting. They may still not play ball, but a court order is a strong deterrent to keep them in line. Good things can come to those who wait. Playing the long game on matters of justice and equality can be frustrating and maddening, but that is why there is a thing called grit. Doing things bigger than yourself will matter in the end, even if you never see who benefits from your deeds in days, months, and years to come. Sometimes, you need to make a stand and stay in the fight because it is the right thing to do. Anything that really matters in life has never been given freely. What matters the most is earned and gained through perseverance, struggle, determination, collaboration, and effort. As Frederick Douglass said, 'Power concedes nothing without a demand. It never did and it never will.'

In my request with my court order, I reminded the state that my mother's release form allowing the state to share my records had been in their files since 1989—a total of twenty-seven years. To preempt the state from ignoring the court order, as the state registrar had threatened it could do, I included two emails I had received in my FOIA records request from two senior state officials. These stated unequivocally my original birth record was to be released with a court order. Even this stubborn agency might be reluctant to deny a court order with such statements on hand.

In the press release I sent the same day to more than two dozen media outlets in Michigan and Media, I explained why this day mattered: "For me, this is an issue of justice and basic fairness, not just for myself, but for millions of adult adoptees who face often hostile, legalized discrimination by Michigan and other states simply because we were adopted at birth. . . . Withholding my original birth certificate is an arbitrary exercise of power and does not serve the people of Michigan and even warps the misguided original intention of these now outdated laws and often harmful legal practices of closed adoptions."

A Detroit Free Press reporter, one of only two who contacted me over three months, called me to ask questions about my case. Her questions challenged my story, and she asked what I wanted. I told her it was simple: my birth certificate and what I want for everyone, including her—equal treatment under the law.

During our conversation, it was clear she had not read the background materials and did not understand the barriers posed by forcing a person to go to a court to petition for their original birth certificates. I tried to tell her how a court hearing was an enormously draining, time-consuming, and offensive demand that is meant to treat adopted persons as second-class persons. I told her, no citizen of Michigan who is not adopted is asked to do this when they ask for their birth certificate. I then challenged her to answer a basic question: was it fair for the state to not treat me the way it treats non-adoptees, such as herself? The question startled her. Flustered, she said she was not well acquainted with the law. She never gave an answer. In the end, the Free Press never covered this story.

The vital-records section called me a week later. It was either an honest call or just another delay tactic. Maybe it was both. The caller said she was confused about the court order and what record it asked for. She even read me the court order, saying it did not specify what birth record was being requested. I told her the judge could not have been clearer on what he had ordered her and the department to do. Did she not read the cover letter, the court form spelling out the required action, or even the order itself? I think she got the message loud and clear. Just to be sure, I alerted the court that the department was confused by the order. The court replied immediately to keep it updated. I called back vital records to again make clear the court ordered the department to release my original birth record and that I had contacted the court to alert them of the possible delay. They got the message.

On July 18, 2016, I found the envelope in my mailbox with a document I had been waiting to receive since April 1989. I was stunned looking at the copy. The state had lived up to its threat, writing three times in big bold letters, "SEALED," as a reminder I was still not a normal person. I was still an adoptee, and thus a bastard, and thus needed to have that brand in my legal documentation when others did not. State law does not require this graffiti.

Underneath those bureaucratic scarlet letters were most of the facts I already had known for three decades. It listed my birth mother's birth name, the name of my hospital—Crittenton General, my birth mother's age when I was born, the date of my birth, and my birth mother's address at the time of my birth. This address was new information. It also listed the full name of the attending physician, another new fact. The document was filed four weeks after my birth, and then put into safekeeping to be hidden from me by law. The document listed my middle name as "Douglass," compared to other original records that say "Douglas." I have no way of knowing which version was the preferred or intended spelling. When I changed my name in 2009 to Rudolf Scott-Douglas Owens, I stuck with the version I saw in more documents.

I shared with my friends that Michigan considered this sheet of paper a state secret to be kept from me only because I was an adoptee. On my blog announcing my victory, I wrote that the only reason I received what was and always had been mine was because I never once recognized the state's legal or moral authority to deny me equal treatment and equal status by law.

After receiving my birth certificate, I published several documents on my blog to share with the media and adoptees seeking information on how to obtain their records. My forensic email summary highlighted how nearly two dozen MDHHS officials worked to deny my request for my birth record. I immediately heard from some open-records advocates in Michigan, who applauded my efforts to document how the department manages adoptee birth records.

I also immediately published a copy of my birth certificate. I whited out all identifying information of my birth mother and medical personnel written on it. Lastly, I shared a press release and told nearly thirty media outlets in Oregon and Michigan how my efforts to secure my original identity document finally forced Michigan to yield, saying, "All my life, I was classified by law as being undeserving of this record, unlike all non-adopted state residents, simply because I was relinquished as an infant to become an adoptee. That is and always has been legalized discrimination, and it's shameful the state treats adoptees as second-class people who have to literally get court orders to get what others receive as a basic records request." No media outlet replied to my release.

My birth certificate also gave me new information that could help me tell a larger story of American adoption. I finally knew the full name of the attending physician who helped to bring me into this world in Detroit, Michigan. The obstetrician's surname was legible in other original birth records I had, but those records never showed his first name. To my great surprise, I learned that the doctor was Moslem, or born Moslem. His first name was Mohammed. I quickly checked for him online, and learned he was still alive. The records showed he was a native of Bangladesh, who completed his first residency in the United States at the now torn-down Crittenton hospital in Detroit—the one created originally to serve single, pregnant women. His story was intrinsically and critically part of my own.

His story made mine more complex. My start in life began with a foreign-trained doctor, from one of the world's poorest countries, who served the needs of unwed mothers like my birth mother. His Moslem heritage added another wrinkle to my tale. I laughed that a man named after the Islamic prophet Mohammed delivered a child who was surrendered to a Lutheran social service agency—probably one among many babies placed with Christian adoption services. My Christian placement service placed me with a Lutheran family, with a Lutheran minister father, who named me after a Protestant reformer, Martin Luther. All of this took place in 1965, long before the influx of South Asian immigrants to the United States. Chasing the facts from my past again showed me how remarkable my odyssey had been for more than five decades.

Holding the certificate in my hand, I again contemplated its exacting price. I had spent two years of searching to find my family when I was in my twenties. I made repeated requests to reluctant Michigan public health officials decades later, completed a FOIA request to put those officials on notice so they would be held accountable for their actions, received a court petition that required months of my time, and devoted uncounted hours to advocacy on behalf of all adoptees denied equal treatment under the law. Some of my friends said I had "won." I never thought about it that way.

Instead, I thought about the hero's journey as described by Joseph Campbell in his classic work on mythology called *The Hero with a Thousand Faces*. That is how I saw my challenge from the start, when I looked to mythical figures like King Arthur and the revered prophet Moses to inspire me. I thought of each stage of the adventure I embarked upon, first as a young man.

I left my ordinary world, the one society expected me to accept as an adoptee. I heard the visceral call to my quest, seeking my identity and kin. I overcame doubt and defiance. I was repeatedly tested by those seeking to keep my identity a secret. I received guidance from strangers who cared. I took leaps of faith into new places, crossing a threshold at key moments in magical ways. I met my family and kin, and had to navigate with them the challenges of our new relationship and with my adoptive family as well. I had disappointments—some I will never share with anyone—when I learned the unfiltered truth about who I really am. I finally received the last prize later in life, my magical and original birth certificate.

In the end, I had confronted my dragons, and slew them. I climbed the mountain and crossed the ring of fire. I reclaimed the person who was taken away. I came back a better person, more committed to those less fortunate than me, who could never slay their dragons and who never found their past and their families at no fault of their own.

My half-sister's prophetic words from September 2014 seemed truer than ever, when she told me, "You don't know how lucky you are." At the end of the journey, I had changed. Good fortune had smiled upon me. The journey taught me that some efforts, even those that take decades, are worth it. I acted decisively and did not waiver over the decades. In the end, I found myself, my past, and my genetic kin. More importantly, I found something bigger than myself, which I had an obligation to share. How lucky I am indeed.

Acknowledgements

My memoir on the institution of American adoption and my lifelong experience as an adoptee, seeking my basic human rights and my ancestral past, is indebted to people who have helped me along this journey throughout my lifetime. Some were strangers who assisted me in my search for my biological relatives. Some were friends who offered counsel when my long quest for justice seemed impossible to complete. For inspiration, I can thank the storytellers in our collective past who showed me that an adoptee's journey of discovery is truly a hero's journey—these stories kept the flame alive when I felt it would be extinguished. Holocaust survivor, psychiatrist, writer, and humanist Viktor Frankl showed me through his writings and life experience why finding meaning matters most in our lives. Frankl's wisdom shows that our freedom and strength comes from within ourselves to decide on our own what our life's meaning will be. Lastly, I especially wish to thank my friend and fellow adoptee Brad Cleveland for providing critical feedback and inspiration as the idea for my memoir took shape and the work emerged as a fully told story about issues far bigger than my own experience. For your assistance and encouragement, Brad, I will always be grateful.

Appendix: Rudy Owens's Original Birth Certificate

Illustration 1: Rudy Owens's Original Birth Certificate

Rudy Owens's original birth certificate was kept from Owens by the state of Michigan for more than 51 years because he was born an adoptee. The state released a copy of the document, slightly adulterated and stamped "SEALED," to Owens in July 2016 following a court hearing a month earlier. The author has intentionally redacted personal information in this photograph.

Chronology of Rudy Owens's Adoption Journey

Birth name: Scott Douglas Owens
Adoptive name: Martin Rudolf Brueggemann
Legal name changed to Rudolf Scott-Douglas Owens in 2009

April 1958
Rudy's future adoptive parents become engaged in Saginaw, Michigan, and get married in New Jersey in July of the same year.

September 1958
Rudy's adoptive parents move to Detroit, on a tree-lined middle-class street not far from River Rouge Park. Rudy's adoptive father begins work as the Lutheran campus minister at Wayne State University. His adoptive mother becomes a homemaker.

February 1963
Rudy's adoptive parents adopt his adoptive sister, who is born in Saginaw, Michigan.

Spring/Summer 1964
Rudy's birth mother and birth father meet in Detroit and his birth mother becomes pregnant.

December 1964
Rudy's birth father marries his wife after having denied paternity for Rudy.

Late 1964, early 1965
Rudy's adoptive father enters into an alcoholic-treatment program. His

addiction and illness is overlooked or hid from social workers who investigated him and Rudy's adoptive mother as prospective adoptive parents.

Mid-April 1965
Scott Douglas Owens is born in Detroit at Crittenton General Hospital, the largest maternity hospital created by the National Florence Crittenton Mission, the organization chartered to serve single mothers and vulnerable women in the 1880s.

Late April 1965
Rudy's birth mother signs documents relinquishing Scott and her legal rights as a parent. It is the last time they will see each other for a quarter century.

Late April 1965 to Late May 1965
Rudy, then still named Scott, becomes a ward of Lutheran Children's Friend Society (later Lutheran Child and Family Services) and become a foster child with a foster family in suburban Detroit.

Late May 1965
The state of Michigan issues an adoption decree, designating Scott the child of his adoptive parents. The state creates an amended birth certificate with the new name, Martin Rudolf Brueggemann, and places Rudy's original birth certificate and birth records into a sealed file for decades.

Fall 1965
Rudy's adoptive parents and family move to Boston for new mission work by Rudy's adoptive minister father. The job lasts barely two years.

October 1967
Rudy's adoptive parents and family move to Clayton, Missouri, where his adoptive father starts a new position as campus minister at Washington University. Rudy's adoptive father's drinking problem begins to affect his family.

1973
Rudy's adoptive parents divorce. Rudy and his adoptive mother and sister move to University City, Missouri.

1974–1979
Rudy and his adoptive sister visit their adoptive father in West Virginia

and southeast Ohio. His adoptive father's alcoholism ends his career in the Lutheran ministry, and his health and life take turns for the worse.

July 1981 and June 1982
Rudy's paternal grandparents, who never knew or met him, die within a year of each other. His paternal grandmother passes away in 1981 and paternal grandfather in 1982.

August 1983
Rudy visits his adoptive father in Cleveland for the last time before his adoptive father's death.

December 1985
Rudy's adoptive father, at age 61, dies from multiple health complications.

August 1987
After graduating from college, Rudy moves to Seattle and begins a full-time search for his biological family and birth records.

Spring 1988
Rudy receives copies of non-identifying information from the Wayne County Probate Court and Lutheran Child and Family Services after extensive delays that sought to deny him records he had legal rights to possess. Rudy learns for the first time basic information about his biological family and ethnic heritage.

April 1989
After nearly two years of searching for his biological family, Rudy flies to Detroit with no identifying information about his birth mother. Within forty-eight hours, Rudy meets his foster parents and birth mother. Rudy learns about his birth mother's family ancestry and meets his birth uncle and birth cousin. Rudy gives Michigan his birth mother's signed statement compelling the state and the adoption agency to release his original medical records, adoption decree, and other file information. The state refuses to surrender his original birth record.

Early May 1989
Rudy meets his maternal birth grandparents in Seattle for first time. They claim him as their long-lost grandson.

Late May 1989
Rudy meets his birth father in San Diego for the first and only time for

less than thirty seconds at his home. His birth father denies paternity and the two never speak to each other again.

September 1994
Rudy's maternal grandmother dies in a nursing home in Michigan. Rudy is listed in her official obituary as her grandson.

September 1998
Rudy speaks by phone for the first time ever to his paternal half-sister, who he met for brief seconds in 1989 at the home of his birth father.

February 2002
Rudy's maternal grandfather dies at his home in northern Michigan. Rudy is listed as his grandson in his obituary.

March 2004
Rudy's birth father dies in Montana from complications from cancer. His official biographies make no reference to his bastard and biological son, Rudy.

May 2007
Rudy obtains genealogical history of his birth father's family in his birth family's hometown. Rudy meets for the first and only time one of his birth father's three older sisters and her daughter—Rudy's biological cousin. They acknowledge him as family.

August 2009
Rudy legally changes his name from Martin Rudolf Brueggemann to Rudolf Scott-Douglas Owens. The name combines his adoptive and original given names to create a new identity that reflects his adoptive heritage.

September 2014
Rudy flies to San Diego and meets his paternal half-sister at her home. The two share information and stories and pictures. She acknowledges Rudy as her biological half-brother. She tells him, "You don't know how lucky you are," in reference to her father and family experiences. Rudy decides that night to write a memoir of his adoption experience with the same name.

November 2015
Rudy begins writing his public health memoir on adoption called *You Don't Know How Lucky You Are*, fifty years after he was relinquished as an adoptee.

March 2016
Rudy petitions Rick Lyon, director of the Michigan Department of Health and Human Services (MDHHS), for his original birth certificate that the state has denied sharing since April 1989. The department refuses to surrender it, illegally claiming it is a sealed record.

June 2016
The Third Judicial Circuit Court of Michigan hears Rudy's petition to have the MDHHS release his certificate and agrees his record is already public knowledge and the state had no grounds to keep it sealed. The judge signs a court order compelling the MDHHS to release his original identity document.

July 2016
Rudy receives his original birth certificate after waiting twenty-seven years and immediately publishes the document online to make it an open and public record.

August 2016
Rudy speaks to his obstetrician who delivered him at Crittenton General Hospital after learning his identity from his original birth certificate. They maintain their correspondence.

December 2017
Rudy completes his public health adoption memoir, ending his adoptee's hero's journey.

Notes

Chapter 1: Meeting My Half-Sister

1 Kim Kozlowski, "John Doe No. 73 Hunts for Birth Parents," *Detroit News*, April 25, 2008.

2 Katarina Wegar, *Adoption, Identity and Kinship: The Debate over Sealed Birth Records* (New Haven, CT: Yale University Press, 1997), 45.

3 "Psychopathology Studies," The Adoption History Project (web page), last modified February 24, 2012, http://pages.uoregon.edu/adoption/topics/psychopathstudies.htm.

4 Liselotte Petersen, Thorkild I. A. Sørensen, Erik Lykke Mortensen, Per Kragh Andersen, "Excess Mortality Rate During Adulthood Among Danish Adoptees," *PLOS ONE* 5, no. 12 (December 16, 2010), http://dx.doi.org/10.1371/journal.pone.0014365.

5 "Effects of Marriage and Fatherhood on Draft Eligibility," Selective Service System (website), accessed July 31, 2016, https://www.sss.gov/About/History-And-Records/Effects.

6 Elizabeth J. Samuels, "The Idea of Adoption: An Inquiry into the History of Adult Adoptee Access to Birth Records," *Rutgers Law Review* 53 (2001): 367.

Chapter 2: The Most Suitable Plan

1 E. Wayne Carp, *Family Matters: Secrecy and Disclosure in the History of Adoption* (Cambridge, MA: Harvard University Press, 1998).

2 Barbara Melosh, *Strangers and Kin: The American Way of Adoption* (Cambridge, MA: Harvard University Press, 2002).

3 Elizabeth J. Samuels, "The Idea of Adoption: An Inquiry into the

History of Adult Adoptee Access to Birth Records," *Rutgers Law Review* 53 (2001).

4   Melosh, *Strangers and Kin*, 52.

5   Child Welfare League of America, *Standards for Adoption Service* (New York: Child Welfare League of America, 1958), 14.

6   Ellen Herman, *Kinship by Design: A History of Adoption in the Modern United States* (Chicago: Chicago University Press, 2008), 148.

7   Child Welfare League of America, *Standards for Adoption Service*, 2.

8   Penelope L. Maza, "Adoption Trends: 1944–1975," Child Welfare Research Notes #9 (US Children's Bureau, August 1984), Child Welfare League of America Papers, Box 65, Folder: "Adoption—Research—Reprints of Articles," 1–4, Social Welfare History Archives, University of Minnesota.

9   Maza, "Adoption Trends."

10   Maza, "Adoption Trends."

11   Ursula M. Gallagher, *Social Workers Look at Adoption* (Washington: US Department of Health, Education, and Welfare, Social Security Administration, Children's Bureau, 1958), 1.

12   Rose M. Kreider and Daphne A. Lofquist, "Adopted Children and Stepchildren: 2010," *Current Population Reports P20-572* (US Census Bureau, Washington, DC. 2014), 4, accessed February 28, 2016, https://www.census.gov/prod/2014pubs/p20-572.pdf.

13   "Adoption Statistics," The Adoption History Project (web page), accessed September 5, 2016, http://pages.uoregon.edu/adoption/topics/adoptionstatistics.htm.

14   Centers for Disease Control and Prevention, *Report to Congress on Out-of-Wedlock Child Bearing* (Hyattsville, MD: September 1995), 83, accessed May 13, 2016, http://www.cdc.gov/nchs/data/misc/wedlock.pdf.

15   Centers for Disease Control and Prevention, *Report to Congress*, 55.

16   Centers for Disease Control and Prevention, *Report to Congress*, 14.

17   Centers for Disease Control and Prevention, *Report to Congress*, xxi, 55.

18   Carp, *Family Matters*, 3.

19   Child Welfare League, *Standards for Adoption Service*, 4.

20   American Academy of Pediatrics, Committee on Adoptions, *Adoption of Children* (Evanston, Illinois: American Academy of Pediatrics, 1960), 2.

21   Melosh, *Strangers and Kin*, 157.

22   Kathryn Joyce, T*he Child Catchers: Rescue, Trafficking, and the New Gospel of Adoption* (New York: Public Affairs, 2013), 92.

23   Regina Kunzel, *Fallen Women, Problem Girls: Unmarried Mothers and*

the Professionalization of Social Work, 1890–1945 (New Haven, CT: Yale University Press, 1993), 147.

24   American Academy of Pediatrics, *Adoption of Children*, 9.

25   State of Illinois, Department of Public Health, *Annual Report of the Department of Public Health* (July 1, 1964 to June 30, 1965) (Springfield: Department of Public Health, 1965), 21, 25, 32.

26   Melosh, *Strangers and Kin*, 132.

27   Joni Mitchell, interviewed on CBC, Q on CBC, "Interview with Joni Mitchell," June 12, 2013, accessed September 29, 2016, http://www.cbc.ca/player/play/2390949611.

28   Ann Fessler, *The Girls Who Went Away: The Hidden History of Women Who Surrendered Children for Adoption in the Decades Before Roe v. Wade* (New York: Penguin Press, 2006), 8.

29   Fessler, *The Girls Who Went Away*, 9.

30   Welfare Council of New York City, Committee on Adoption, *Adoption In New York City: Report of an Inquiry into Adoptions and Related Services* (New York: Welfare Council of New York City, 1948), 1.

31   Child Welfare League of America, *Standards for Services for Unmarried Parents* (New York: Child Welfare League of America, 1960), 2.

32   Gallagher, *Social Workers Look at Adoption*, 8.

Chapter 3: A Place for Unwed Mothers

1   Otto Wilson, Robert South Barrett, and National Florence Crittenton Mission, *Fifty Years Work With Girls, 1883–1933: A Story of the Florence Crittenton Homes* (Alexandria: The National Florence Crittenton Mission, 1933), 270.

2   University of Minnesota, *National Florence Crittenton Mission Records*, last modified 2006, http://archives.lib.umn.edu/repositories/11/resources/736#.

3   Kunzel, *Fallen Women, Problem Girls*, 89.

4   Fessler, *The Girls Who Went Away*, 144–145.

5   Fessler, *The Girls Who Went Away*, 150.

6   Fessler, *The Girls Who Went Away*, 155.

7   Melosh, *Strangers and Kin*, 134.

8   Joyce, *The Child Catchers*, 89.

9   Susan Daly, "A life unlived: 35 years of slavery in a Magdalene Laundry," *The Journal.ie*, last modified September 30, 2012,

http://www.thejournal.ie/magdalene-laundry-true-story-margaret-bullen-samantha-long-614350-Sep2012/.

10   Joyce, *The Child Catchers*, 90.

11   *Rochester Clarion*, "A Salute to Crittenton Hospital" (supplemental), August 3, 1967. Item provided to author by Ascension Crittenton Hospital.

12   Wilson, Barrett, and Crittenton, *Fifty Years Work With Girls*, 276.

13   Wilson, Barrett, and Crittenton, *Fifty Years Work With Girls*, 276.

14   *Rochester Clarion*, "A Salute to Crittenton Hospital."

15   Joyce, *The Child Catchers*, 89.

16   Melosh, *Strangers and Kin*, 125.

17   Fessler, *The Girls Who Went Away*, 155.

18   Florence Crittenton Association of America, "Services to and Characteristics of Unwed Mothers, 1965," (August 1966), Box 67, Folder 6, 11, Social Welfare History Archives, University of Minnesota Libraries, Florence Crittenton.

19   "Crittenton Becomes Ascension Crittenton Hospital," Ascension (website), last modified August 2, 2017, https://ascension.org/news/news-articles/2017/08/02/16/06/crittenton-becomes-ascension-crittenton-hospital.

20   "The History of Ascension Crittenton," Ascension Crittenton (website), accessed August 20, 2017, http://www.crittenton.com/about-crittenton/history-of-crittenton/.

21   "The History of Ascension Crittenton," Ascension Crittenton (website).

22   Jenny Teichman, *Illegitimacy: An Examination of Bastardy* (Ithaca, NY: Cornell University Press, 1982), 129.

23   "History of Woodridge," Woodridge Professional Building, accessed August 13, 2016, http://www.woodridgeprofessionalbuilding.com/history.shtml.

24   Peter Romanofsky, ed., *The Greenwood Encyclopedia of American Institutions, Social Service Organizations*, vol. 1 (Westport, CT: Greenwood Press, 1978), 310.

25   Florence Crittenton Association of America, "Services to and Characteristics of Unwed Mothers," 17.

26   Florence Crittenton Association of America, "Services to and Characteristics of Unwed Mothers," 16.

27   Florence Crittenton Association of America, "Services to and Characteristics of Unwed Mothers," 5, 6, 10.

28   Florence Crittenton Association of America, "Services to and Characteristics of Unwed Mothers," 10.

29   Florence Crittenton Home Reunion Registry, accessed January 31, 2017, http://www.florencecrittentonhome.com/aboutus.html.

30   Karen Wilson-Buterbaugh, "Not By Choice," *Eclectica Magazine*, July/August 2001, 6, no. 1, http://www.eclectica.org/v6n1/buterbaugh.html.

31   Wilson-Buterbaugh, "Not By Choice," 2001.

32   Katherine Harmon, "How Important Is Physical Contact with Your Infant?," *Scientific American*, May 6, 2010, https://www.scientificamerican.com/article/infant-touch/.

33   Florence Crittenton Association of America, "Services to and Characteristics of Unwed Mothers," 15.

34   Helen C. Chase, "Ranking Countries by Infant Mortality Rates," *Public Health Reports* 84, no. 1 (1969), 22.

35   Florence Crittenton Association of America, "Services to and Characteristics of Unwed Mothers," 11.

36   "Forced Adoption Practices," Government of Australia (website), accessed January 14, 2017, https://www.dss.gov.au/our-responsibilities/families-and-children/programs-services/forced-adoption-practices.

37   Giselle Wakatama, "Church Says Sorry Over Forced Adoptions," Australian Broadcasting Corporation, July 24, 2016, http://www.abc.net.au/news/2011-07-25/catholic-church-apologises-over-forced-adoptions/2808672.

38   Dan Rather, "Adopted or Abducted?," *Dan Rather Reports*, May 1, 2012, https://itunes.apple.com/us/tv-season/adopted-or-abducted/id485436827?i=524245986.

39   Fessler, *The Girls Who Went Away*, 102.

Chapter 4: How Scott Became Martin: A Life Told in Records

1   Carp, *Family Matters*, 2.

2   Gallagher, *Social Workers Look at Adoption*, 1.

3   Gallagher, *Social Workers Look at Adoption*, 12.

4   American Academy of Pediatrics, *Adoption of Children*, 12.

5   American Academy of Pediatrics, *Adoption of Children*, 16.

6   United States Children's Bureau, *The Physician's Part in Adoption* (Washington, DC: US Government Printing Office, 1958), 7.

7   Carp, Family Matters, 55.

8   "State Adoption Legislation," (webpage), American Adoption Congress, accessed August 20, 2016, http://www.americanadoptioncongress.org/state.php.

9   Kirk Johnson, "'Gertie's Babies,' Sold at Birth, Use DNA to Unlock Secret Past," *New York Times*, April 4, 2015, http://www.nytimes.com/2015/04/05/us/gerties-babies-sold-at-birth-use-dna-to-unlock-secret-past.html.

10   Carp, Family Matters, 66.

11   "Arnold Gessell," Adoption History Project (website), accessed September 5, 2016, http://pages.uoregon.edu/adoption/topics/adoptionstatistics.htm.

12   "US Children's Service Bureau," Adoption History Project (website), accessed March 15, 2016, http://pages.uoregon.edu/adoption/people/uscb.html.

Chapter 5: Knowing You Are Adopted: Just Look in the Mirror

1   Peter Conn, *Adoption: A Brief Social and Cultural History* (New York: Palgrave Macmillan, 2013), 95.

2   Melosh, *Strangers and Kin*, 54.

3   Child Welfare League of America, *Standards for Adoption Service*, 36.

4   Child Welfare League of America, *Standards for Adoption Service*, 36.

5   Herman, *Kinship by Design*, 202.

6   Herman, *Kinship by Design*, 203.

7   Gallagher, *Social Workers Look at Adoption*, 10.

8   Herman, *Kinship by Design*, 109.

9   Child Welfare League of America, *Standards for Adoption Service*, 25.

10   Melosh, *Strangers and Kin*, 34.

11   Child Welfare League of America, *Standards for Adoption Service*, 1.

Chapter 6: Blood Is Thicker Than Water

1   Trish Foxwell, *A Visitor's Guide to the Literary South* (New York: W. W. Norton, 2013), 157.

2   Betty Jean Lifton, *Lost and Found: The Adoption Experience* (New York: Harper and Row, 1988), 6.

3   David Brodzinsky, Marshall Schechter, and Robin Henig, *Being Adopted: The Lifelong Search for Self* (New York: Doubleday, 1992), 79.

4   Rather, "Adopted or Abducted?," 2012.

5   Joanne Wolf Small, "Adopted in America: A Study of Stigma," *SSRN*, (June 17, 2013), 14, http://dx.doi.org/10.2139/ssrn.2280517.

6   Claudia Corrigan D'Arcy, "About Musings of the Lame," *Musings of the Lame* (website), accessed March 11, 2016, http://www.adoptionbirthmothers.com/about-musings-of-the-lame/.

7   The Donaldson Adoption Institute, "For the Records: Restoring a Legal Right for Adult Adoptees," *Executive Summary*, accessed March 11, 2016, http://adoptioninstitute.org/old/publications/2007_11_For_Records_Executive_Summary.pdf.

8   "Mission," The National Council for Adoption (website), accessed February 28, 2016, https://www.adoptioncouncil.org/who-we-are/mission.

9   "Defenders of the Status Quo," Bastard Nation (website), accessed February 28, 2016, http://bastards.org/defenders-of-the-status-quo/.

10   Mark Schaller and Jeffry Simpson, eds., *Evolution and Social Psychology* (New York: Psychology Press, 2006), 243.

11   Margarete Vollrath, ed., *Handbook of Personality and Health* (Hoboken, NJ: John Wiley & Sons, 2008), 208.

12   Margo Daly and Martin Wilson, "The Cinderella Effect: Parental Discrimination Against Stepchildren," *Samfundsøkonomen* 4 (2002): 39.

13   Daly and Wilson, "The Cinderella Effect," 40.

14   Daly and Wilson, "The Cinderella Effect," 41–44.

15   Daly and Wilson, "The Cinderella Effect," 45.

16   Sebastian Schnettler and Anja Steinbach, "An Evolutionary Perspective on Perceived Parental Care and Closeness in Adolescents: How Do Biological and Social Kinship Play out within Families in the U.S.?," (working paper), *Max Planck Institute for Demographic Research*, accessed March 17, 2016, http://www.demogr.mpg.de/papers/working/wp-2011-002.pdf.

17   Kyle Gibson, "Differential parental investment in families with both adopted and genetic children," *Evolution and Human Behavior* 30, no. 3 (May 2009): 184–189.

18   Katherine S. Button et al., "Power failure: why small sample size undermines the reliability of neuroscience," *Nature Reviews Neuroscience* 14, (April 2013), 365.

19   Nigel Barber, "Do Parents Favor Natural Children over Adopted Ones?," *The Human Beast* (blog), *Psychology Today*, June 1, 2009, https://www.psychologytoday.com/blog/the-human-beast/200906/do-parents-favor-natural-children-over-adopted-ones.

20   Melosh, *Strangers and Kin*, 12.

21   Carp, *Family Matters*, 100.

22   Deborah Gray, *Attaching in Adoption: Practical Tools for Today's Parents*, 2nd ed. (Philadelphia: Jessica Kingsley, 2012).

23   Sally Bacchetta, "Adoptive Parents Don't Love Their Children the Same Way Biological Parents Do," *Adoption Voices*, accessed February 28, 2016, http://adoptionvoicesmagazine.com/parents-perspective/adoptive-parents-dont-love-their-children-the-same-way-biological-parents-do/#.

24   Lisette Petersen et al., "Excess Mortality Rate During Adulthood Among Danish Adoptees," *PLOS ONE* 5 no. 12 (2010): http://dx.doi.org/10.1371/journal.pone.0014365.

25   Herman, *Kinship by Design*, 7.

26   Carp, *Family Matters*, 3.

27   Conn, *Adoption*, 28–65.

28   Conn, *Adoption*, 92.

29   Carp, *Family Matters*, 3.

30   "Adoption Records," Government of United Kingdom (website), accessed February 27, 2016, https://www.gov.uk/adoption-records/accessing-your-birth-records.

31   "Relating to Adoption Records, H.B. 2082, H.D. 1, S.D. 1," Hawaii State Legislature, 2016, http://www.capitol.hawaii.gov/measure_indiv.aspx?billtype=HB&billnumber=2082&year=2016.

Chapter 7: Legalized Discrimination Against Adoptees: The Demon Behind the Problem

1   Carp, *Family Matters*, 144–45.

2   Carp, *Family Matters*, 178–181.

3   Carp, *Family Matters*, 180.

4   United Nations, *Universal Declaration of Human Rights* (United Nations: 1948), accessed March 5, 2017, http://www.un.org/en/universal-declaration-human-rights/.

5   Gregory D. Luce, "New Jersey," Adoptee Rights Law Center (website), accessed June 11, 2017, https://adopteerightslaw.com/new-jersey-obc/.

6   Donaldson Adoption Institute and J. Walter Thompson Worldwide & Research, *Adoption Perceptions Study*, 26, December 15, 2016, http://www.adoptioninstitute.org/wp-content/uploads/2016/12/DAI-Adoption-Perceptions-Study.pdf.

7   E. Wayne Carp, "How Tight Was the Seal? A Reappraisal of Adoption Records in the United States, England and New Zealand, 1851–1955," in *International Advances in Research Adoption for Practice*,

ed. G. M. Wrobel and E. Neil (Chichester, UK: John Wiley & Sons, 2012).

8   Carp, "How Tight Was the Seal?"

9   "Mission Statement," Bastard Nation, accessed March 27, 2016, http://bastards.org/mission-statement/.

10   Marianne Novy, "Novy on Carp, 'Adoption Politics: Bastard Nation and Ballot Initiative 58,'" Humanities and Social Sciences Online, August 2006, https://networks.h-net.org/node/18732/reviews/ 18972/novy-carp-adoption-politics-bastard-nation-and-ballot-initiative-58.

11   "Oregon Ballot Measure 58, 1998," Adoption History Project (website), accessed February 1, 2017, http://pages.uoregon.edu/ adoption/archive/BallotMeasure58.htm.

12   E. Wayne Carp, *Adoption Politics: Bastard Nation & Ballot Initiative 58* (Lawrence: University Press of Kansas, 2004).

13   Gregory D. Luce, "Bastards in the Room," Adoptee Rights Law Center (website), June 5, 2017, https://adopteerightslaw.com/ bastards-in-the-room/.

14   Gregory D. Luce, "OBC Access Maps," Adoptee Rights Law Center (website), accessed January 2, 2018, https://adopteerightslaw.com/ interactive-maps/.

15   E. Wayne Carp, *Jean Paton and the Struggle to Reform American Adoption* (Ann Arbor: University of Michigan Press, 2014), 115.

16   Jean Paton, *The Adopted Break Silence: The Experiences and Views of Forty Adults Who Were Once Adopted Children* (Philadelphia: Life History Study Center, 1954).

17   Paton, *The Adopted Break Silence*, 54.

18   "Search and Reunion," The Adoption History Project (website), accessed March 25, 2016, http://darkwing.uoregon.edu/~adoption/ topics/search&reunion.htm.

19   Carp, *Jean Paton.*

20   Carp, *Jean Paton*, 292.

21   Ruthena Hill Kittson, [Jean Patton], *Orphan Voyage* (New York: Vantage Press, 1968), 51-52.

22   Carp, *Family Matters*, 100.

23   Carp, *Family Matters*, 100.

24   United States Children's Bureau, *Essentials of Adoption Law and Procedure* (Washington, DC: US Government Printing Office, 1949), 23.

25   United States Children's Bureau, *Essentials of Adoption Law*, 24.

26   Melosh, *Strangers and Kin*, 107.

27   Samuels, "The Idea of Adoption," 367.

28   Child Welfare League of America, *Standards for Adoption Service*, 48.

29   Child Welfare League of America, *Standards for Adoption Service*, 64.

30   Elizabeth J. Samuels, "The Strange History of Adult Adoptee Access to Original Birth Records," *Adoption Quarterly* 5, no. 2 (2001): 67.

31   Samuels, "The Strange History of Adult Adoptee Access," 67.

32   Elizabeth J. Samuels, "How Adoption in America Grew Secret; Birth Records Weren't Closed for the Reasons You Might Think," *Washington Post*, October 21, 2001, B05.

33   Samuels, "The Idea of Adoption," 409.

34   Melosh, *Strangers and Kin*, 109.

35   Margaret A. Yelloly, "Factors relating to an adoption decision by the mothers of illegitimate infants," *The Sociological Review* 13, no. 1, (March 1965), 5.

36   Samuels, "The Idea of Adoption," 410.

37   Carp, *Family Matters*, 134.

38   "National Committee for Adoption, 'About Adoption and Privacy of Records,' 1982," Adoption History Project (website), accessed March 26, 2016, http://pages.uoregon.edu/adoption/archive/NCFAAAPR.htm.

39   Child Welfare League of America, *Standards for Adoption Service*, 110.

40   Child Welfare League of America, *Standards for Adoption Service*, 97.

41   Samuels, "The Idea of Adoption," 424.

42   Elizabeth J. Samuels, "Adoption," in the *Encyclopedia of Privacy*, vol. 1, A--M, ed. William G. Staples (Santa Barbara, CA: Greenwood Press, 2007), 11–12.

43   Carp, *Family Matters*, 200.

44   Elizabeth J. Samuels, "Surrender and Subordination: Birth Mothers and Adoption Law Reform," *Michigan Journal of Gender and Law* 20 (2013): 35–36.

45   Carp, *Family Matters*, 201.

46   Carp, *Family Matters*, 202.

47   "Bastard Nation, 'Open Records: Why It's an Issue,' 1999," The Adoption History Project (website), accessed April 2, 2016, http://pages.uoregon.edu/adoption/archive/BNOR.htm.

48   Carp, *Family Matters*, 36.

49   Carp, *Jean Paton*, 199.

50   Elizabeth J. Samuels, "Proponent Testimony on State of Ohio,

House Bill 61," March 6, 2013,http://www.adoptionnetwork.org/media/documents/document-gallery/roar/hb61-testimony-samuels-elizabeth.pdf.

51   Samuels, "Proponent Testimony."

52   Reid Wilson, "Republicans in State Governments Plan Juggernaut of Conservative Legislation," *Washington Post*, January 2, 2015, https://www.washingtonpost.com/politics/republicans-in-state-governments-plan-juggernaut-of-conservative-legislation/2015/01/02/6a0a82be-92bd-11e4-a900-9960214d4cd7_story.html.

53   Tim Storey, "Moving Ahead: Legislatures cruised through the anything but ho-hum election largely unchanged," National Conference of State Legislatures (website), December 2016, http://www.ncsl.org/Portals/1/Statevote/Election_Wrapup_SL_December_3.pdf.

54   Wilson, "Republicans in State Governments."

55   The Republican Party, *The Republican Party Platform* (2012), accessed April 3, 2016, https://prod-static-ngop-pbl.s3.amazonaws.com/docs/2012GOPPlatform.pdf, 14, 32.

56   Claudia Corrigan D'Arcy, "Finally! Accurate Data on Profits in Adoption," *Musings of the Lame* (website), last modified February 22, 2015, http://www.adoptionbirthmothers.com/adoption-industry-profit-data-2015/.

57   David M. Smolin, "Of Orphans and Adoption, Parents and the Poor, Exploitation and Rescue: A Scriptural and Theological Critique of the Evangelical Christian Adoption and Orphan Care Movement," *Regent Journal of International Law* 8, no. 2 (2012): 270.

58   Smolin, "Of Orphans and Adoption," 319.

59   Claudia Corrigan D'Arcy, "Re-Marketing Adoption," *Musings of the Lame* (website), last modified May 8, 2013, http://www.adoptionbirthmothers.com/marketing-adoption-indusrty-business/.

60   E. J. Graff, "They Steal Babies, Don't They?," *Pacific Standard*, November 24, 2014, http://www.psmag.com/politics-and-law/they-steal-babies-dont-they-international-adoption-schuster-institute-95027.

61   Joyce, The Child Catchers, 3–10.

62   Joyce, The Child Catchers, 3–10.

63   Melosh, *Strangers and Kin*, 202.

64   Barbara Stark, *International Family Law: An Introduction* (Abingdon, United Kingdom: Ashgate, 2013).

65   Sandy Musser, "An Executive Order to Restore Original Birth Certificates to Adult Adoptees by Enacting the Adoptees National

Restoration Act," (online petition), accessed April 16, 2016, http://petitions.moveon.org/sign/an-executive-order-to-1.fb52?source=s.icn.fb&r_by=10829605.

Chapter 8: Who Am I?

1   Ezra Hall Gillett, *God in Human Thought: Or, Natural Theology Traced in Literature, Ancient and Modern, to the Time of Bishop Butler*, vol. 1 (Whitefish, MT: Kessinger Publishing, 2010), 130.

2   Marshall D. Schechter, "Observations on Adopted Children," *Archives of General Psychiatry* 3 (July 1960): 21, 29, 31.

3   Carp, *Jean Paton*, 290.

4   Renea Nilsson and others, "Conduct Problems in Adopted and Non-Adopted Adolescents and Adoption Satisfaction as a Protective Factor" *Adoption Quarterly* 14, no. 3 (2011): 181.

5   University of Connecticut School of Social Work, "Training for Adoption Competency (TAC)," last modified January 16, 2014, http://ssw.uconn.edu/2014/01/16/training-for-adoption-competency-tac/.

6   American Academy of Pediatrics, Committee on Adoptions, "Identity Development in Adopted Children," *Pediatrics* 47 no. 5 (1971): 949.

7   American Academy of Pediatrics, *Adoption of Children*, 9.

8   American Academy of Pediatrics, "Identity Development," 949.

9   D. Borders & Committee on Early Childhood, Adoption, and Dependent Care, "Families and Adoption: The Pediatricians' Role in Supporting Communication," *Pediatrics* 112, no. 6 (2003): 1440.

10   "Questions About Biological Parents," American Academy of Pediatrics, last modified November 21, 2015, https://www.healthychildren.org/English/family-life/family-dynamics/adoption-and-foster-care/Pages/Questions-About-Biological-Parents.aspx.

11   American Academy of Pediatrics, "Statement of Endorsement: National Adoption Center: Open Records," Pediatrics (2014), May 26, 2014, http://pediatrics.aappublications.org/content/pediatrics/133/6/e1808.full.pdf.

12   American Academy of Pediatrics, "Questions About Biological Parents."

13   Donaldson Adoption Institute, "For the Records II: An Examination of the History and Impact of Adult Adoptee Access to Original Birth Certificates. Policy & Practice Perspective," July

2010,   http://www.adoptedforthelifeofme.com/resources/
DonaldsonInstitute%20-%20ForTheRecordsII_ExSum.pdf.

14   "The Genetics of Cancer," National Cancer Institute (website), accessed January 31, 2017, http://www.cancer.gov/about-cancer/causes-prevention/genetics.

15   W. Gregory Feero, "National Family History Day 2015: Thinking Globally and Acting Locally," *Genomics and Health Impact Blog, Centers for Disease Control and Prevention,* November 20, 2015, http://blogs.cdc.gov/genomics/2015/11/20/national-family-history-day-2015-thinking-globally-and-acting-locally/.

16   "Genetics Home Reference: Inheriting Genetic Conditions," US National Library of Medicine (website), accessed February 8, 2016, http://ghr.nlm.nih.gov/handbook/inheritance?show=all.

17   Feero, "National Family History Day 2015."

18   "Melanoma Causes and Risk Factors," Skin Cancer Foundation (website), accessed February 16, 2016, http://www.skincancer.org/skin-cancer-information/melanoma/melanoma-causes-and-risk-factors.

19   Luce, "OBC Access Maps."

20   Brian Johnston, "For Adoptees, Envelopes Put End to Decades of Waiting," *Ashbury Park Press,* January 9, 2017, http://www.app.com/story/news/local/new-jersey/2017/01/09/adoptees-envelopes-put-end-decades-waiting/96368186/.

21   Luce, "OBC Access Maps."

22   "State Legislation," American Adoption Congress (website), accessed February 16, 2016, http://www.americanadoptioncongress.org/state.php.

23   Kim Kozlowski, "Adoptees: Unseal Birth Records," *Detroit News,* March 5, 2008.

24   American Adoption Congress, "Statistics for States Implementing Access to Original Birth Certificate (OBC) Laws Since 2000," March 12, 2015, http://www.americanadoptioncongress.org/docs/Stats_for_States_with_access_3.12.15.pdf.

25   Leland Meitzler, "Rhode Island Makes Adoption Records Available," *Genealogy Blog,* July 2, 2012, http://www.genealogyblog.com/?p=20105.

Chapter 9: The Paper Chase

1   Frederick Douglass, "The Significance of Emancipation in the West Indies" (Speech, Canandaigua, New York, August 3, 1857),

collected in pamphlet by author, in *The Frederick Douglass Papers: Series One: Speeches, Debates, and Interviews*. Volume 3: 1855-63, ed. John W. Blassingame (New Haven, CT: Yale University Press, 1985), 204.

2   Sarah Yang, "X-rays linked to increased childhood leukemia risk," *UC Berkeley News*, October 4, 2010, http://news.berkeley.edu/2010/10/04/x-ray/.

3   Elizabeth J. Samuels, "The Idea of Adoption," 367.

4   Samuels, "The Idea of Adoption," 411.

5   Carp, *Family Matters*, 151.

6   Herman, *Kinship by Design*, 282.

7   Carp, *Family Matters*, 188.

8   Wegar, *Adoption, Identity, and Kinship*, 69.

9   Joanne Wolf Small, "Adopted in America: A Study of Stigma," *SSRN*, June 17, 2013, 25, http://dx.doi.org/10.2139/ssrn.2280517.

10   Chris Kirk, "The Most Popular Swear Words on Facebook," *Lexicon Valley* (blog), *Slate Magazine*, last modified September 11, 2013, http://www.slate.com/blogs/lexicon_valley/2013/09/11/top_swear_words_most_popular_curse_words_on_facebook.html.

11   Sara McDougall, "How Do You Say 'Bastard' in Medieval Latin?," *Institute for Advanced Study, the Institute Letter* (Spring 2015), https://www.ias.edu/ideas/2015/mcdougall-latin.

12   McDougall, "How Do You Say 'Bastard.'"

13   Teichman, *Illegitimacy: An Examination of Bastardy*, 129.

14   "Illegitimacy: The Shameful Secret," *Guardian*, April 14, 2007, http://www.theguardian.com/news/2007/apr/14/guardianspecial4.guardianspecial215.

15   Teichman, *Illegitimacy: An Examination of Bastardy*, 28.

16   Teichman, *Illegitimacy: An Examination of Bastardy*, 89.

17   Peter Laslett, "Introduction: Comparing Illegitimacy Over Time and Between Cultures," in *Bastardy and Its Comparative History*, ed. Peter Laslett, Karla Oosterveen, and Richard M. Smith (Cambridge, MA: Harvard University Press, 1980), 5.

18   Shirley Foster Hartley, *Illegitimacy* (Berkeley: University of California Press, 1975), 5.

19   Laslett, *Bastardy*, 5.

20   Laslett, *Bastardy*, 2.

21   Teichman, *Illegitimacy: An Examination of Bastardy*, 62.

22   Susan Stewart, "Bastardy and the Family Reconstitution Studies of Banbury and Hartland," in *Bastardy and Its Comparative History*, ed. Peter Laslett, Karla Oosterveen, and Richard M. Smith (Cambridge, MA: Harvard University Press, 1980), 127.

23   Teichman, *Illegitimacy: An Examination of Bastardy*, 105.

24   Robert V. Wells, "Illegitimacy and Bridal Pregnancy in Colonial America," in *Bastardy and Its Comparative History*, ed. Peter Laslett, Karla Oosterveen, and Richard M. Smith (Cambridge, MA: Harvard University Press, 1980), 360.

25   Hartley, *Illegitimacy*, 8.

26   Hartley, *Illegitimacy*, 8.

27   Reid Alice et al., "Vulnerability Among Illegitimate Children in Nineteenth Century Scotland," *Annales de démographie historique* 1, no. 111 (2006): 89.

28   Reid Alice et al., "Vulnerability Among Illegitimate Children, 90.

29   George Walker, *The Traffic in Babies: An Analysis of the Conditions Discovered During an Investigation Conducted in the Year 1914* (Baltimore, MD: The Norman, Remington Co., 1918), 3.

30   Melosh, *Strangers and Kin*, 19.

31   Walker, *The Traffic in Babies*, 16.

32   "Prenatal Care," US Department of Health and Human Services (website), last modified June 12, 2017, http://www.womenshealth.gov/publications/our-publications/fact-sheet/prenatal-care.html.

33   David M. Amodio, "The Neuroscience of Prejudice and Stereotyping," *Nature Reviews Neuroscience* 15, no. 10 (2014), 670, http://doi.org/10.1038/nrn3800.

Chapter 10: Flying to Detroit

1   American Academy of Pediatrics, *Adoption of Children*, 13.

Chapter 11: Out of the Darkness:
The Son Emerges from the Shadows

1   Kreider, "Adopted Children and Stepchildren," 13.

Chapter 12: After the Discovery:
Figuring out a New Identity

1   "Jean M. Paton, Orphan Voyage, 1968," Adoption History Project (website), accessed December 9, 2016, http://pages.uoregon.edu/adoption/archive/PatonOV.htm.

Chapter 13: Battling Michigan for Records

1   Carp, *Family Matters*, 144.
2   Sally Moore, "An Adopted Woman Who Finally Found Her Real Parents Helps Others Search for Theirs," *People Magazine*, August 18, 1975, http://www.people.com/people/archive/article/0,,20065554,00.html.
3   Niki Kelly, "Adoptee: Help us 'Feel Whole': Man Who Found Birth Mom advocates Simplifying Process," *Journal Gazette*, March 16, 2016, http://www.journalgazette.net/news/local/indiana/Adoptee–Help-us–feel-whole–5021302.
4   Joyce, *The Child Catchers*, 122.
5   "Know Thine Enemies," Bastard Nation (website), accessed July 10, 2016, http://bastards.org/bb-know-thine-enemies/.
6   Smolin, "Of Orphans and Adoption," 270.
7   Smolin, "Of Orphans and Adoption," 312.
8   Joyce, *The Child Catchers*, 315.
9   Christian Family Services (website), accessed July 16, 2016, http://www.cfs-michigan.org.
10   Michigan Adoption Resource Exchange (website), accessed February 4, 2018, https://mare.org/.
11   Michigan Department of Health and Human Services (website), "Community and Faith-Based Initiative on Foster Care and Adoption," accessed February 4, 2018, http://www.michigan.gov/mdhhs/0,5885,7-339-71551_61719—,00.html.
12   Mark Brush, "Gov. Snyder signs law allowing adoption agencies to deny services over 'sincere religious objection," *Michigan Radio*, June 11, 2015, http://michiganradio.org/post/gov-snyder-signs-law-allowing-adoption-agencies-deny-services-over-sincere-religious-objection#stream/0.
13   Laura Biehl (Senior Communications Advisor, Governor Rick Snyder, State of Michigan) email message to author, July 25, 2016.
14   "Section 710.67: Probate Code of 1939 Act 288 of 1939," Michigan Legislature (website), accessed March 5, 2016, http://legislature.mi.gov/doc.aspx?mcl-710-67.
15   Carp, *Family Matters*, 178.
16   Samuels, "The Idea of Adoption, 367.
17   E. Wayne Carp, "Jean Paton on Confidential Intermediary Legislation in Colorado," *The Biography of Jean Paton* (website), last modified February 18, 2014, http://jeanpaton.com/2014/02/18/jean-paton-on-confidential-intermediary-legislation-in-colorado/.

18 Samuels, "The Idea of Adoption," 432.
19 "Closed Adoption Records," Michigan Department of Health and Human Services (website), accessed March 5, 2016, http://www.michigan.gov/mdhhs/ 0,5885,7-339-73971_7116_7125-14884–,00.html.
20 "Closed Adoption Records." Michigan Department of Health and Human Services.
21 Samuels, "The Idea of Adoption," 367.
22 Jennifer Eisner (Press Officer, Michigan Department of Health and Human Services), email to author, July 27, 2016.
23 Eisner, email to author, July 27, 2016.
24 "Adoption Statistics," The Adoption History Project.
25 Eisner, email to author, July 27, 2016.
26 State of Illinois, Department of Public Health, *Annual Report of the Department of Public Health* (July 1, 1964 to June 30, 1965) (Springfield: Department of Public Health, 1965), 21, 25, 32.
27 "What is Bastard Nation?," Bastard Nation, accessed July 10, 2016, http://bastards.org/what-is-bastard-nation/.
28 Lauren Sabina Kneisly, "WTF?," *Baby Love Child* (blog), accessed July 15, 2016, http://www.babylovechild.org/wtf/.
29 Government of Australia, Attorney General's Department, "National Apology for Forced Adoptions," (delivered on March 21, 2013, by then-Prime Minister Julia Gillard), https://www.ag.gov.au/ About/ForcedAdoptionsApology/Documents/ Nationalapologyforforcedadoptions.PDF.
30 Joyce, *The Child Catchers*, 94.
31 John Bingham, "Cardinal's Apology to Mothers Over Babies Handed Over for Adoption," *Telegraph*, November 3, 2016, http://www.telegraph.co.uk/news/2016/11/03/cardinals-apology-to-mothers-over-babies-handed-over-for-adoptio/.
32 Joyce, *The Child Catchers*, 95.
33 Joyce, *The Child Catchers*, 100.

Chapter 14: Birth Certificate, the Final Battle

1 "Birth Registration," International Observatory on Statelessness, accessed April 8, 2016, http://www.nationalityforall.org/birth-registration.
2 Tamara Weaver, email to Glenn Copeland, "Subject: Re: Story of Interest: Michigan Not Releasing Original Birth Certificate to Adult Adoptee," March 21, 2016 and March 22, 2016.

3   Tamara Weaver, email to Glenn Copeland, "Subject: Re: Story of Interest: Michigan Not Releasing Original Birth Certificate to Adult Adoptee," March 21, 2016.

4   Eisner, email sent to author, July 27, 2016.

5   Tamara Weaver (Deputy State Registrar, Michigan Department of Health and Human Services), email to Connie Stevens (Analyst, Central Adoption Registry), "Subject: Re: Question," March 23, 2016.

6   Glenn Copeland (State Registrar, Michigan Department of Health and Human Services), email to Tamara Weaver (Deputy State Registrar, Michigan Department of Health and Human Services), Angela Minicuci (Communications Director, Michigan Department of Health and Human Services), Nancy Grijalva (Michigan Department of Health and Human Services), "Subject: Story of Interest: Michigan Not Releasing Original Birth Certificate to Adult Adoptee," March 22, 2016.

7   Tamara Weaver, email to Glenn Copeland, "Subject: Story of Interest: Michigan Not Releasing Original Birth Certificate to Adult Adoptee," March 22, 2016.

8   Tamara Weaver, email to Glenn Copeland, "Subject: Story of Interest: Michigan Not Releasing Original Birth Certificate to Adult Adoptee," March 22, 2016.

9   Glenn Copeland, email to Angela Minicuci, Nancy Grijalva, "Subject: Story of Interest: Michigan Not Releasing Original Birth Certificate to Adult Adoptee," March 24, 2016.

10   Tamara Weaver, email to Paula Anderson (Executive Secretary, Michigan Department of Health and Human Services), "Subject: Story of Interest: Michigan Not Releasing Original Birth Certificate to Adult Adoptee," March 31, 2016.

11   Glenn Copeland, letter to author, March 29, 2016.

12   Glenn Copeland, letter to author, March 29, 2016.

13   Glenn Copeland, letter to author, March 29, 2016.

14   Third Judicial Circuit Court of Michigan, *2014 Annual Report*, May 2015, https://www.3rdcc.org/Documents/Administration/General/AnnualReports/2014%5EAnnual%20Report%20for%202014%5E%5E.pdf, 20.

Bibliography

Adoption History Project (website). "Adoption Statistics." Accessed September 5, 2016. http://pages.uoregon.edu/adoption/topics/adoptionstatistics.htm.

Adoption History Project (website). "Arnold Gessell." Accessed September 5, 2016. http://pages.uoregon.edu/adoption/people/gesell.html.

Adoption History Project (website). "Bastard Nation, 'Open Records: Why It's an Issue,' 1999." Accessed April 2, 2016. http://pages.uoregon.edu/adoption/archive/BNOR.htm.

Adoption History Project (website). "Jean M. Paton, Orphan Voyage, 1968." Accessed December 9, 2016. http://pages.uoregon.edu/adoption/archive/PatonOV.htm.

Adoption History Project (website). "National Committee for Adoption, 'About Adoption and Privacy of Records,' 1982." Accessed March 26, 2016. http://pages.uoregon.edu/adoption/archive/NCFAAAPR.htm.

Adoption History Project (website). "Oregon Ballot Measure 58, 1998." Accessed February 1, 2017. http://pages.uoregon.edu/adoption/archive/BallotMeasure58.htm.

Adoption History Project (website). "Psychopathology Studies," Accessed April 2, 2016. http://pages.uoregon.edu/adoption/topics/psychopathstudies.htm.

Adoption History Project (website). "Search and Reunion." Accessed March 25, 2016. http://darkwing.uoregon.edu/~adoption/topics/search&reunion.htm.

Adoption History Project (website). "U.S. Children's Service Bureau." Accessed March 15, 2016. http://pages.uoregon.edu/adoption/people/uscb.html.

American Academy of Pediatrics. "Questions About Biological Parents." Last modified November 21, 2015. https://www.healthychildren.org/English/family-life/family-dynamics/adoption-and-foster-care/Pages/Questions-About-Biological-Parents.aspx.

American Academy of Pediatrics. "Statement of Endorsement: National Adoption Center: Open Records." *Pediatrics* (2014). May 26, 2014. http://pediatrics.aappublications.org/content/pediatrics/133/6/e1808.full.pdf.

American Academy of Pediatrics, Committee on Adoptions. *Adoption of Children*. Evanston, IL: American Academy of Pediatrics, 1960.

American Academy of Pediatrics, Committee on Adoptions. "Identity Development in Adopted Children." *Pediatrics* 47, no. 5 (1971): 948–950.

American Adoption Congress. "State Legislation." Accessed March 11, 2017. http://www.americanadoptioncongress.org/state.php.

American Adoption Congress. "Statistics for States Implementing Access to Original Birth Certificate (OBC) Laws Since 2000." March 12, 2015. http://www.americanadoptioncongress.org/docs/Stats_for_States_with_access_3.12.15.pdf.

Amodio, David M. "The Neuroscience of Prejudice and Stereotyping." *Nature Reviews Neuroscience* 15, no. 10 (2014): 670–682. http://doi.org/10.1038/nrn3800.

Ascension Crittenton Hospital (website). "Crittenton Becomes Ascension Crittenton Hospital." August 2, 2017. https://ascension.org/news/news-articles/2017/08/02/16/06/crittenton-becomes-ascension-crittenton-hospital.

Ascension Crittenton Hospital (website). "The History of Ascension Crittenton." Accessed August 20, 2017. http://www.crittenton.com/about-crittenton/history-of-crittenton/.

Avery, Wayne. Interview with author. March 19, 2016.

Bacchetta, Sally. "Adoptive Parents Don't Love Their Children the Same Way Biological Parents Do." *Adoption Voices*. Accessed February 28, 2016. http://adoptionvoicesmagazine.com/parents-perspective/adoptive-parents-dont-love-their-children-the-same-way-biological-parents-do/#.

Barber, Nigel. "Do Parents Favor Natural Children Over Adopted Ones?" *The Human Beast* (blog). *Psychology Today*. June 1, 2009. https://www.psychologytoday.com/blog/the-human-beast/200906/do-parents-favor-natural-children-over-adopted-ones.

Bastard Nation (website). "Defenders of the Status Quo." Accessed February 28, 2016. http://bastards.org/defenders-of-the-status-quo/.

Bastard Nation (website). "Know Thine Enemies." Accessed July 10, 2016. http://bastards.org/bb-know-thine-enemies/.

Bastard Nation (website). "What is Bastard Nation?" Accessed July 10, 2016. http://bastards.org/what-is-bastard-nation/.

Bingham, John. "Cardinal's Apology to Mothers Over Babies Handed Over for Adoption." *Telegraph*. November 3, 2016. http://www.telegraph.co.uk/news/2016/11/03/cardinals-apology-to-mothers-over-babies-handed-over-for-adoptio/.

Borders, D. and Committee on Early Childhood, Adoption, and Dependent Care. "Families and Adoption: The Pediatricians' Role in Supporting Communication." *Pediatrics* 112, no. 6 (2003): 1437–1441.

Brodzinsky, David, Marshall Schechter, and Robin Henig. *Being Adopted: The Lifelong Search for Self*. New York: Doubleday, 1992.

Brush, Mark. "Gov. Snyder signs law allowing adoption agencies to deny services over sincere religious objection." *Michigan Radio*, June 11, 2015.

http://michiganradio.org/post/gov-snyder-signs-law-allowing-adoption-agencies-deny-services-over-sincere-religious-objection#stream/0.

Button, Katherine S., John P. A. Ioannidis, Claire Mokrysz, Brian A. Nosek, Jonathan Flint, Emma S. J. Robinson, and Marcus R. Munafò. "Power Failure: Why Small Sample Size Undermines the Reliability of Neuroscience." *Nature Reviews Neuroscience* 14, (May 2013): 365–376.

Canadian Broadcasting Corporation. "Interview with Joni Mitchell." *Q on CBC*, June 12, 2013. http://www.cbc.ca/player/play/2390949611.

Carp, E. Wayne. *Adoption Politics: Bastard Nation & Ballot Initiative 58*. Lawrence: University Press of Kansas, 2004.

Carp, E. Wayne. *Family Matters: Secrecy and Disclosure in the History of Adoption*. Cambridge, MA: Harvard University Press, 1998.

Carp, E. Wayne. "How Tight Was the Seal? A Reappraisal of Adoption Records in the United States, England, and New Zealand, 1851–1955." In *International Advances in Research Adoption for Practice*. Edited by G. M. Wrobel and E. Neil. Chichester, UK: John Wiley & Sons, 2012.

Carp, E. Wayne. *Jean Paton and the Struggle to Reform American Adoption*. Ann Arbor: University of Michigan Press, 2014.

Carp, E. Wayne. "Jean Paton on Confidential Intermediary Legislation in Colorado." *The Biography of Jean Patton* (website). Last modified February 18, 2014. http://jeanpaton.com/2014/02/18/jean-paton-on-confidential-intermediary-legislation-in-colorado/.

Chase, Helen C. "Ranking Countries by Infant Mortality Rates." *Public Health Reports* 84, no. 1 (1969): 19–27.

Centers for Disease Control and Prevention. *Report to Congress on Out-of-Wedlock Child Bearing*. Hyattsville, MD: US Government Printing Office, 1995.

Child Welfare League of America. *Standards for Adoption Service*. New York: Child Welfare League of America, 1958.

Child Welfare League of America. *Standards for Adoption Service*. New York: Child Welfare League of America, 1971.

Child Welfare League of America. *Standards for Services for Unmarried Parents*. New York: Child Welfare League of America, 1976.

Christian Family Services (website). Accessed July 16, 2016. http://www.cfs-michigan.org.

Conn, Peter. *Adoption: A Brief Social and Cultural History*. New York: Palgrave Macmillan, 2013.

Connolly, Elizabeth. "An Ethnicity Conversation Your Adoptive Child Wants You to Have." *The Blog. Huffington Post.* November 12, 2014. http://www.huffingtonpost.com/elizabeth-connolly/an-ethnicity-conversation-your-adoptive-child-wants-to-have_b_5768150.html.

Corrigan D'Arcy, Claudia. "About Musings of the Lame." *Musings of the Lame* (website). Accessed March 11, 2016. http://www.adoptionbirthmothers.com/about-musings-of-the-lame/.

Corrigan D'Arcy, Claudia. "Finally! Accurate Data on Profits in Adoption." *Musings of the Lame* (website). Last modified February 22, 2015.

http://www.adoptionbirthmothers.com/adoption-industry-profit-
data-2015/.

Corrigan D'Arcy, Claudia. "Re-Marketing Adoption." *Musings of the Lame*
(website).   Last   Modified   May   8,   2013.
http://www.adoptionbirthmothers.com/marketing-adoption-indusrty-
business/.

Daly, Margo and Martin Wilson. "The Cinderella Effect: Parental Discrimination
Against Stepchildren." *Samfundsøkonomen* 4 (2002): 39–46.

Daly, Susan. "A life unlived: 35 years of slavery in a Magdalene Laundry." *The
Journal.ie*. Last modified September 30, 2012. http://www.thejournal.ie/
magdalene-laundry-true-story-margaret-bullen-samantha-
long-614350-Sep2012/.

Detroit Free Press. "Silent Halls, Empty Beds at Crittenton." January 24, 1974: 64.

Donaldson Adoption Institute (website). "Board." Accessed February 28, 2016.
http://adoptioninstitute.org/about/board-of-directors/.

Donaldson Adoption Institute. "For the Records II: An Examination of the
History and Impact of Adult Adoptee Access to Original Birth Certificates.
Policy & Practice Perspective." Last modified July 2010.
http://www.adoptedforthelifeofme.com/resources/
DonaldsonInstitute%20-%20ForTheRecordsII_ExSum.pdf.

Donaldson Adoption Institute. "For the Records: Restoring a Legal Right for
Adult   Adoptees."   Last   modified   November   2007.
http://adoptioninstitute.org/old/publications/
2007_11_For_Records_Executive_Summary.pdf.

Donaldson Adoption Institute and J. Walter Thompson Worldwide. "Adoption
Perceptions   Study."   Last   modified   December   2016.
http://www.adoptioninstitute.org/wp-content/uploads/2016/12/DAI-
Adoption-Perceptions-Study.pdf.

Douglass, Frederick. "The Significance of Emancipation in the West Indies."
Speech, Canandaigua, New York, 3 August 1857; collected in pamphlet by
author. In *The Frederick Douglass Papers. Series One: Speeches, Debates, and
Interviews. Volume 3: 1855–63*. Edited by John W. Blassingame. New Haven,
CT: Yale University Press, 1985.

Fessler, Ann. *The Girls Who Went Away: The Hidden History of Women Who
Surrendered Children for Adoption in the Decades Before Roe v. Wade*. New York:
Penguin Press, 2006.

Feero, W. Gregory. "National Family History Day 2015: Thinking Globally and
Acting Locally." *Genomics and Health Impact Blog*. Centers for Disease
Control and Prevention. November 20, 2015. http://blogs.cdc.gov/
genomics/2015/11/20/national-family-history-day-2015-thinking-
globally-and-acting-locally/.

Florence Crittenton Association of America. "Services to and Characteristics
of Unwed Mothers, 1965." August 1966. Box 67, folder 6. Social Welfare
History Archives, University of Minnesota Libraries, Florence Crittenton.

Florence Crittenton Home Reunion Registry. Accessed January 31, 2017.
http://www.florencecrittentonhome.com/aboutus.html.

Foxwell, Trish. *A Visitor's Guide to the Literary South*. New York: W. W. Norton, 2013.

Frankl, Viktor. *Man's Search for Meaning*. Boston: Beacon Press, 2006.

Gallagher, Ursula M. *Social Workers Look at Adoption*. Washington, DC: U.S. Dept. of Health, Education, and Welfare, Social Security Administration, Children's Bureau, 1958.

Gibson, Kyle. "Differential parental investment in families with both adopted and genetic children." *Evolution and Human Behavior* 30, no. 3 (2009): 184–189.

Gillett, Ezra Hall. *God in Human Thought: Or, Natural Theology Traced in Literature, Ancient and Modern, to the Time of Bishop Butler, Volume 1*. Whitefish, MT: Kessinger Publishing, 2010.

Gillman, Matthew W. "Developmental Origins of Health and Disease." *New England Journal of Medicine* 353, no. 17 (2005): 1848–1850.

Government of Australia (website). "Forced Adoption Practices." Accessed January 14, 2017. https://www.dss.gov.au/our-responsibilities/families-and-children/programs-services/forced-adoption-practices.

Government of Australia. Attorney General's Department. "National Apology for Forced Adoptions." Delivered on March 23, 2013 by former Prime Minister Julia Gillard. https://www.ag.gov.au/About/ForcedAdoptionsApology/Pages/default.aspx.

Government of the United Kingdom. "Adoption Records." Accessed February 27, 2016. https://www.gov.uk/adoption-records/accessing-your-birth-records.

Graff, E. J. "They Steal Babies, Don't They?" *Pacific Standard*. November 24, 2014. http://www.psmag.com/politics-and-law/they-steal-babies-dont-they-international-adoption-schuster-institute-95027.

Gray, Jessica. *Attaching in Adoption: Practical Tools for Today's Parents*. 2nd ed. Philadelphia: Jessica Kingsley, 2012.

Guardian. "Illegitimacy: The Shameful Secret." April 14, 2007. http://www.theguardian.com/news/2007/apr/14/guardianspecial4.guardianspecial215.

Hartley, Shirley Foster. *Illegitimacy*. Berkeley: University of California Press, 1975.

Harmon, Katherine. "How Important Is Physical Contact with Your Infant?" *Scientific American*. May 6, 2010. https://www.scientificamerican.com/article/infant-touch/.

Hawaii State Legislature. "Relation to Adoption Records, H.B. 2082, H.D. 1, S.D. 1." 2016. http://www.capitol.hawaii.gov/measure_indiv.aspx?billtype=HB&billnumber=2082&year=2016.

Herman, Ellen. *Kinship by Design: A History of Adoption in the Modern United States of America*. Chicago: University of Chicago Press, 2008.

Higgins, Daryl. *Impact of Past Adoption Practices: Summary of Key Issues from Australian Research/Final Report, A Report to the Australian Government Department of Families, Housing, Community Services and Indigenous Affairs*. Melbourne: Australian Institute of Family Studies, March 2010. Last modified April 30, 2010. https://www.dss.gov.au/sites/default/files/documents/pastadoptionreport.pdf.

International Observatory on Statelessness. "Birth Registration." Accessed April 8, 2016. http://www.nationalityforall.org/birth-registration.

Johnston, Brian. "For Adoptees, Envelopes Put End to Decades of Waiting." *Ashbury Park Press*, January 9, 2017. http://www.app.com/story/news/local/new-jersey/2017/01/09/adoptees-envelopes-put-end-decades-waiting/96368186/.

Johnson, Kirk. "'Gertie's Babies,' Sold at Birth, Use DNA to Unlock Secret Past." *New York Times*, April 4, 2015. http://www.nytimes.com/2015/04/05/us/gerties-babies-sold-at-birth-use-dna-to-unlock-secret-past.html.

Joyce, Kathryn. *The Child Catchers: Rescue, Trafficking, and the New Gospel of Adoption*. New York: Public Affairs, 2013.

Kelly, Niki. "Adoptee: Help Us 'Feel Whole': Man Who Found Birth Mom Advocates Simplifying Process." *The Journal* Gazette, February 15, 2015. http://www.journalgazette.net/news/local/indiana/Adoptee—Help-us—feel-whole–5021302.

Kim, JaeRan. "About Me." *Harlow's Monkey: An Unapologetic Look at Transracial and Transnational Adoption* (blog). Accessed February 21, 2016. https://harlows-monkey.com/home/.

Kirk, Chris. "The Most Popular Swear Words on Facebook." *Lexicon Valley* (blog). *Slate Magazine*. Last modified September 11, 2013. http://www.slate.com/blogs/lexicon_valley/2013/09/11/top_swear_words_most_popular_curse_words_on_facebook.html.

Kittson, Ruthena Hill [Jean Paton]. *Orphan Voyage*. New York: Vantage Press, 1968.

Kneisly, Lauren Sabina. "On So Called 'the Primal Wound': 'Personal Problems' vs. Political Solutions." *Baby Love Child* (blog). Accessed July 16, 2016. http://www.babylovechild.org/2008/01/30/on-so-called-the-primal-wound-personal-problems-vs-political-solutions/.

Kneisly, Lauren Sabina. "WTF?" *Baby Love Child* (blog). Accessed July 15, 2016. http://www.babylovechild.org/wtf/.

Kozlowski, Kim. "Adoptees: Unseal Birth Records." *Detroit News*. March 5, 2008.

Kozlowski, Kim. "John Doe No. 73 Hunts for Birth Parents." *Detroit News*. April 25, 2008.

Kreider, Rose M. and Daphne Lofquist. "Adopted Children and Stepchildren: 2010, Population Characteristics." *U.S. Census Bureau*, April 2014. https://www.census.gov/prod/2014pubs/p20-572.pdf.

Kunzel, Regina. *Fallen Women, Problem Girls. Unmarried Mothers and the Professionalization of Social Work, 1890–1945*. New Haven, CT: Yale University Press, 1993.

Laslett, Peter. "Introduction: Comparing Illegitimacy Over Time and Between Cultures." *Bastardy and Its Comparative History*. Edited by Peter Laslett, Karla Oosterveen, and Richard M. Smith. Cambridge, MA: Harvard University Press, 1980.

Lifton, Betty Jean. *Lost and Found: The Adoption Experience*. 2nd ed. New York: Harper and Row, 1988.

Lifton, Betty Jean. *Lost and Found: The Adoption Experience*. 3rd ed. Ann Arbor: University of Michigan Press, 2009.

Luce, Gregory D. "Bastards in the Room." Adoptee Rights Law Center (website). June 5, 2017. https://adopteerightslaw.com/bastards-in-the-room/.

Luce, Gregory D. "New Jersey." Adoptee Rights Law Center (website). Accessed June 11, 2017, https://adopteerightslaw.com/new-jersey-obc/.

Luce, Gregory D. "OBC Access Maps." Adoptee Rights Law Center (website). Accessed January 2, 2018. https://adopteerightslaw.com/interactive-maps/.

Maza, Penelope L. "Adoption Trends: 1944–1975." Child Welfare Research Notes, no. 9, U.S. Children's Bureau, August 1984. Child Welfare League of America Papers. Box 65, folder: "Adoption—Research—Reprints of Articles," Social Welfare History Archives, University of Minnesota.

McDougall, Sara. "How Do You Say 'Bastard' in Medieval Latin?" *Institute for Advanced Study, the Institute Letter* (Spring 2015). https://www.ias.edu/ideas/2015/mcdougall-latin.

Meitzler, Leland, "Rhode Island Makes Adoption Records Available." *Genealogy Blog*. Last modified July 2, 2012. http://www.genealogyblog.com/?p=20105.

Melosh, Barbara. *Strangers and Kin: The American Way of Adoption*. Cambridge, MA: Harvard University Press, 2002.

Michigan Adoption Resource Exchange (website). Accessed February 4, 2018. https://mare.org/.

Michigan Department of Health and Human Services (website). "Closed Adoption Records." Accessed March 5, 2016. http://www.michigan.gov/mdhhs/0,5885,7-339-73971_7116_7125-14884–,00.html.

Michigan Department of Health and Human Services (website). "Community and Faith-Based Initiative on Foster Care and Adoption." Accessed February 4, 2018. http://www.michigan.gov/mdhhs/0,5885,7-339-71551_61719—,00.html.

Michigan Legislature (website). "Section 710.67: Probate Code of 1939 Act 288 of 1939." Accessed March 5, 2016. http://legislature.mi.gov/doc.aspx?mcl-710-67.

Michigan Legislature (website). "Section 710.68: Probate Code of 1939 Act 288 of 1939." Accessed March 5, 2016. http://legislature.mi.gov/doc.aspx?mcl-710-68.

Moore, Sally. "An Adopted Woman Who Finally Found Her Real Parents Helps Others Search for Theirs." *People Magazine* (August 18, 1975). http://www.people.com/people/archive/article/0,,20065554,00.html.

Musser, Sandy. "An Executive Order to Restore Original Birth Certificates to Adult Adoptees by Enacting the Adoptees National Restoration Act" (online petition). Accessed April 16, 2016. http://petitions.moveon.org/sign/an-executive-order-to-1.fb52?source=s.icn.fb&r_by=10829605.

National Cancer Institute (website). "The Genetics of Cancer." Accessed January 31, 2017. http://www.cancer.gov/about-cancer/causes-prevention/genetics.

Nilsson, Renea, Soo Hyun Rhee, Robin P. Corley, Sally-Ann Rhea, Sally J. Wadsworth, and John C. DeFries. "Conduct Problems in Adopted and Non-Adopted Adolescents and Adoption Satisfaction as a Protective Factor." *Adoption Quarterly* 14, no. 3 (2011): 181–198.

Novy, Marianne. "Novy on Carp, 'Adoption Politics: Bastard Nation and Ballot

Initiative 58.'" *Humanities and Social Sciences Online* (August 2006). https://networks.h-net.org/node/18732/reviews/18972/novy-carp-adoption-politics-bastard-nation-and-ballot-initiative-58.

National Council for Adoption (website). "Mission." Accessed February 28, 2016. https://www.adoptioncouncil.org/who-we-are/mission.

Paton, Jean. *The Adopted Break Silence: The Experiences and Views of Forty Adults Who Were Once Adopted Children.* Philadelphia: Life History Study Center, 1954.

Petersen, Lisette, Thorkild I.A. Sørensen, Erik Lykke Mortensen, and Per Kragh Andersen. "Excess Mortality Rate During Adulthood Among Danish Adoptees," *PLOS ONE* 5 no. 12 (2010). http://dx.doi.org/10.1371/journal.pone.0014365.

Rather, Dan. "Adopted or Abducted." *Dan Rather Reports*, May 1, 2012. http://www.tv.com/shows/dan-rather-reports/adopted-or-abducted-2451587/.

Reid, Alice, Davies Ros, Garrett Eilidh, and Andrew Blaikie. "Vulnerability Among Illegitimate Children in Nineteenth Century Scotland." *Annales de Démographie Historique* 111, (2006): 89–113.

Republican Party. *The Republican Party Platform (2012).* Accessed April 3, 2016. https://prod-static-ngop-pbl.s3.amazonaws.com/docs/2012GOPPlatform.pdf.

Rochester Clarion. "A Salute to Crittenton Hospital (supplemental)." August 3, 1967.

Romanofsky, Peter, ed. *The Greenwood Encyclopedia of American Institutions. Social Service Organizations,* vol. 1. Westport, CT: Greenwood Press, 1978.

Samuels, Elizabeth J. "Adoption." *Encyclopedia of Privacy, vol. 1, A–M.* Santa Barbara, CA: Greenwood Press, 2007.

Samuels, Elizabeth J. "How Adoption in America Grew Secret; Birth Records Weren't Closed for the Reasons You Might Think." *Washington Post,* October 21, 2001.

Samuels, Elizabeth J. "The Idea of Adoption: An Inquiry into the History of Adult Adoptee Access to Birth Records." *Rutgers Law Review* 53, no. 2 (2001): 367–437.

Samuels, Elizabeth J. "Proponent Testimony on State of Ohio, House Bill 61," March 6, 2013. http://www.adoptionnetwork.org/media/documents/document-gallery/roar/hb61-testimony-samuels-elizabeth.pdf.

Samuels, Elizabeth J. "The Strange History of Adult Adoptee Access to Original Birth Records." *Adoption Quarterly* 5 no. 2 (2001): 63–74.

Samuels, Elizabeth J. "Surrender and Subordination: Birth Mothers and Adoption Law Reform." Michigan Journal of Gender and Law 20 (2013): 33–81.

Schaller, Mark and Jeffry Simpson, eds. *Evolution and Social Psychology.* New York: Psychology Press, 2006.

Schechter, Marshall D. "Observations on Adopted Children." *Archives of General Psychiatry* 3 (1960): 21–32.

Schnettler, Sebastian and Anja Steinbach. "An Evolutionary Perspective on

Perceived Parental Care and Closeness in adolescents: How Do Biological and Social Kinship Play Out Within Families in the U.S.?" (Unpublished working paper.) *Max Planck Institute for Demographic Research*. Accessed March 17, 2016. http://www.demogr.mpg.de/papers/working/wp-2011-002.pdf.

Selective Service System (website), "Effects of Marriage and Fatherhood on Draft Eligibility." Accessed July 31, 2016. https://www.sss.gov/About/History-And-Records/Effects.

Skin Cancer Foundation (website). "Melanoma Causes and Risk Factors." Accessed February 16, 2016. http://www.skincancer.org/skin-cancer-information/melanoma/melanoma-causes-and-risk-factors.

Small, Joanne Wolf. "Adopted in America: A Study of Stigma." *SSRN* June 17, 2013. Accessed June 9, 2017. http://dx.doi.org/10.2139/ssrn.2280517.

Smolin, David M. "Of Orphans and Adoption, Parents and the Poor, Exploitation and Rescue: A Scriptural and Theological Critique of the Evangelical Christian Adoption and Orphan Care Movement." *Regent Journal of International Law* 8, no. 2 (2012): 267–324.

State of Illinois, Department of Public Health. *Annual Report of the Department of Public Health (July 1, 1964 to June 30, 1965)*. Springfield: Department of Public Health, 1965.

Stark, Barbara. *International Family Law: An Introduction*. Abingdon, UK: Ashgate, 2013.

Stewart, Susan. "Bastardy and the Family Reconstitution Studies of Banbury and Hartland." *Bastardy and Its Comparative History*. Edited by Peter Laslett, Karla Oosterveen, and Richard M. Smith. Cambridge, MA: Harvard University Press, 1980.

Storey, Tim. "Moving Ahead: Legislatures Cruised Through the Anything but Ho-hum Election Largely Unchanged." National Conference of State Legislatures (website), December 2016. Accessed December 17, 2016. http://www.ncsl.org/Portals/1/Statevote/Election_Wrapup_SL_December_3.pdf.

Teichman, Jenny. *Illegitimacy: An Examination of Bastardy*. Ithaca, NY: Cornell University Press, 1982.

Third Judicial Circuit Court of Michigan. *2014 Annual Report*. May 2015. https://www.3rdcc.org/Documents/Administration/General/AnnualReports/2014%5EAnnual%20Report%20for%202014%5E%5E.pdf.

United Nations. *Universal Declaration of Human Rights*. United Nations, 1948. Accessed March 5, 2017. http://www.un.org/en/universal-declaration-human-rights/.

United States Children's Bureau. *Essentials of Adoption Law and Procedure*. Washington, DC: U.S. Government Printing Office, 1949.

United States Children's Bureau. *The Physician's Part in Adoption*. Washington, DC: U.S. Government Printing Office, 1958.

United States Department of Health and Human Services. "Prenatal Care." Last modified June 12, 2017. http://www.womenshealth.gov/publications/our-publications/fact-sheet/prenatal-care.html.

United States National Library of Medicine. "Genetics Home Reference: Inheriting Genetic Conditions." Accessed February 8, 2016. http://ghr.nlm.nih.gov/handbook/inheritance?show=all.

University of Connecticut School of Social Work. "Training for Adoption Competency (TAC)." Last modified January 16, 2014. http://ssw.uconn.edu/2014/01/16/training-for-adoption-competency-tac/.

University of Minnesota. *National Florence Crittenton Mission Records.* Accessed September 5, 2016. http://archives.lib.umn.edu/repositories/11/resources/736#.

Verrier, Nancy N. *The Primal Wound* (website). Accessed February 21, 2016. http://nancyverrier.com/.

Vollrath, Margarete, ed. *Handbook of Personality and Health.* Hoboken, NJ: John Wiley & Sons, 2008.

Wakatama, Giselle. "Church Says Sorry Over Forced Adoptions." *Australian Broadcasting Corporation.* July 24, 2016. http://www.abc.net.au/news/2011-07-25/catholic-church-apologises-over-forced-adoptions/2808672.

Walker, George. *The Traffic In Babies: An Analysis of the Conditions Discovered During an Investigation Conducted In the Year 1914.* Baltimore: The Norman, Remington Co., 1918.

Wegar, Katarina. *Adoption, Identity, and Kinship: The Debate over Sealed Records.* New Haven, CT: Yale University Press, 1997.

Welfare Council of New York City, Committee on Adoption. *Adoption in New York City: Report of an Inquiry into Adoptions and Related Services.* New York: Welfare Council of New York City, 1948.

Wells, Robert V. "Illegitimacy and Bridal Pregnancy in Colonial America." *Bastardy and Its Comparative History.* Edited by Peter Laslett, Karla Oosterveen, and Richard M. Smith. Cambridge, MA: Harvard University Press, 1980.

Wilson, Otto, Robert South Barrett, and National Florence Crittenton Mission. *Fifty Years Work With Girls, 1883–1933: A Story of the Florence Crittenton Homes.* Alexandria: The National Florence Crittenton Mission, 1933.

Wilson, Reid. "Republicans in State Governments Plan Juggernaut of Conservative Legislation." *Washington Post,* January 2, 2015. https://www.washingtonpost.com/politics/republicans-in-state-governments-plan-juggernaut-of-conservative-legislation/2015/01/02/6a0a82be-92bd-11e4-a900-9960214d4cd7_story.html.

Wilson-Buterbaugh, Karen. "Not By Choice." *Eclectica Magazine* 6, no. 1, July/August 2001. http://www.eclectica.org/v6n1/buterbaugh.html.

Woodridge Professional Building. "History of Woodridge." Accessed August 13, 2016. http://www.woodridgeprofessionalbuilding.com/history.shtml.

Yang, Sarah. "X-Rays Linked to Increased Childhood Leukemia Risk." *UC Berkeley News,* October 4, 2010. http://news.berkeley.edu/2010/10/04/x-ray/.

Yelloly, Margaret A. "Factors relating to an adoption decision by the mothers of illegitimate infants." *The Sociological Review* 13, no. 1 (March 1965): 5-14.

Index

McDaniels, Darryl, 30
McLachlan, Sarah, 30
MDHHS (Michigan Department of
    Health and Human Services), 93,
    122, 182, 185–87, 197, 199–201,
    207–8, 210, *215*, 220
media: Adopted Child Syndrome
    and the, 127–28; adoptees and
    the, 117, 193; adoption and the, 2,
    4–5, 84, 92; adoption laws and
    the, 4–5, 84, 112; adoption
    searches and the, 98; black-
    market adoptions and the, 53;
    closed records and the, 4–5, 209;
    discrimination and the, 4–5;
    equal rights and the, 84; global
    adoptions and the, 4; legislatures/
    legislation and the, 84; Owens,
    Rudolf (Rudy) and the, 200–201,
    205, 206, 208–9, 210; reunions
    and the, 4–5, 84, 120
Medicaid, 42
medical care, 35, 42, 47, 76, 81,
    135–36, 145. *See also* birth doctors;
    health risks; medical
    professionals
medical groups, 4, 25–26, 140, 178,
    189. *See also* medical professionals
medical histories: adoptees and, 79,
    109–12; adoptee-search websites
    and, 40; adoption laws and, 109;
    American Academy of Pediatrics
    (AAP) and, 109; birth defects and,
    111; birth records and, 109;
    Casebere, Jon and, 179; genetics
    and, 111; medical professionals
    and, 48–49, 109–12; non-
    identifying information and, 96;
    open records and, 81, 112; Owens,
    Rudolf (Rudy) and, 110, 112, 158,
    162, 167, 170–71; policies and, 112;
    public health and, 111–12; uncles
    (birth) and, 170–71; United States
    Preventive Services Task Force/
    United States Surgeon General

and, 111. *See also* health risks;
    individual illnesses
medical professionals: adoptees and,
    109–12; adoption agencies and,
    47, 48–49, 53; adoption and,
    25–26, 33–34, 35, 47–49, 52, 53,
    54–55, 109–12, 136, 178, 190–91;
    American Academy of Pediatrics
    (AAP) and, 25–26; apologies and,
    190–91, 192–93; Australia and,
    191; baby shops and, 135; birth
    records and, 49, 51–52; CDC
    (Centers for Disease Control and
    Prevention) and, 24; Crittenton
    General Hospital (Detroit) and,
    36; family histories and, 111–12,
    136; *The Girls Who Went Away: The
    Hidden History of Women Who
    Surrendered Children for Adoption
    in the Decades Before Roe v. Wade*
    (Fessler) and, 28; medical
    histories and, 48–49, 109–12;
    medical specialists, 21, 42;
    Owens, Rudolf (Rudy) and,
    52–53, 110; public health and,
    111–12; secrecy and, 46; single
    mothers and, 47–48, 49; social
    service agencies and, 49; social
    workers and, 27; vital records
    and, 49. *See also* birth doctors;
    physicians; psychiatrists
medical records, 48, 49, 124, 198, 218.
    See also medical histories
Medicare, 42
Melosh, Barbara, 20–21, 26, 27,
    28–29, 36, 60, 78, 90, 101
mental health, 12–13, 17, 21, 77, 88, 89,
    105–7, 108–9, 165, 170
mental health professionals:
    adoptees and, 89; adoption and,
    25, 66, 109; as adoption
    intermediaries, 147; adoption
    searches and, 179–80; apologies
    and, 106; births outside marriage
    and, 27, 92; gratitude and, 12–13;
    identity and, 105–7; mental

Hospital (Detroit) and, 39; CWLA
(Child Welfare League of
America) and, 25; data and,
39–40; Florence Crittenton
Home and Hospital (Detroit) and,
35, 47; Florence Crittenton
Homes and, 32, 33–34, 36,
135–36; Florence Crittenton
Maternity Home and, 35; *The
Girls Who Went Away: The Hidden
History of Women Who Surrendered
Children for Adoption in the Decades
Before Roe v. Wade* (Fessler) and,
27–28; health outcomes and, 134;
illegitimacy and, 130–31, 193–94;
maternity homes and, 33–34;
medical professionals and, 47–48,
49; mental pathologies and, 97;
National Florence Crittenton
Mission and, 217; neuroses and,
27; 1980s and, 24, 97; policies
and, 100; post–World War II and,
180–81; prenatal care and,
135–36; social workers and, 26,
48, 191; societies and, 29;
stigmatization and, 193–94;
triads and, 120; United States
Children's Bureau and, 29–30.
See also birth mothers
single white mothers: adoption and,
24, 26, 33, 39, 47–48, 95, 177;
adoptive families and, 48; births
outside marriage and, 25; CDC
(Centers for Disease Control and
Prevention) and, 24; illegitimacy
and, 21, 95; mental health and, 21;
National Florence Crittenton
Mission and, 33; 1990s and, 95;
1960s and, 24, 48; shame and, 15,
28, 39, 91–92; *Standards for
Adoption Service* (CWLA, 1958)
and, 21; stereotypes and, 21;
stigmatization and, 21
sisters. *See* adoptive sister; half-
sisters (paternal); stepsisters
Sixsmith, Martin, 43

slavery, 3, 72, 83, 117, 118
Smolin, David, 99, 181
Snyder, Rick, 182–83, 197, 200–201,
203, 208
social engineering, ix, 14, 20–21, 25,
62, 92, 177, 192, 196
social media, 183, 188, 205, 208
Social Security, 50, 68, 197
social service agencies, 49, 58–59, 73,
91, 92, 108, 144, 198. *See also
individual agencies*
social service agencies (Christian), 6,
58, 59–60, 191. *See also individual
agencies*
social services, 24, 25, 124, 176, 180,
192–93. *See also* National
Florence Crittenton Mission
social workers: adoptee rights and,
26; adoptees and, 26, 78, 107–8;
adoption and, 22–23, 26–30,
32–34, 35, 48, 52, 54–55, 56, 92,
95, 107–8, 109, 178, 191; adoption
competency and, 107–8; as
adoption intermediaries, 147;
adoption laws and, 100, 151;
adoption searches and, 142;
adoptive families and, 58–59;
adoptive mother and, 26;
adoptive parents and, 29, 56,
58–59, 78, 107, 216–17; American
adoption and, 22–23, 48;
apologies and, 191; Arnett, Jeanne
N., 124; birth mothers and, 26, 29,
45, 78, 107–8; birth parents/
families and, 29–30, 107; birth
records and, 108; Florence
Crittenton Homes and, 32–33;
home studies and, 58–59;
identity and, 92, 107–8;
illegitimacy and, 28; kin and, 90;
kinship and, 78, 107; Lutheran
Child and Family Services
(Michigan) and, 100, 142, 143–44,
151; maternity homes and, 32, 41;
medical professionals and, 27;
Melosh, Barbara and, 26, 28–29,

About the Author

Rudy Owens is a Detroit native who grew up in the Midwest and attended public schools in University City, Missouri, just outside of St. Louis. He spent most of his adult life in the West Coast states of Oregon, Washington, and Alaska. He has a professional background in communications, international relations, and public health. He earned a master's degree from the University of North Carolina at Chapel Hill in journalism and a master of public health degree from the University of Washington School of Public Health. Owens has worked as a reporter, editor, and political and public affairs officer for the Government of Canada. Owens also has worked in community-based public health in Washington State. Owens has been blogging about current affairs, policy, and public health issues since 2012. *You Don't Know How Lucky You Are* is his first nonfiction work. Owens currently lives in Portland, Oregon.

Made in United States
Troutdale, OR
09/05/2023

12654676R00164